THE PRINCETON REVIEW

High School
Math I Review

THE PRINCETON REVIEW

High School Math I Review

BY JONATHAN SPAIHTS

RANDOM HOUSE, INC.
New York 1998
www.randomhouse.com

Princeton Review Publishing, L.L.C.
2315 Broadway
New York, NY 10024

Copyright © 1998 by Princeton Review Publishing, L.L.C.

ISBN 0-375-75073-8

Editor: Lesly Atlas
Production Editor: James Petrozzello
Designer: Illeny Maaza
Production Coordinator: Robert McCormack
Illustrations: Scott Harris, Adam Hurwitz, and Iam Williams

9 8 7 6 5 4

First Edition

ACKNOWLEDGMENTS

The author would like to thank Annette Arguros of the New York State Education Department Testing Unit, for her cordial assistance; reviewers, Doreen Adelman, Kenneth Butka, and Ann Dolan for their invaluable expertise; Lesly Atlas and James Petrozzello, for their editorial prowess; and Patricia Acero, Greta Englert, Scott Harris, Mike Hollitscher, Rainy Orteca, Matt Reilly, Dave Spalding, Spencer Sweeney, Chris Thomas, and Iam Williams, for their excellence in the difficult work of producing this book.

CONTENTS

CHAPTER 1

Logic

Logic is the study of the principles of reasoning, especially the ways in which logical statements are related. You use the principles of logic every day, in ordinary conversation. In this chapter, you'll review some basic rules of logic that allow you to proceed from simple statements to complex conclusions.

1.1 STATEMENTS AND OPEN SENTENCES

In the study of logic, a statement is a special kind of sentence. Specifically, a statement is any sentence that is either true or false. Here are some examples of statements:

- My cat weighs more than your cat.
- 2 + 3 = 5
- Magnets attract iron.
- Harrisburg is the capital of Pennsylvania.
- 5 > 6

Some of these are mathematical sentences, and some are English sentences. What they have in common is a definite meaning that can be true or false, but not both. Another way to say this is that these sentences have definite *truth values*. The truth value of a statement is its truth or falsity. A statement has one and only one truth value—either true or false.

The two mathematical sentences above have different truth values. The first mathematical statement, 2 + 3 = 5, is true, and the second, 5 > 6, is false.

A statement is a sentence that is true or false, but not both.

In the study of logic, statements are commonly represented by letters such as *p*, *q*, *r*, and so on.

Sometimes, however, a sentence contains a placeholder or variable. This variable represents an unknown value. It's impossible to judge the truth or falsity of such a sentence until you know what the variable represents. A sentence with a variable or placeholder is called an *open sentence*. Here are some examples of open sentences:

- That is more than three feet long.

- $n > 16$

- $x - 4 = 3$

- It became an American state after 1950.

It's impossible to say whether these open sentences are true or false, because we don't know enough. The variables in the mathematical sentences, *n* and *x*, and the placeholders in the English sentences, "It" and "That," represent unknowns. We can consider these sentences true or false only when we know what the variables represent.

An open sentence is a sentence that contains one or more variables.

The variable in an open sentence may be replaced by any member of the *domain* or *replacement set*.

The set of replacement values that make an open sentence true is called the *solution set*. For example, the solution set of "It became an American state after 1950" is {Alaska, Hawaii}. The solution set of $x - 4 = 3$ is {7}. Only these values make the sentences true.

Decide whether each of the following is a statement or an open sentence.

1. Seven is a prime number.

2. Jenny is taller than Fred.

3. That is the class president.

4. *n* is greater than zero.

5. It's a bright red hat.

6. $x + y = 12$

7. Benjamin Franklin was President of the United States.

8. $5 < 6$

1.2 NEGATIONS

The opposite of a statement is called its *negation*. The negation of the statement, "It is raining," for example, can be written in English as

"It is not true that it is raining."

or, more simply,

"It is not raining."

Both of these statements represent the negation of the original statement, "It is raining." The truth value of the negation is the opposite of the truth value of the original statement. We can write this symbolically as well.

Let *p* represent the statement, "It is raining."

The negation of this statement, "It is not raining," is represented by *not p*. This can be written as $\sim p$, which is read "not *p*." The symbol $\sim$ is used to mean *not*. The negation of *p* is therefore $\sim p$.

The negation of a statement is its opposite. If a statement is represented by p, then the negation of that statement is ~p. A statement and its negation have opposite truth values.

For example let *q* represent the statement, "The moon is made of cheese."

Written symbolically, the negation of this statement is $\sim q$.

Written in English, the negation of this statement is "The moon is not made of cheese."

The original statement is false, and the negation is true.

It is sometimes helpful to use a table to show the truth values of two or more related statements. Here, for example, is a simple truth table for the statements p and $\sim p$.

Truth Table for $\sim p$	
p	$\sim p$
T	F
F	T

The first column contains the possible truth values of p: either true (T) or false (F). The second column contains the corresponding truth values for $\sim p$. When p is true, then $\sim p$ must be false. When p is false, then $\sim p$ must be true. This is reflected in the table. More complicated truth tables can be made with more columns to reflect the truth values of additional statements.

EXERCISES

Write the negations of the following statements.

1. Eight is an odd number.
2. Gold is heavier than lead.
3. Marie Curie discovered radium.
4. My pants are not on fire.
5. Venus is the planet nearest the sun.
6. Zero is not a negative number.
7. $2 + 3 = 5$
8. $7 - 4 = 3$
9. $7 > 3$
10. $3 \times 4 \neq 1.2$

1.3 CONJUNCTION

In everyday speech, we often combine more than one statement into a single sentence, like "That's a flying saucer or I'm seeing things," or "My babysitter has fangs and I'm afraid." These sentences are called *compound statements*. The words used to create these compound statements, such as "and" and "or," are called *logical connectives*.

CONJUNCTION

A compound statement formed by joining two statements with the word "and" is called a *conjunction*. The statement "Seven is a prime number and six is an even number" is a conjunction. The two statements that make up a conjunction are called *conjuncts*. The conjuncts in this case are the statements "Seven is a prime number" and "Six is an even number."

A conjunction is a compound statement formed by joining two statements with the word "and."

In logic, the word "and" is represented by the symbol ∧. Suppose that *p* represents "Seven is a prime number" and *q* represents "Six is an even number." The conjunction of these two statements could be written as $p \wedge q$, which would be read, "*p* and *q*."

The truth value of a compound statement depends on the truth values of its parts. A conjunction is true only when *both* of its conjuncts are true. A conjunction is false when one of its conjuncts is false, or when both of its conjuncts are false.

A conjunction is true only when both of its conjuncts are true.

Truth Table for Conjunction $p \wedge q$		
p	*q*	$p \wedge q$
T	T	T
T	F	F
F	T	F
F	F	F

This rule can be illustrated with a truth table. The table has four rows because there are four possible combinations of truth values for the statements *p* and *q*. These four combinations are shown in the first two columns. The conjunction is true only in the case shown in the first row, in which *p* and *q* are both true. In every other case, the conjunction is false.

If b *represents "My babysitter has fangs" and* a *represents "I am afraid," write each of the following sentences in symbolic form.*

1. My babysitter has fangs and I am not afraid.

2. My babysitter does not have fangs and I am afraid.

3. My babysitter has fangs and I am afraid.

4. I am not afraid and my babysitter does not have fangs.

If p *is true and* q *is false, state the truth value of each of the following statements.*

5. $\sim p \wedge q$

6. $q \wedge p$

7. $p \wedge \sim q$

8. $q \wedge \sim q$

Make a truth table for each of the following statements.

9. $p \wedge q$

10. $p \wedge \sim q$

11. $\sim (p \wedge q)$

12. $\sim p \wedge \sim q$

1.4 DISJUNCTION

A compound statement formed by joining two statements with the word "or" is called a *disjunction*. The statement "It is raining or it is snowing" is a disjunction. The two statements that make up a disjunction are called *disjuncts*. The disjuncts in this case are the statements "It is raining" and "It is snowing."

A disjunction is a compound statement formed by joining two statements with the word "or."

In logic, the word "or" is represented by the symbol $\vee$. If p represents "It is raining" and q represents "It is snowing," then the disjunction of these two statements can be written as $p \vee q$, which is read "p or q."

A disjunction is true when one or both of its parts are true. The statement is true if p is true, q is true, or both p and q are true. Note that both *p* and *q* can be true at the same time—not just one or the other. The statement is false when *p* and *q* are both false.

A disjunction is false only when both of its disjuncts are false.

Truth Table for Disjunction $p \lor q$		
p	*q*	$p \lor q$
T	T	T
T	F	T
F	T	T
F	F	F

In this truth table, the disjunction is false only in the fourth row, which represents the case in which both disjuncts are false. In all other cases, the disjunction is true.

EXERCISES

If p *represents "Jennifer is moving out,"* q *represents "Jason is moving in," and* r *represents "Leigh is running away," write the following sentences in symbolic form.*

1. Jennifer is moving out or Leigh is running away.

2. Jennifer is moving out and Jason is moving in

3. Either Jennifer is moving out or Jason is moving in and Leigh is running away.

4. Jason is not moving in or Jennifer is moving out.

If m *is true and* n *is false, state the truth values of the following statements.*

5. $m \lor n$

6. $n \lor \sim m$

7. $\sim(\sim n \lor m)$

8. $m \land (n \lor m)$

Make truth tables for the following statements.

9. $s \lor \sim s$

10. $s \lor \sim t$

11. $\sim(s \lor t)$

12. $t \lor (s \land \sim t)$

1.5 THE CONDITIONAL

A compound statement formed by joining two statements with the words "if...then" is called a *conditional*. The statement "If it snows, then I get cold," is a conditional. The first statement in a conditional is called the *antecedent,* or *hypothesis,* and the second statement is called the *consequent,* or *conclusion.* In this case, the antecedent is the statement "It snows," and the consequent is the statement, "I get cold."

A conditional is a compound statement formed by joining two statements with the words "if...then."

In logic, the words "if...then" are represented by the symbol $\rightarrow$. This symbol replaces the words "if...then," and appears in place of the word "then." If p represents the antecedent "It snows" and q represents the consequent "I get cold," then the conditional can be written $p \rightarrow q$ "if p then q."

In English, a conditional statement can take a number of different forms, although its meaning never changes. Here are several sentences that are equivalent to the statement "If it snows, I get cold":

"I get cold if it snows."

"The fact that it is snowing implies that I am cold."

"I always get cold when it snows."

All of these statements have the same logical meaning, and all would be symbolized $p \rightarrow q$.

A conditional is false when its antecedent is true but its consequent is false. This can be tricky. Take a look at our conditional example to see how the truth values of p, q, and $p \rightarrow q$ are related.

"If it snows, I get cold."

If it snows, and you get cold, then the statement $p \rightarrow q$ is clearly true.

If it doesn't snow, and you get cold, then $p \rightarrow q$ is still true. Nothing has happened to disprove the statement.

If it doesn't snow, and you don't get cold, then $p \rightarrow q$ is still true. Once again, nothing has happened to disprove the statement.

If it snows, and you don't get cold, then $p \rightarrow q$ is false. This case directly contradicts the conditional statement.

A conditional statement is false only when its antecedent is true and its consequent is false.

Truth Table for Conditional $p \rightarrow q$		
p	q	$p \rightarrow q$
T	T	T
T	F	F
F	T	T
F	F	T

This rule can be illustrated with a truth table. In this table, the statement $p \rightarrow q$ is false only in row 2. This row represents the case in which p is true and q is false. In every other case, $p \rightarrow q$ is true.

EXERCISES

If l *represents "I am pursued by a lion,"* m *represents "Monkeys laugh at me," and* n *represents "I take shelter in a tree," write the following statements in symbolic form.*

1. If I am pursued by a lion, then I take shelter in a tree.

2. If I take shelter in a tree, then monkeys do not laugh at me.

3. I take shelter in a tree if monkeys laugh at me or I am pursued by a lion.

4. If I am pursued by a lion and do not take shelter in a tree, then monkeys laugh at me.

If f *is true and* g *is false, state the truth values of the following statements.*

5. $f \rightarrow g$

6. $g \rightarrow f$

7. $g \rightarrow (f \wedge g)$

8. $\sim g \rightarrow \sim f$

Make truth tables for the following statements.

9. $p \rightarrow \sim p$

10. $\sim p \rightarrow \sim p$

11. $(p \rightarrow q) \vee \sim p$

12. $(p \wedge q) \rightarrow (p \vee q)$

1.6 TAUTOLOGIES

Some compound statements are always true. One of the simplest statements of this kind takes the form $p \to p$. For example:

Let p represent "The fire engine is red."

"If the fire engine is red, then the fire engine is red."

It's hard to argue with this sentence. If p is true (the fire engine is red), then the sentence is true. If p is false (the fire engine is *not* red), then the sentence is still true. A statement that is always true, like $p \to p$, is called a tautology.

A tautology is a compound statement that is always true, regardless of the truth values of its component statements.

Another simple tautology takes the form $p \lor \sim p$. For example:

Let p represent "Ted is asleep."

"Ted is asleep or Ted is not asleep."

Once again, it's tough to argue with this one. If p is true (Ted is asleep), then the sentence is true. If p is false (Ted is not asleep), then the sentence is still true. The statement $p \lor \sim p$ is a tautology.

Truth Table for the Disjunction $p \lor \sim p$		
p	$\sim p$	$p \lor \sim p$
T	F	T
F	T	T

You can use a truth table to determine whether a statement is a tautology. In Table 1.5, the statement $p \lor \sim p$ is shown to be true for every possible truth value of p. The statement is therefore a tautology.

Exercises

Make a truth table for each of the following statements and determine whether the statement is a tautology.

1. $c \to c$
2. $(c \land d) \to d$
3. $d \to \sim d$
4. $(c \lor d) \lor \sim d$
5. $(c \to d) \lor (\sim d \to \sim c)$

1.7 CONVERSE, INVERSE, AND CONTRAPOSITIVE

For every conditional statement, there are three related statements called the *converse, inverse,* and *contrapositive*. These related statements are formed by negating or interchanging the parts of a conditional statement, or both, according to the following rules:

For any conditional statement $p \to q$:		
To form the:	**Procedure**	**Symbolic Form**
Converse	Interchange p and q.	$q \to p$
Inverse	Negate both p and q.	$\sim p \to \sim q$
Contrapositive	Interchange and negate both p and q.	$\sim q \to \sim p$

As an example, here are the converse, inverse, and contrapositive of the conditional statement, "If I am swimming, I am wet":

Original: "If I am swimming, I am wet."

Converse: "If I am wet, I am swimming."

Inverse: "If I am not swimming, I am not wet."

Contrapositive: "If I am not wet, I am not swimming."

You might notice that some of these statements make more sense than others. Special relationships exist between the truth values of these statements. Some of these statements have essentially identical meanings. Some are very different. This will be addressed in the following section.

EXERCISES

Write the converse, inverse, and contrapositive of each of the following statements in English.

1. If I see peaches, I get hungry.

2. If Holly isn't on the bus, then Holly is lost.

3. If the camel doesn't spit at you, then the camel is not dangerous.

4. I don't go swimming if it's dark.

Write the converse, inverse, and contrapositive of each of the following statements in symbolic form.

5. $r \to s$

6. $\sim r \to s$

7. $r \rightarrow (s \wedge t)$

8. $(q \rightarrow r) \rightarrow \sim (s \wedge t)$

If p is true and q is false, state the truth values of the following statements.

9. $p \rightarrow q$

10. The converse of $p \rightarrow q$

11. The inverse of $p \rightarrow q$

12. The contrapositive of $p \rightarrow q$

1.8 LOGICAL EQUIVALENCY AND THE BICONDITIONAL

If two statements always have the same truth value, they are considered *logically equivalent*. Some interesting equivalencies exist between a conditional statement and its related statements. A truth table makes these relationships clear:

				Original	Converse	Inverse	Contrapositive
p	q	$\sim p$	$\sim q$	$p \rightarrow q$	$q \rightarrow p$	$\sim p \rightarrow \sim q$	$\sim q \rightarrow \sim p$
T	T	F	F	T	T	T	T
T	F	F	T	F	T	T	F
F	T	T	F	T	F	F	T
F	F	T	T	T	T	T	T

Truth Table for the conditional $p \rightarrow q$ and its related statements

If you examine the columns for the original statement and the contrapositive, you'll see that the truth values listed in both columns are the same. In other words, the statements $p \rightarrow q$ and $\sim q \rightarrow \sim p$ are logically equivalent. Regardless of the truth values of p and q, the truth values of $p \rightarrow q$ and $\sim q \rightarrow \sim p$ are always the same. This is true for any conditional statement and its contrapositive.

A conditional statement and its contrapositive are logically equivalent.

Similarly, the truth values of the converse and the inverse are the same in every row of the truth table. These statements too are logically equivalent, and always have the same truth values regardless of the truth or falsity of p and q.

> *The converse and inverse of a conditional statement are logically equivalent.*

THE BICONDITIONAL

If a conditional $p \rightarrow q$ and its converse are both true, then we can say that the statement $(p \rightarrow q) \wedge (q \rightarrow p)$ is true. This statement, the conjunction of a conditional and its converse, is called a *biconditional*. A biconditional statement is true when p and q are both true or both false.

> *A biconditional is a compound statement formed by the conjunction of a conditional and its converse.*

In logic, the biconditional relationship is represented by the symbol $\leftrightarrow$. The biconditional $(p \rightarrow q) \wedge (q \rightarrow p)$ can be written as $p \leftrightarrow q$, which is read, "*p* if and only if *q*."

Truth Table for the Biconditional $p \leftrightarrow q$		
p	q	$p \leftrightarrow q$
T	T	T
T	F	F
F	T	F
F	F	T

A truth table shows that the biconditional $p \leftrightarrow q$ is true when p and q are both true or both false. In other words, when a biconditional is true, then its two parts are logically equivalent. A true biconditional can also be called an *equivalency*.

> *A biconditional is true when both of its component statements have the same truth values.*

A conditional and its contrapositive, for example, are logically equivalent. This relationship can be symbolized as follows.

$(p \rightarrow q) \leftrightarrow (\sim q \rightarrow \sim p)$

This biconditional is always true, because its two component statements are equivalent. In other words, this biconditional is a tautology.

EXERCISES

If p *represents "Brendan is happy,"* q *represents "Valerie is happy,"* *and* r *represents "Business is good," write the following sentences in symbolic form.*

1. Brendan is happy if and only if business is good.

2. Business is good if and only if Brendan is happy and Valerie is happy.

3. Brendan is happy if Valerie is happy, and Valerie is happy if Brendan is happy.

4. Business is not good and Valerie is happy if and only if Brendan is happy.

5. Which of the following is logically equivalent to $\sim a \rightarrow b$?
   (a) $\sim a \rightarrow \sim b$
   (b) $b \rightarrow \sim a$
   (c) $a \rightarrow \sim b$
   (d) $\sim b \rightarrow a$

6. Which of the following is logically equivalent to the statement "If Jessica has received too many compliments, she is consumed with vanity"?
   (a) If Jessica is not consumed with vanity, she has not received too many compliments.
   (b) If Jessica is consumed with vanity, she has received too many compliments.
   (c) If Jessica has received too many compliments, she is not consumed with vanity.
   (d) If Jessica has not received too many compliments, she is not consumed with vanity.

7. Which of the following is logically equivalent to the *converse* of $p \rightarrow \sim q$
   (a) $q \rightarrow p$
   (b) $q \rightarrow \sim p$
   (c) $\sim p \rightarrow q$
   (d) $\sim q \rightarrow \sim p$

8. Which of the following is logically equivalent to the *inverse* of the statement "If the lunch special is not expensive, then I buy the lunch special"?
   (a) If I do not buy the lunch special, then the lunch special is expensive.
   (b) If I buy the lunch special, then the lunch special is not expensive.
   (c) If I do not buy the lunch special, then the lunch special is not expensive.
   (d) If the lunch special is expensive, then I buy the lunch special.

Construct a truth table for each of the following statements. Determine whether each statement is a tautology.

9. $(a \lor \sim b) \leftrightarrow a$
10. $(a \rightarrow b) \leftrightarrow (b \rightarrow a)$
11. $\sim(a \land b) \leftrightarrow (\sim a \lor \sim b)$
12. $[(a \land b) \rightarrow (a \lor b)] \leftrightarrow \sim a$

SUMMARY

- A statement is a sentence that is true or false, but not both.

- An open sentence is a sentence that contains one or more variables.

- The negation of a statement is its opposite. If a statement is represented by p, then the negation of that statement is $\sim p$. A statement and its negation have opposite truth values.

- A conjunction is a compound statement formed by joining two statements with the word "and." A conjunction is true only when both of its conjuncts are true.

- A disjunction is a compound statement formed by joining two statements with the word "or." A disjunction is false only when both of its disjuncts are false.

- A conditional is a compound statement formed by joining two statements with the words "if...then." A conditional statement is false only when its antecedent is true and its consequent is false.

- A tautology is a compound statement that is always true, regardless of the truth values of its component statements.

- A conditional statement and its contrapositive are logically equivalent.

- The converse and inverse of a conditional statement are logically equivalent.

- A biconditional is a compound statement formed by the conjunction of a conditional and its converse.

- A biconditional is true when both of its component statements have the same truth values.

2

Numbers and Operations

In algebra, letters known as variables are used to represent numbers. The use of variables allows mathematicians to write "general" equations that describe a variety of situations. The operations employed in algebraic equations can be written in a number of different ways. Understanding the rules governing these operations and the properties of numbers in general is the beginning of algebra.

2.1 VARIABLES AND CONSTANTS

In algebra, an ordinary number is known as a *constant*. The value of a constant never changes. Numbers like 7, 0, and −0.4 are constants.

A *variable* is a symbol—usually a letter—whose value is not fixed. A statement containing a variable is called an *open sentence*. The set of possible replacements for a variable is called the domain or *replacement set*.

Replacements for the variable that make an open sentence true are called *solutions* for that sentence. The set of all such replacements is called the *solution set*.

Example

Consider the sentence $x > 4$ when the domain is {2, 3, 4, 5, 6}. There are two values in the domain that make this sentence true:

$5 > 4$ $6 > 4$

The values 5 and 6 are solutions of the sentence $x > 4$. Together, they make up the solution set. The solution set is therefore {5, 6}.

An algebraic expression is an expression that contains at least one variable and at least one operation (such as addition or division). Here are some examples of algebraic expressions:

$k + 8$ $3xy$ $ab - 7$ $3(a + b)$

Expressions like these can be *evaluated* when the values of the variables are known.

Example

To evaluate $k + 8$ when $k = 3$, replace k with the number 3.

The value of the expression $k + 8$ is 11 when $k = 3$.

In algebra, the way some operations are written is different from the ways that they are written in simple arithmetic. Addition and subtraction are represented with the old familiar plus (+) and minus (–) signs, but multiplication and division are sometimes written differently.

MULTIPLICATION

In arithmetic, the phrase "three times five" would be written as 3×5. Multiplication may also be written in the following ways.

- A dot may be used between numbers or variables to indicate multiplication. For example,

$3 \cdot 5$	is equivalent to	"three times five"
$4 \cdot x$	is equivalent to	"four times x"
$x \cdot y$	is equivalent to	"x times y"

- Parentheses used without other operation symbols may be used to represent multiplication. For example,

$3(5)$	is equivalent to	"three times five"
$(3)(5)$	is equivalent to	"three times five"
$4(x)$	is equivalent to	"four times x"
$(x)(y)$	is equivalent to	"x times y"

- Placing a number and a variable, or two variables, side by side without any operation symbol indicates multiplication. For example,

$4x$	is equivalent to	"four times x"
xy	is equivalent to	"x times y"

When a number is placed beside a variable to indicate multiplication, as in $4x$, the number is called a *coefficient*. The coefficient of $7n$ is 7, and the coefficient of $5xy$ is 5. A variable with no written coefficient actually has a coefficient of 1. For example, $1x$ and x are equivalent expressions. The coefficient of x is 1.

EXPONENTS

Repeated multiplication may be represented by an exponent. An exponent is a number that tells you how many times to multiply a factor by itself. For example:

$$x = x^1$$

$$x \cdot x = x^2$$

$$x \cdot x \cdot x = x^3$$

$$x \cdot x \cdot x \cdot x = x^4$$

$$x \cdot x \cdot x \cdot x \cdot x = x^5$$

In each of the expressions above, the exponential term is equal to a series of factors multiplied together. The expression x, which is read "x to the fifth power," is equal to the product of five x^5's. Exponents may be used with constant factors as well as variables.

The expression 2^5 is equal to $2 \cdot 2 \cdot 2 \cdot 2 \cdot 2$ or 32.

In the expression x^5, the number 5 is called an *exponent*. The number 2 is called the base. The expression is called a *power* of 2.

Notice that a number or variable with no written exponent is said to have an exponent of 1:

$$x = x^1 \quad 4 = 4^1 \quad 0.7 = (0.7)^1$$

Any quantity raised to the first power equals itself.

DIVISION

In algebra, the symbol $\div$ for division is rarely used. Division is most often represented by the fraction bar. The meaning of the fraction bar is the same as the meaning of the division sign ($\div$).

$$12 \div 3 = \frac{12}{3} \quad x \div 6 = \frac{x}{6} \quad m \div n = \frac{m}{n} \quad 2 \div (x+5) = \frac{2}{x+5}$$

EXERCISES

Write each of the following expressions in two other ways.

1. Four times x
2. a multiplied by b
3. The product of x, y, and z
4. Four times the product of n and m

Write each of the following expressions in exponential form.

5. $10 \cdot 10 \cdot 10 \cdot 10 \cdot 10 \cdot 10$
6. $x \cdot x \cdot x \cdot x$

Write each of the following expressions as a series of multiplied factors.

7. z^8
8. 5^3

Write each of the following in fractional form.

9. $5 \div 3$
10. $x \div y$
11. $(n+5) \div 8$
12. $(x+y) \div (x-y)$

2.2 THE ORDER OF OPERATIONS

When evaluating expressions with more than one operation, like $3 \times 4 + 5$, the order in which you perform the operations can make a difference in the answer you get.

Example

Evaluate $3 \times 4 + 5$

If you multiply first and then add, you get

$$3 \times 4 + 5 = 12 + 5$$
$$= 17$$

But if you add first and then multiply, you get

$$3 \times 4 + 5 = 3 \times 9$$
$$= 27$$

That's a big difference.

Obviously, it's unacceptable to assign a mathematical expression more than one numerical value. The value of each numerical expression should be unique. To find the correct value of an expression, you must perform the operations according to a certain order.

- *Evaluate all exponents*
- *Do all multiplication and division from left to right*
- *Do all addition and subtraction from left to right*

Example

Evaluate $4 + 3^2 \cdot 2$

Do the exponent first: $4 + 3^2 \cdot 2 = 4 + 9 \cdot 2$

Then the multiplication: $= 4 + 18$

And finally, the addition: $= 22$

The value of $4 + 3^2 \cdot 2$ is 22.

PARENTHESES

The order of operations is affected by parentheses. Any expression in parentheses must be evaluated first, before it undergoes any operation outside the parentheses.

For example, in evaluating the expression $(7 - 3)^2$, it's necessary to perform the subtraction first, because it's inside the parentheses. Only then can the exponent be applied correctly: $(7 - 3)^2 = 4^2 = 16$.

The complete order of operations must therefore take parentheses into account. The order of operations can be written this way:

The Order of Operations

- *Parentheses*
- *Exponents*
- *Multiplication and Division (left to right)*
- *Addition and Subtraction (left to right)*

This order of operations is sometimes remembered by the word PEMDAS, in which each letter represents one operation.

Exercises

Evaluate the following expressions.

1. $5 - 2 + 3$
2. $4 \times 3 - 2$
3. $6(-2) + 3$

4. $10(5-3)$

5. $4^2 - 6 \div 2$

6. $(7-5)^3 \times 3$

7. $(6 \times 4 \div 2)^2$

8. $\dfrac{8-3^2}{5-3}$

2.3 SETS

A set is a group of elements or values. Most often, a set is a collection of things of a similar type—like a collection of numbers, or a collection of points, or a collection of Presidents' names. Sets are often named with capital letters.

A set may be listed or described in words. For example, the following descriptions of set S are equivalent:

Set S contains only the positive factors of 12.

$S = \{1, 2, 3, 4, 6, 12\}$

The sequence of elements in a set does not matter. The set $\{2, 4, 5\}$ is identical to the set $\{5, 2, 4\}$. A set may be finite, like set S above, or infinite. If set T is defined as the set of all positive multiples of four, then T will contain an infinite number of elements, because there is an infinite number of positive multiples of four.

UNION

A new set may be formed by combining two sets into one. This new set is called the union of the two sets. The union contains every element from each of the two original sets. The union of two sets is indicated by the symbol $\cup$. The sentence $C = A \cup B$ means that set C is the union of sets A and B.

The **union** of two sets is the set consisting of every element from each of the two original sets. Union is represented by the symbol $\cup$.

Example

For the sets $R = \{2, 4, 8, 16\}$ and $S = \{1, 3, 5, 7\}$, $T = R \cup S$. List set T.

$T = \{1, 2, 3, 4, 5, 7, 8, 16\}$

It is convenient but not necessary to list the element of set T in order. It would be equally correct to write

$T = \{2, 4, 8, 16, 1, 3, 5, 7\}$

INTERSECTION

A new set may also be formed from the elements common to two other sets. This new set is called the *intersection* of the original sets. The intersection of two sets is indicated by the symbol ∩. The sentence $P = M \cap N$ means that set P is the intersection of sets M and N.

The intersection of two sets is the group of elements common to both sets. Intersection is represented by the symbol ∩.

Example

For the sets $A = \{1, 2, 3, 4, 5, 6, 7, 8, 9\}$ and $B = \{0, 2, 4, 6, 8, 10\}$, $C = A \cap B$. List set C.

$C = \{2, 4, 6, 8\}$

Only these four numbers are present in **both** A and B.

The intersection of two sets is always a *subset* of each of the two original sets. A subset is a set that is completely contained within another set. The set of positive multiples of 5, for example, is a subset of the set of positive integers.

NULL SET

It is possible for a set to contain no elements. For example, suppose that $X = \{1, 2, 3\}$, $Y = \{4, 5, 6\}$, and $Z = X \cap Y$. Set Z is the intersection of X and Y, but X and Y have no elements in common. Set Z therefore contains no elements. The intersection of X and Y is said to be the *empty set*, or the *null set*. This can be represented in two ways:

$Z = \{ \}$

$Z = \varnothing$

DOMAIN AND SOLUTION SET

For any open sentence, the set of values that can replace the variable is called the *replacement set* or the *domain*.

Replacements for the variable that make the sentence true are called *solutions*. The set of all solutions is called the *solution set*. The solution set is always a subset of the domain.

Example

State the solution set of $x \geq 6$ for the domain $\{3, 4, 5, 6, 7, 8\}$.

Only three values in the domain make the sentence true:

$6 \geq 6 \quad 7 \geq 6 \quad 8 \geq 6$

The solution set is $\{6, 7, 8\}$.

EXERCISES

List the set resulting from each of the following unions and intersections.

1. $\{3, 4, 6\} \cup \{5, 7, 9\}$

2. {even factors of 60} $\cup$ {odd factors of 60}

3. $\{1, 2, 3,...\} \cup \{...,-3, -2, -1, 0\}$

4. $\{10, 20, 30\} \cap \{30, 40, 50\}$

5. $\{1, 2, 3\} \cap \{-3, -2, -1\}$

6. {whole numbers} $\cap$ {integers}

Find the solution set of each of the following open sentences for the domain given.

7. Find the solution set of $n > 3$ for the domain $\{2, 3, 4\}$.

8. Find the solution set of $x + 3 = 7$ for the domain {rational numbers}.

9. Find the solution set of $5a > 25$ for the domain $\{1, 3, 5, 7, 9\}$.

10. Find the solution set of $p = p + 1$ for the domain {integers}.

2.4 CLASSIFICATION OF NUMBERS

By convention, numbers are organized into sets that are referred to frequently in algebra.

COUNTING NUMBERS

The counting numbers are the members of the infinite set $\{1, 2, 3, 4, 5, ...\}$. All positive numbers that are evenly divisible by 1 are counting numbers. (In other words, all positive numbers that are not fractions or decimals.) The counting numbers are sometimes called the *natural numbers*.

WHOLE NUMBERS

The set of whole numbers is the set of counting numbers, with the addition of zero. Whole numbers are the members of the set $\{0, 1, 2, 3, 4, 5, ...\}$. There are no negative whole numbers.

INTEGERS

The set of integers contains all whole numbers, including zero, and their opposites. Integers are the members of the set {..., –3, –2, –1, 0, 1, 2, 3, ...}. Certain subsets of the set of integers are often referred to. For example, *positive integers* are members of the set {1, 2, 3, ...}, which is equivalent to the set of counting numbers. *Negative integers* are members of the set {–1, –2, –3, ...}. Finally, *non-negative integers* are members of the set {0, 1, 2, 3, ...}, which is also known as the set of whole numbers.

RATIONAL NUMBERS

Rational numbers are numbers that can be written in fractional form so that the numerator and denominator are both integers. All integers are rational numbers, since any integer may be expressed as a fraction with a denominator of 1: $7 = \frac{7}{1}$, $-2 = \frac{-2}{1}$, and so on. All fractions whose numerators and denominators are integers are rational: $\frac{3}{5}$, $\frac{1}{100}$, and $\frac{11}{4}$ are all rational numbers.

Decimal numbers that can be expressed as the quotient of two integers are also rational numbers. For example, $0.4 = \frac{4}{10}$, $0.125 = \frac{1}{8}$, and $0.333333... = \frac{1}{3}$. All three of these decimal numbers are therefore rational.

The sets of counting numbers, whole numbers, and integers are all subsets of the set of rational numbers.

IRRATIONAL NUMBERS

Irrational numbers are numbers that cannot be expressed as the quotient of two integers. In decimal form, irrational numbers appear as numbers that go on forever without repeating. There are several kinds of irrational numbers. Some of the most common examples of irrational numbers are square roots that can't be simplified into integers, like $\sqrt{3}$. The number $\sqrt{3}$ cannot be expressed as the quotient of two integers. Another common irrational number is π, which is approximately equal to 3.14. The exact value of π cannot be expressed as the quotient of two integers.

Irrational numbers will be dealt with in more detail in a later chapter.

REAL NUMBERS

The set of real numbers is the union of the set of rational numbers and the set of irrational numbers. Virtually all of the numbers in everyday algebra are real numbers.

{Counting Numbers} = {1, 2, 3, ...} (positive integers)
{Whole Numbers} = {0, 1, 2, 3, ...} (non–negative integers)
{Integers} = {..., –3, –2, –1, 0, 1, 2, 3, ...}
{Rational Numbers} = {Numbers that can be expressed as

the quotient of two integers, in the form $\frac{a}{b}$ where $b \neq 0$.}

{Irrational Numbers} = {Numbers that cannot be expressed as the quotient of two integers}
{Real Numbers} = {All rational numbers and all irrational numbers}

EXERCISES

1. The set of integers is a subset of which of the following sets?
   (a) Irrational numbers
   (b) Counting numbers
   (c) Whole numbers
   (d) Rational numbers

2. The set of rational numbers is a subset of which of the following sets?
   (a) Irrational numbers
   (b) Real numbers
   (c) Integers
   (d) Whole numbers

Identify each of the following as a rational number or an irrational number.

3. 7

4. 0

5. $\frac{9}{8}$

6. $\sqrt{11}$

7. $\sqrt{64}$

8. -1

9. $0.666...$

10. π

2.5 SIGNED NUMBERS

The number line is commonly used to represent the set of real numbers. It's a horizontal line that extends forever in both directions.

The number given to any point on the number line is called a *coordinate*. The point with a coordinate of zero is called the *origin*. All points to the right of the origin represent positive numbers. All points to the left of the origin are negative.

On a number line, numbers increase to the right and decrease to the left. Every number on a number line is greater than every number to its left. This is known as the *Order Property of Numbers*.

ABSOLUTE VALUE

The distance between a point on a number line and the origin is equal to the *absolute value* of that point. An absolute value is always positive, because distance cannot be negative. The absolute value of a number n is written as $|n|$.

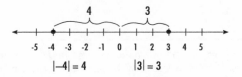

---

*The **absolute value** of a number is the distance between the number and zero on the number line.*

In numerical terms, the absolute value of a number is simply the positive version of that number, the number without a negative sign. The absolute value of a positive number is itself. The absolute value of a negative number is its opposite. For example, $|6| = 6$, $|-8| = 8$, and $|0| = 0$.

OPPOSITES

Every real number has an *opposite*. The opposite of any positive number is the negative number that has the same absolute value. Likewise, the opposite of any negative number is the positive number with the same absolute value.

For example, the opposite of 5 is –5, and the opposite of –12 is 12. The opposite of zero is zero.

ADDING SIGNED INTEGERS

The idea of absolute value can be helpful in doing addition with signed numbers.

Adding two positive integers is simple: Just add the numbers together to produce a positive sum. Adding two negative integers is just as simple: Add the absolute values of the numbers together, and add a negative sign.

To add two integers with the same sign, add their absolute values. The sum will have the same sign as the two numbers.

Example

$3 + 4 = 7$ $-2 + -8 = -10$

Adding integers with different signs is a little more complicated. When you add a positive and a negative, the sum might be positive or negative. For example, $6 + -2 = 4$, but $-6 + 2 = -4$. In each case, the sum is equal to the difference of the absolute values of the two numbers. The number with the greater absolute value determines the sign of the sum.

To add two integers with different signs, find the difference of their absolute values. Give the sum the sign of the number with the greater absolute value.

Example

$-10 + 4 = -6$ $4 + -3 = 1$ $7 + -12 = -5$ $-3 + 5 = 2$

SUBTRACTING SIGNED INTEGERS

Subtracting an integer is the same thing as adding its opposite. For example, $10 - 3$ is equal to $10 + (-3)$. This approach can make it easier to subtract negative integers. For example, the expression $9 - (-4)$ is equal to $9 + 4$.

> To subtract an integer, add its opposite. Subtracting a
> negative number is like adding a positive.

Example

$22 - (-8) = 22 + 8 = 30 \qquad 4 - (-4) = 4 + 4 = 8$

MULTIPLYING AND DIVIDING SIGNED INTEGERS

Multiplying two signed integers is straightforward. Simply multiply the absolute values of the integers together. If the two integers have the same sign, the product will be positive. If the two integers have different signs, the product will be negative. For example, $3 \times 4 = 12$, and $-3 \times -4 = 12$, while $-3 \times 4 = -12$, and $3 \times -4 = -12$.

> The product of two numbers with the same sign is positive.
> The product of two numbers with different signs is negative.

EXERCISES

Complete the following equations.

1. $15 - (-3) =$
2. $-6x - (-2x) =$
3. $(12)(-3) + 6 =$
4. $(-3n)(-5) =$
5. $|27| =$
6. $|-6| - |9| =$

2.6 FRACTIONS

A fraction represents a quotient of two integers. Some fractions, like $\frac{6}{3}$, may represent integer values ($\frac{6}{3}$—that is, six divided by three for example,—$\frac{6}{3}$ equals 2). Others, like $\frac{3}{4}$, cannot be expressed as integers. There are other ways to express the number $\frac{3}{4}$, however. For every fraction, there's an infinite number of equivalent fractions.

The fraction $\frac{3}{4}$, for example, is equal to all of the following fractions: $\frac{6}{8}$, $\frac{9}{12}$, $\frac{30}{40}$, and $\frac{300}{400}$. Each of these fractions is obtained by multiplying the numerator and denominator of the fraction by the same factor: $\frac{2}{2}\left(\frac{3}{4}\right) = \frac{6}{8}$.

If the numerator and denominator of a fraction have a factor in common, then that fraction can be *reduced*. To reduce a fraction, simply divide the numerator and denominator by a common factor. In the fraction $\frac{10}{15}$, for example, the numerator and denominator are both multiples of 5. To reduce the fraction, divide the top and bottom by 5: $\frac{10}{15} = \frac{10 \div 5}{15 \div 5} = \frac{2}{3}$

The fraction $\frac{10}{15}$ reduces to $\frac{2}{3}$. The numerator and denominator of $\frac{2}{3}$ have no factors in common, so the fraction can't be reduced any farther. The fraction $\frac{2}{3}$ is therefore expressed in its *simplest form*.

FRACTIONS AND DECIMALS

To find the decimal value of a fraction, do the division represented by the fraction bar. For example, the fraction $\frac{3}{4}$ is equivalent to the expression $3 \div 4$. To find its decimal value, do the division: $3 \div 4 = 0.75$. The decimal value of $\frac{3}{4}$ is therefore 0.75.

Example

$$\frac{3}{5} = 3 \div 5 = 0.6 \qquad \frac{9}{4} = 9 \div 4 = 2.25 \qquad \frac{1}{8} = 1 \div 8 = 0.125$$

To express a decimal as a fraction, rewrite the number as an integer divided by a power of 10. Count the number of decimal places in the original number. The denominator should be a 1 followed by the same number of zeroes. For example, the number 0.256, which has three decimal places, would be written as $\frac{256}{1000}$, with three zeroes in the denominator.

Example

$$2.3 = \frac{23}{10} \qquad 0.125 = \frac{125}{1000} \qquad 0.6 = \frac{6}{10}$$

Often, the fractions produced in this way can be reduced. The fraction $\frac{125}{1000}$, for example, reduces to $\frac{1}{8}$, because 125 goes into 1000 eight times. The decimal number 0.125 therefore equals $\frac{1}{8}$.

COMPARING FRACTIONS

It's easy to compare the values of fractions with the same denominator. Just look at the numerator. The following fractions, for example, are arranged in order: $..., \frac{-3}{7}, \frac{-2}{7}, \frac{-1}{7}, \frac{1}{7}, \frac{2}{7}, \frac{3}{7}, ...$

When fractions have different denominators, however, it's more difficult to compare their values. To compare fractions, find the *Lowest Common Denominator* (L.C.D.) of the two fractions. This will be the lowest multiple that the fractions' denominators have in common.

To **compare** fractions with unlike denominators, find the L.C.D. of the fractions and rewrite each fraction using the L.C.D. The fraction with the larger numerator will then be the larger fraction.

Example

Compare $\frac{5}{3}$ and $\frac{7}{4}$.

The lowest common multiple of 3 and 4 is 12. The L.C.D. of the two fractions is therefore 12. Rewrite each fraction using the L.C.D.:

$$\frac{4}{4}\left(\frac{5}{3}\right) = \frac{20}{12} \qquad \frac{3}{3}\left(\frac{7}{4}\right) = \frac{21}{12}$$

The second fraction has a greater numerator when both are written with a common denominator. Of the two original fractions, $\frac{7}{4}$ is greater.

ADDING AND SUBTRACTING FRACTIONS

Fractions may be combined by addition or subtraction only when they have the same denominator. To add or subtract fractions, find the L.C.D. and rewrite the fractions in terms of this common denominator, just as if you were comparing the fractions. Then add or subtract the fractions normally.

Adding or subtracting fractions once their denominators are the same is simple. Just add or subtract the numerators, leaving the denominator the same. For example, $\frac{4}{9} + \frac{3}{9} = \frac{7}{9}$ and $\frac{15}{14} - \frac{2}{14} = \frac{13}{14}$.

To add or subtract fractions, rewrite the fractions using the L.C.D. Then add or subtract their numerators, leaving the denominator the same.

MULTIPLYING FRACTIONS

The product of two fractions is obtained by multiplying the numerators together to find the numerator of the product, and multiplying the denominators together to find the denominator of the product. For example, $\frac{2}{3} \times \frac{4}{5} = \frac{2 \times 4}{3 \times 5} = \frac{8}{15}$.

To multiply two fractions, multiply the numerators by each other and multiply the denominators by each other.

DIVIDING FRACTIONS

The quotient of two fractions is obtained by flipping the second fraction (the divisor) and multiplying the fractions together. The expression $\frac{4}{3} \div \frac{2}{5}$, for example, can also be written as $\frac{4}{3} \times \frac{5}{2}$. Do the multiplication normally to find the answer: $\frac{4}{3} \times \frac{5}{2} = \frac{4 \times 5}{3 \times 2} = \frac{20}{6}$. Once a fraction has been flipped it is referred to as the *reciprocal* of the original fraction. So $\frac{3}{4}$ is the reciprocal of $\frac{4}{3}$.

To divide by a fraction, multiply by the fraction's reciprocal.

Example

$$\dfrac{\frac{7}{10}}{\frac{2}{3}} = \frac{7}{10} \div \frac{2}{3} = \frac{7}{10} \times \frac{3}{2} = \frac{21}{20} \qquad \frac{15}{2} \div \frac{3}{4} = \frac{15}{2} \times \frac{4}{3} = \frac{60}{6} = 10$$

EXERCISES

Reduce the following fractions completely.

1. $\dfrac{18}{10}$

2. $\dfrac{33}{121}$

3. $\dfrac{300}{48}$

4. $\dfrac{12}{90}$

5. Express the fraction $\dfrac{3}{8}$ as a decimal number.

6. Express the number 1.48 as a fraction in simplest form.

Complete the following equations.

7. $\dfrac{3}{8} + \dfrac{4}{5} =$

8. $\dfrac{1}{4} \times \dfrac{5}{6} =$

9. $\dfrac{x}{4} - \dfrac{x}{7} =$

10. $\dfrac{5}{12} \div \dfrac{1}{3} =$

11. $\left(\dfrac{1}{4}\right)^3 =$

12. $\dfrac{\frac{3}{5}}{\frac{7}{8}} =$

2.7 EXPONENTS

Exponents, as we've seen, represent repeated multiplication. The expression 4^3, in which 4 is called the *base* and 3 is the *exponent*, represents the multiplication $4 \cdot 4 \cdot 4$ —three fours multiplied together. The term 4^3, containing a base and an exponent, is called a *power*. Performing operations on powers is a little different from ordinary arithmetic, but it's not difficult. Just learn the following simple laws.

POWERS OF SIGNED NUMBERS

Exponents indicate multiplication, so naturally the rules for the multiplication of signed numbers apply to exponents. A positive times a positive is a positive; a negative times a negative is a positive; and a negative times a positive is a negative. You can see the effects of these mathematical facts in the powers of a negative number:

$(-2)^1 = -2$

$(-2)^2 = -2 \cdot -2 = 4$

$(-2)^3 = -2 \cdot -2 \cdot -2 = -8$

$(-2)^4 = -2 \cdot -2 \cdot -2 \cdot -2 = 16$

$(-2)^5 = -2 \cdot -2 \cdot -2 \cdot -2 \cdot -2 = -32$

$(-2)^6 = -2 \cdot -2 \cdot -2 \cdot -2 \cdot -2 \cdot -2 = 64$

When an odd number of negative factors are multiplied together, the product is negative. When an even number of factors are multiplied together, the product is positive. These rules apply only to powers of negative bases. All powers of a positive base are also positive.

Any number raised to an even power has a positive value. Any number raised to an odd power keeps the sign of its base.

Multiplying and Dividing Powers

In multiplying powers of the same base, the product is obtained by multiplying the exponents together and leaving the base the same. The reason for this is clearly seen by writing the powers as a series of factors multiplied together:

$$3^3 \cdot 3^4 = (3 \cdot 3 \cdot 3)(3 \cdot 3 \cdot 3 \cdot 3)$$
$$= 3 \cdot 3 \cdot 3 \cdot 3 \cdot 3 \cdot 3 \cdot 3$$
$$= 3^7$$

The product of three to the third power and three to the fourth power is three to the seventh power: 3 + 4 = 7.

> To multiply two powers of the same base, add the exponents and leave the base unchanged.

The same process works in reverse when dividing powers of the same base. The quotient is obtained by subtracting the exponents and leaving the base the same. Once again, writing out the repeated multiplication represented by the exponents makes this clearer:

$$\frac{5^6}{5^2} = \frac{5 \cdot 5 \cdot 5 \cdot 5 \cdot 5 \cdot 5}{5 \cdot 5}$$

Cancel out the factors common to the numerator and denominator to simplify the fraction.

$$= \frac{5 \cdot 5 \cdot 5 \cdot 5 \cdot \cancel{5} \cdot \cancel{5}}{\cancel{5} \cdot \cancel{5}}$$
$$= 5 \cdot 5 \cdot 5 \cdot 5$$
$$= 5^4$$

The value of five to the sixth power divided by five squared is five to the fourth power: 6 − 2 = 4.

> To divide powers of the same base, subtract the exponents and leave the base unchanged.

ZERO EXPONENT

Consider the fraction $\frac{2^4}{2^4}$. Its numerator and denominator are equal, which means that the fraction equals 1 (just as $\frac{5}{5} = 1$ and $\frac{1}{1} = 1$). The fraction $\frac{2^4}{2^4}$ can also be evaluated, however, by subtracting exponents to divide powers: $\frac{2^4}{2^4} = 2^{4-4} = 2^0$. This fraction cannot have two different numerical values. The implication is that $2^0 = 1$, and this is in fact the case.

> Any nonzero number raised to the zero power equals 1.

NEGATIVE EXPONENTS

Consider the fraction $\dfrac{3^2}{3^5}$. Evaluated according to the rule for the quotient of two powers, it should be equal to 3^{2-5}, or 3^{-3}. What does this negative exponent mean? Writing out the exponents makes things clearer.

$$\frac{3^2}{3^5} = \frac{3 \cdot 3}{3 \cdot 3 \cdot 3 \cdot 3 \cdot 3}$$

$$= \frac{\cancel{3} \cdot \cancel{3}}{3 \cdot 3 \cdot 3 \cdot \cancel{3} \cdot \cancel{3}}$$

$$= \frac{1}{3 \cdot 3 \cdot 3}$$

$$= \frac{1}{3^3}$$

The expression 3^{-3} equals $\dfrac{1}{3^3}$. This illustrates a general rule.

A number raised to a negative exponent is equal to its reciprocal raised to the opposite (positive) exponent.

If and , then if $n \neq 0$ and $x > 0$, then $n - x = \dfrac{1}{n^x}$

SCIENTIFIC NOTATION

In scientific notation, a number is expressed as a value between 1 and 10 multiplied by a power of 10. The number 3,000, for example, is expressed in scientific notation as 3.0×10^3. The number 0.016 is expressed as 1.6×10^{-2}.

Here's how to convert an ordinary decimal number into scientific notation:

1. Move the decimal point until there is only one digit (a nonzero digit) to the left of the decimal point.

2. Count the number of places the decimal point must be moved to return the number to its original value. If the decimal point must move to the right, make this number positive. If the decimal point must move to the left, make this number negative. This number is the power of 10 by which the number must be multiplied.

For example, to convert the number 0.0034 into scientific notation, you would first move the decimal point until the number was between 1 and 10, producing the number 3.4. Next, you would note that the decimal must move three places to the left to turn 3.4 back into 0.0034. That means that the power of ten you should use is 10^{-3}.

The number 0.0034 in scientific notation is 3.4×10^{-3}.

EXERCISES

Evaluate the following expressions.

1. 8^0

2. $(-5)^3$

3. 3^{-4}

4. 2^{-3}

Rewrite each of the following expressions using a single exponent.

5. $\dfrac{x^3}{x^6} =$

6. $n^2\left(n^5\right) =$

7. $\left(a^4\right)^5 =$

8. $\left(m^2\right)^{-3} =$

Express the following numbers in scientific notation.

9. 3,400

10. 0.0019

11. 531,000

12. 1.68

2.8 MATHEMATICAL PROPERTIES

INVERSES

The *additive inverse* of a number is its opposite. Any number plus its additive inverse equals zero. The additive inverse of 3 is –3. The additive inverse of –12 is 12, and so on.

The *multiplicative inverse* of a number is its reciprocal. Any number times its multiplicative inverse equals 1. The multiplicative inverse of 5 is $\dfrac{1}{5}$. The multiplicative inverse of $\dfrac{2}{3}$ is $\dfrac{3}{2}$, and so on.

COMMUTATIVE PROPERTIES

The commutative law holds only for the operations of addition and multiplication. Basically, it states that when performing an operation on two numbers, it doesn't matter what order the numbers are in. You get the same answer either way. The commutative law does *not* hold for subtraction or division.

---

*The Commutative Laws for Addition
and Multiplication*

For any rational numbers a and b,
$$a + b = b + a \quad \text{and} \quad a \cdot b = b \cdot a$$

ASSOCIATIVE PROPERTIES

The associative law also holds only for addition and multiplication. It states that when adding or multiplying three or more numbers, it doesn't matter how the numbers are grouped; you'll get the same answer either way. The associative property does *not* hold for subtraction or division.

---

*The Associative Laws for Addition
and Multiplication*

For any rational numbers a, b, and c,
$$a + (b + c) = (a + b) + c \quad \text{and} \quad a(bc) = (ab)c$$

DISTRIBUTIVE PROPERTIES

The *distributive property* applies to the specific situation in which an expression of several terms combined by addition or subtraction is multiplied by another factor. It states that you can add the numbers up and then multiply the sum by the outside factor, or multiply each term by the outside factor, and then add them up. You get the same number either way.

The Distributive Property

For any rational numbers a, b, and c,
$$a(b + c) = ab + ac \quad \text{and} \quad (b + c)a = ba + ca$$

EXERCISES

State the additive inverse of each number.

1. 14

2. −1

State the multiplicative inverse of each number.

3. 32

4. −2

State the value represented by the box in each equation.

5. $a + b = b + \square$

6. $\square(yz) = (xy)z$

7. $r + (s + 5) = (r + \square) + 5$

8. $8x = x\square$

Identify the property illustrated in each of the following statements.

9. $(m)(n) = (n)(m)$

10. $xz + yz = z(x + y)$

11. $f(gh) = (fg)h$

12. $n + (o + p) = (n + o) + p$

SUMMARY

The Order of Operations (PEMDAS)

- Parentheses
- Exponents
- Multiplication and Division (left to right)
- Addition and Subtraction (left to right)
- {Counting Numbers} = 1, 2, 3, ...} (positive integers)
  {Whole Numbers} = {0, 1, 2, 3, ...} (non-negative integers)
  {Integers} = {..., −3, −2, −1, 0, 1, 2, 3, ...}
  {Rational Numbers} = {Numbers that can be expressed as the quotient of two integers}
  {Irrational Numbers} = {Numbers that cannot be expressed as the quotient of two integers}
  {Real Numbers} = {All rational numbers and all irrational numbers}

- The absolute value of a number is the distance between the number and zero on the number line.

- The product of two numbers with the same sign is positive. The product of two numbers with different signs is negative.

- To add or subtract fractions, rewrite the fractions using the L.C.D. Then add or subtract their numerators, leaving the denominator the same.

  To multiply two fractions, multiply the numerators and multiply the denominators.

  To divide by a fraction, multiply by the fraction's reciprocal.

- To multiply two powers of the same base, add the exponents and leave the base unchanged.

  To divide powers of the same base, subtract the exponents and leave the base unchanged.

  Any nonzero number raised to the zero power equals 1.

  A number raised to a negative exponent is equal to its reciprocal raised to the opposite (positive) exponent.

  If $n \neq 0$ and $x > 0$, then

$$n^{-x} = \frac{1}{n^x}$$

- **The Commutative Laws for Addition and Multiplication**
  For any rational numbers a and b,
  $a + b = b + a$ and $a \cdot b = b \cdot a$

- **The Associative Laws for Addition and Multiplication**
  For any rational numbers a, b, and c,
  $a + (b + c) = (a + b) + c$ and $a(bc) = (ab)c$

- **The Distributive Property**
  For any rational numbers a, b, and c,
  $a(b + c) = ab + ac$ and $(b + c)a = ba + ca$

3

Algebra Basics

Algebra is used to solve problems that are mathematical in nature. This chapter will show you how to write equations to describe real-world situations, and how to solve these equations to find solutions.

3.1 TRANSLATING ENGLISH INTO ALGEBRA

When mathematical relationships are described in English, certain words and phrases indicate certain mathematical operations. Here are some commonly encountered terms:

Terms indicating addition: *sum, plus, more than, increased by, exceeded by*

Terms indicating subtraction: *difference, less than, decreased by, taken from, diminished by*

Terms indicating multiplication: *product, twice, times*

Terms indicating division: *quotient, divided by*

Also important in writing equations based on English sentences is the indicator of equality, which separates the two equivalent sides of an equation. Equality is also represented by a few telltale words and phrases:

Terms indicating equality: *is, equals, is equal to, the result is*

Using terms like these as your guide, you can translate English sentences into algebra.

Examples

Let n represent the number of dollars Kara has saved. Suppose that Kara's sister, Janey, has saved an amount of money that is described in terms of Kara's savings. Here are some written descriptions of Janey's savings and the corresponding algebraic expressions in terms of n:

JANEY HAS...	JANEY'S SAVINGS
Seven more dollars than Kara has.	$n + 7$
Three times Kara's savings.	$3n$
Kara's savings decreased by 5 dollars.	$n - 5$
Eight more than twice Kara's savings.	$2n + 8$

Let x represent the smaller of two positive integers. Suppose that the larger integer is described in terms of *the smaller integer*. Here are some written descriptions of the second integer and the corresponding algebraic expressions in terms of x:

THE LARGER INTEGER IS...	THE LARGER INTEGER
Five times the smaller integer.	$5x$
Five more than half the smaller integer.	$\frac{1}{2}x + 5$
Twice the sum of the smaller integer and 6.	$2(x + 6)$
Three less than twice the smaller integer.	$2x - 3$

When one quantity is defined in terms of another, you can represent both quantities in terms of one variable. This can make it easy to write an equation that describes a relationship between the two quantities.

Suppose, for example, you are told that the larger of two numbers is five less than twice the smaller integer. Letting x represent the smaller integer, you can express the larger integer as $2x - 5$. Once you have expressed both numbers in terms of one variable, you can easily write an equation to describe any relationship between the two numbers:

The sum of the two numbers is twenty-seven.

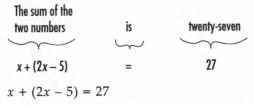

$x + (2x - 5) = 27$

The product of the larger number and the smaller number is twelve.

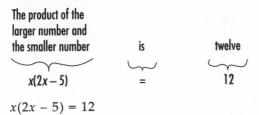

$x(2x - 5) = 12$

Once you've written an equation in terms of a single variable, you're ready to solve the problem. Techniques for solving equations will be reviewed in the following pages.

EXERCISES

Rewrite each of the following as an algebraic expression.

1. five more than x

2. twelve less than z

3. the product of 6 and b

4. n divided by eight

5. twenty more than half of y

6. twice the sum of m and 1

7. two more than the product of a and seven

8. three less than five times c

State the answer to each of the following questions in algebraic terms.

9. What is the number of cents in d dollars?

10. How many days are there in $n + 1$ weeks?

11. Jared is g years old. How old was he seven years ago?

12. Salma has n cookies. If she eats twelve of them, how many are left?

13. Melanie weighs p pounds, and Harold weighs twice as much as Melanie. How much does Harold weigh?

14. A candle is 12 inches tall when it is lit. While it is lit, its height decreases 1.5 inches each hour. What is its height x hours after it is lit?

15. Today, Snooks has $450.00 in savings. If he saves an additional $20.00 each week, how much will he have t weeks from today, in dollars?

16. Barvis spent $23.00 for dinner and a movie. If the movie cost m dollars, how much did dinner cost, in dollars?

3.2 SOLVING EQUATIONS BY ADDITION

The *solution set* of an equation is the set of all replacements for the variable that make the equation true. Each of these replacement values is called a *solution*, or *root*, of the equation.

Equations that have the same solution set are called *equivalent equations*. For example, the equations $x = 3$ and $2x = 6$ are equivalent, because they have the same solution set. The solution set of each equation is {3}.

Sometimes, changing an equation into another, equivalent equation can help you find the equation's solution. One of the most basic ways to change an equation into an equivalent equation is to add some number (positive or negative) to both sides of the equation. Both sides of the equation will change, but the equation will remain true, and its solution set will not change.

Adding the same number to both sides of an equation produces a new equation that is equivalent to the original.

Equations involving addition and subtraction may be solved using this rule. To solve an equation, try to *isolate* the variable—that is, to get the variable alone on one side of the equation. When the variable is isolated, the equation will state its value. In the equation

a = 5, for example, the variable a has been isolated, and its value is obvious: The value of a is 5. To isolate a variable, undo whatever is being done to it.

Example

Solve: $x - 7 = 5$

To isolate the variable, undo what is being done to it. In this case, 7 is being subtracted from the variable, so you should add 7 to both sides of the equation.

$$
\begin{array}{rl}
x - 7 = & 5 \\
+7 & +7 \\
\hline
x \quad = & 12
\end{array}
$$

You're left with the equation $x = 12$, which gives you the equation's solution. To check this solution, replace x in the original equation with the value $x = 12$. If the original equation proves true, your solution is correct.

$x - 7 = 5$

$12 - 7 = 5$

$5 = 5$

The solution is 12.

The same technique may be applied in reverse when a number is being added to a variable. In that case, simply subtract that number—or, in other words, add its opposite.

Example

Solve: $9 = n + 6$

To isolate the variable n in this case, you must subtract 6 from both sides. This can also be thought of as adding –6 to both sides.

$$
\begin{array}{rl}
9 = & n + 6 \\
-6 & -6 \\
\hline
3 = & n
\end{array}
$$

Once again, check the solution by replacing n in the original equation with 3.

$9 = n + 6$

$9 = 3 + 6$

$9 = 9$

The solution is 3.

Practice solving simple equations by addition and subtraction.

EXERCISES

In each of the following exercises, determine whether the pair of equations is equivalent.

1. $x + 3 = 5$ and $x = 2$
2. $n - g10$
   $5 = 5$ and $n = 0$
3. $t + 4 = 3$ and $t = -7$
4. $2 - p = -4$ and $p = 6$

Solve each equation. Check your answer.

5. $x + 8 = 13$
6. $b + (-5) = 8$
7. $c + 11 = -5$
8. $y - 13 = -6$
9. $n + 242 = -356$
10. $p - (-4) = 3$
11. $t + 12 = -7$
12. $\dfrac{1}{3} + h = \dfrac{4}{3}$

3.3 SOLVING EQUATIONS BY MULTIPLICATION

Another way of converting an equation into another, equivalent equation is by multiplying both sides of the equation by some non-zero number. Once again, both sides of the equation will change, but the equation will remain true, and its solution set will not change.

Notice that, by implication, dividing both sides of an equation by the same number will also produce an equivalent equation. For example, multiplying both sides of an equation by $\dfrac{1}{4}$ is the same things as dividing both sides of the equation by 4. Likewise, multiplying both sides of the equation by 4 is the same as dividing both sides by $\dfrac{1}{4}$. Multiplication and division are closely related operations, and both may be used to isolate variables in equations containing multiplication or fractions.

> *Multiplying or dividing both sides of an equation by the same nonzero number will produce an equation that is equivalent to the original.*

This rule may be used to isolate variables in equations containing multiplication or fractions. Once again, your goal is to isolate a variable by undoing the operations that are being done to it. For example, to isolate s in the equation $4s = 12$, in which s is multiplied by 4, you would *divide* each side by 4, or multiply by $\frac{1}{4}$.

Example

Solve: $5x = 30$

In this equation, x is multiplied by 5. To isolate x, divide by 5 or multiply by $\frac{1}{5}$.

$$5x = 30$$

$$\frac{5x}{5} = \frac{30}{5}$$

$$\frac{\cancel{5}x}{\cancel{5}} = \frac{30}{5}$$

$$x = 6$$

$$5x = 30$$

$$\frac{1}{5} \cdot 5x = \frac{1}{5} \cdot 30$$

$$1x = \frac{30}{5}$$

$$x = 6$$

Check:

$$5x = 30$$

$$5(6) = 30$$

$$30 = 30$$

The solution is 6.

This technique of isolating the variable can be used just as well when the variable is being *divided* by some number. In that case, simply multiply both sides of the equation by that number, to produce an equivalent equation in which the variable is alone.

Examples

Solve: $\dfrac{x}{8} = -3$

In this equation, x is divided by 8. Multiply both sides of the equation by 8 to isolate the variable.

$\dfrac{x}{8} = -3$

$8\left(\dfrac{x}{8}\right) = 8(-3)$

$1x = -24$

$x = -24$

Check:

$\dfrac{x}{8} = -3$

$\dfrac{-24}{8} = -3$

$-3 = -3$

The solution is -24.

Solve: $\dfrac{3}{4}n = 12$

In this equation, n is multiplied by $\dfrac{3}{4}$. To isolate n, multiply both sides of the equation by the multiplicative inverse of $\dfrac{3}{4}$, which is $\dfrac{4}{3}$.

$\dfrac{3}{4}n = 12$

$\dfrac{4}{3}\left(\dfrac{3}{4}n\right) = \dfrac{4}{3}(12)$

$n = \dfrac{48}{3}$

$n = 16$

Check:

$\dfrac{3}{4}n = 12$

$\dfrac{3}{4}(16) = 12$

$12 = 12$

The solution is 16.

Practice using these techniques to solve equations.

Solve each of the following equations.

1. $7v = 14$

2. $6b = 54$

3. $12n = 0$

4. $9x = -72$

5. $-34a = 2$

6. $8g = 104$

7. $\frac{1}{5}t = 7$

8. $-3l = 0.6$

9. $\frac{2f}{5} = 14$

10. $-r = -15$

11. $-\frac{3}{4} = \frac{2d}{3}$

12. $0.48 = 0.06n$

3.4 EQUATIONS WITH MULTIPLE OPERATIONS

An equation containing a single operation is solved by undoing the operation–that is, by performing the opposite operation to isolate the variable. Equations that contain more than one operation are solved the same way.

Remember the order of operations. To isolate the variable in an equation with multiple operations, undo the operations in reverse order. Begin by undoing addition and subtraction, and then undo multiplication and division. Take a look at this example:

Example

Solve: $4b + 7 = 15$

Begin by subtracting 7 from both sides of the equation to undo the addition:

$$
\begin{array}{r}
4b + 7 = 15 \\
-7 \quad -7 \\
\hline
4b \quad\ \ = 8
\end{array}
$$

Next, divide both sides by 4 to undo the multiplication.

$$\frac{4b}{4} = \frac{8}{4}$$

$1b = 2$

$b = 2$

Check:

$4b + 7 = 15$

$4(2) + 7 = 15$

$8 + 7 = 15$

$15 = 15$

The solution is 2.

If an equation contains parentheses, remove the parentheses first. Likewise, if a fraction contains an operation in its numerator or denominator, remove the fraction before attempting other inverse operations. Take a look at these examples:

Examples

Solve: $3(n - 3) = 6$

First, remove the parentheses by distributing the 3.

$3(n - 3) = 6$

$3n - 9 = 6$

Next, add 9 to both sides.

$$\begin{array}{r} 3n - 9 = 6 \\ +9 \ +9 \\ \hline 3n \ \ = 15 \end{array}$$

Finally, divide both sides by 3 to isolate the variable.

$$\frac{3n}{3} = \frac{15}{3}$$

$n = 5$

Check:

$3(n - 3) = 6$

$3(5 - 3) = 6$

$3(2) = 6$

$6 = 6$

The solution is 5.

Solve: $\dfrac{2x+7}{3} = 1$

Begin by multiplying both sides by 3 to remove the fraction.

$$\frac{2x+7}{3} = 1$$

$$3\left(\frac{2x+7}{3}\right) = 3(1)$$

$2x + 7 = 3$

Next, undo the addition by subtracting 7 from both sides.

$$2x + 7 = 3$$
$$\underline{-7 -7}$$
$$2x = -4$$

Finally, divide both sides by 2 to undo the multiplication.

$$\frac{2x}{4} = \frac{-4}{2}$$

$x = -2$

Check:

$$\frac{2x+7}{3} = 1$$

$$\frac{2(-2)+7}{3} = 1$$

$$\frac{-4+7}{3} = 1$$

$$\frac{3}{3} = 1$$

$1 = 1$

The solution is –2.

Using these techniques will help you solve equations with multiple operations with a minimum of fuss.

To Solve Equations with Multiple Operations:

- *Undo the operations one at a time, beginning with addition and subtraction and ending with multiplication and division.*
- *If operations are contained within fractions or parentheses, remove the fraction or parentheses first.*

EXERCISES

Solve each equation and check your answer.

1. $3x - 4 = 11$

2. $5 - 2a = 17$

3. $7y + 28 = 0$

4. $16 - 5b = 1$

5. $\frac{1}{4}t - 7 = -6$

6. $23 - \frac{1}{6}n = 16$

7. $\frac{5}{4}x - 30 = 0$

8. $\frac{2}{3}s + 100 = 78$

9. $3(k - 7) = 24$

10. $6\left(\frac{1}{3}m + 5\right) = 37$

11. $\frac{h + 6}{9} = -3$

12. $\frac{6j - 13}{4} = -3$

3.5 WORD PROBLEMS

Consider this problem:

Lance has 24 Humongous Guy comic books. So far, he has read 17 of the books. How many of the books does he have left to read?

To solve word problems like this one, follow a four-step plan to express the problem algebraically, solve, and check.

To Solve a Word Problem:

1. Figure out what piece of information you must find. Use a variable to represent this information.
2. Write an equation using this variable.
3. Solve the equation.
4. Check your solution.

Let's take a look at how these four steps would apply to our word problem.

Example

Lance has 24 Humongous Guy comic books. So far, he has read 17 of the books. How many of the books does he have left to read?

STEP	WHAT YOU DO
1. Assign a variable.	You must find out how many books Lance has not read. Let x = books Lance has not read.
2. Write an equation.	books read plus books not read equals total books read plus books not read equals total 17 + x = 24 $17 + x = 24$
3. Solve the equation.	$17 + x = 24$ $-17 \quad -17$ $x = 7$
4. Check your answer.	Check the solution, $x = 7$, in the statement of the original problem: Since Lance has read 17 out of 24 books, he should have 7 left to read. The answer is correct.
Lance has 7 Humongous Guy comic books left to read.	

This four-step plan will guide you through any simple word problem. Practice writing equations and solving them in the following exercises.

EXERCISES

For each of the following, define a variable and write the equation you would use to solve the problem.

1. In seven years, Pooky will be 22 years old. How old is Pooky now?

2. A toy costs $3.50. How many toys can be purchased for $42.00?

3. The product of a number and 6 is −78. What is the number?

4. A number decreased by 32 is −12. Find the number.

Solve each of the following problems. Define a variable, write and solve an equation, and clearly state the solution.

5. Kaiser wants to buy a bike that costs $120.00. He has $86.00. How much money must Kaiser earn before he can buy the bike?

6. Lana rides the Ferris wheel five times, which costs her a total of $12.50. What is the cost in dollars of one ride on the Ferris wheel?

7. If Jamal were three years younger, he would be 16. How old is Jamal?

8. Benson bought a stereo for ten dollars more than half its original price. If Benson paid $46.00 , what was the stereo's original price?

9. Lucy has $360.00, and saves an additional $20.00 each week. How much money will she have after 8 weeks?

10. A candle is ten inches tall when it is lit. The candle's height decreases by 1.5 inches every hour as it burns. In how many hours will the candle be 2.5 inches tall?

11. Jeff is two years older than Ellen, and Tyler is twice as old as Ellen. If the sum of their three ages is 26, how old is Ellen?

12. One side of a triangle is two inches more than half as long as the longest side. The third side is 4 inches shorter than the longest side. If the perimeter of the triangle is 33 inches, how long is the longest side of the triangle?

3.6 CONSECUTIVE INTEGERS

The key to solving many algebra problems easily is expressing more than one quantity in terms of a single variable. For example, if Deborah is eight years younger than Kelly, their ages can be expressed as d and $d + 8$, respectively. This makes it possible to describe the relationship between their ages in an equation with a single variable. This is very important, because an equation with more than one variable cannot be solved by itself.

Algebra problems concerning *consecutive numbers* present a unique challenge. Consecutive numbers are numbers in a sequence presented in ascending order, without skipping any. For example:

Consecutive integers:	{..., –3, –2, –1, 0, 1, 2, 3, ...}
Consecutive odd integers:	{..., –5, –3, –1, 1, 3, 5, ...}
Consecutive even integers:	{..., –4, –2, 0, 2, 4, ...}
Consecutive multiples of 5:	{5, 10, 15, 20, 25, ...}

The important quality of consecutive numbers is that they are separated by constant intervals. In the lists above, you can see that *consecutive integers* are separated by 1. *Consecutive odd integers* and *consecutive even integers* are separated by 2. And *consecutive multiples of 5*, naturally, are separated by intervals of 5.

Consecutive numbers are separated by 1 unit. Consecutive elements in a series are separated by equal intervals.

The meaning of this is that consecutive numbers can easily be represented in terms of a single variable. Three consecutive integers, for example, may be represented as x, $x + 1$, and $x + 2$. Four consecutive even integers may be represented as n, $n + 2$, $n + 4$, and $n + 6$.

Example

The sum of three consecutive even integers is 60. List the integers.

Let x = the smallest integer.

Then $x + 2$ = the next integer

and $x + 4$ = the biggest integer.

The sum of the three integers is 60, so you can write an equation:

$x + (x + 2) + (x + 4) = 60$

Simplify the equation by combining like terms.

$x + x + 2 + x + 4 = 60$

$3x + 6 = 60$

Subtract 6 from both sides of the equation.

$$\begin{aligned} 3x + 6 &= 60 \\ -6 \quad &-6 \\ \hline 3x \quad &= 54 \end{aligned}$$

Divide both sides by 3 to find the value of x.

$$\frac{3x}{3} = \frac{54}{3}$$

$x = 18$

The three integers, represented by x, $x + 2$, and $x + 4$, are 18, 20, and 22.

Practice solving problems algebraically be representing consecutive numbers in terms of a single variable.

EXERCISES

For each problem, define a variable and write the equation that you would use to solve the problem. Do not solve.

1. The sum of two consecutive integers is 17. List the integers.

2. The sum of two consecutive odd integers is 140. List the integers.

3. The sum of three consecutive integers is –24. List the integers.

4. Three consecutive multiples of six add up to 54. List the numbers.

Solve each problem. Define a variable, write and solve an equation, and state the solution clearly.

5. If two consecutive integers add up to 31, what is the smaller integer?

6. The sum of three consecutive even integers is 48. List the integers.

7. The sum of two consecutive multiples of 3 is –51. List the numbers.

8. If three consecutive integers add up to 132, what is the largest of the three integers?

3.7 VARIABLES ON BOTH SIDES

Sometimes variables occur on both sides of an equation. To solve equations of this kind, eliminate the variable term on one side of the equation by addition or subtraction. Remember that each operation you perform must be performed on both sides of the equation.

Example

Solve: $6n + 5 = 3n - 7$

Begin by eliminating the $3n$ term on the right of the equal sign by subtracting $3n$ from both sides of the equation.

$$6n + 5 = 3n - 7$$
$$\underline{-3n \qquad - 3n}$$
$$3n + 5 = \quad -7$$

Next, subtract 5 from both sides of the equation to undo the addition.

$$3n + 5 = -7$$
$$\underline{-5 \quad -5}$$
$$3n \quad = -12$$

Finally, divide both sides by 3 to find the value of n.

$$n = -4$$

Some equations of this type have no solution. The solution set of such equations are said to be the empty set or the null set, represented by the symbol $\varnothing$.

Example

Solve: $6x - 4 = 3(2x - 1)$

Distribute through the parentheses on the right side of the equation.

$6x - 4 = 6x - 3$

Subtract $6x$ from both sides of the equation.

$$6x - 4 = 6x - 3$$
$$\underline{-6x \quad\quad - 6x}$$
$$-4 = \quad -3$$

The resulting equation is $-4 = -3$, which is not true. No replacement value of x will ever make this equation true. The solution set of this equation is the empty set.

Other equations of this type are true for every replacement value of the variable. Such an equation is called an *identity*. The solution set of an identity is all real numbers.

Example

Solve: $4(x + 3) = 2(2x + 6)$

Distribute through the parentheses on each side of the equation.

$4(x + 3) = 2(2x + 6)$

$4x + 12 = 4x + 12$

Subtract $4x$ from both sides of the equation.

$$4x + 12 = 4x + 12$$
$$\underline{-4x \quad\quad - 4x}$$
$$12 = \quad 12$$

You're left with the equation $12 = 12$, which is always true.

Every real replacement value of x will make the equation true. The equation is an identity, and its solution set is the entire set of real numbers.

Practice solving equations with variables on both sides of the equal sign in the following exercises.

EXERCISES

Solve each equation and check your answer.

1. $23d = 14d - 9$

2. $2x = 6 + 3x$

3. $y + 5 = 3y - 7$

4. $6 - 7x = 17 + 4x$

5. $\dfrac{1}{2}n = \dfrac{3}{2}n + 14$

6. $3(h - 5) + 1 = h$

7. $4(x + 2) = 2(2x + 3) + 2$

8. $5x = 4(x + 1) + x$

Solve each problem. Define a variable, write and solve an equation, and state the solution clearly.

9. The difference of two numbers is 7. Their sum is 25. What are the numbers?

10. Janet's age two years ago was half of her age five years from now. How old is Janet now?

11. Three times the sum of two consecutive integers is equal to the smaller integer decreased by 17. What are the integers?

12. A collection of 16 coins consists entirely of pennies and nickels. If the value of the collection is $0.44, how many pennies are in the collection?

SUMMARY

- Terms indicating addition: *sum, plus, more than, increased by, exceeded by*

  Terms indicating subtraction: *difference, less than, decreased by, taken from, diminished by*

  Terms indicating multiplication: *product, twice, times*

  Terms indicating division: *quotient, divided by*

  Terms indicating equality: *is, equals, is equal to, the result is*

- Adding the same number to both sides of an equation produces a new equation that is equivalent to the original.

- Multiplying or dividing both sides of an equation by the same nonzero number will produce an equation that is equivalent to the original.

- **To Solve a Word Problem:**
  1. Figure out what piece of information you must find. Use a variable to represent this information.
  2. Write an equation using this variable.
  3. Solve the equation.
  4. Check your solution.

- **To Solve Equations with Multiple Operations:**

  Undo the operations one at a time, beginning with addition and subtraction and ending with multiplication and division.

  If operations are contained within fractions or parentheses, remove the fraction or parentheses first.

- Consecutive numbers are separated by fixed intervals.

- The solution set of an equation that has no solution is said to be the empty set or the null set ($\varnothing$).

- An equation that is true for every replacement value is called an identity, and its solution set is the set of real numbers.

4

Formulas
and Inequalities

A formula expresses a relationship between two or more quantities. They are commonly used in geometry, as you will see later in this book. For example, the area (A) of a rectangle is related to the rectangle's length (l) and width (w) by the formula $A = lw$. Formulas are used to describe many other relationships in geometry and elsewhere.

4.1 FORMULAS

A formula uses different variables to represent distinct quantities. For example, for any object moving along a straight line at a constant speed, the distance traveled by the object after a given time is given by the formula $d = rt$, where d is the distance traveled, r is the rate at which the object is moving, and t is the time spent traveling.

Example

If a car travels for 4 hours at 35 miles per hour, how far does it travel?

$d = rt$

Replace r and t with the values given in the question.

$d = (35)(4)$

$d = 140$

The car travels 140 miles.

How long does it take a cyclist to pedal 6 miles at 12 miles per hour?

$d = rt$

Replace d and r with the values given in the question.

$6 = 12t$

$$\frac{6}{12} = \frac{12t}{12}$$

$$\frac{1}{2} = t$$

It takes the cyclist half an hour.

It's possible to determine the value of any quantity in the formula, as long as you know the values of the other quantities.

Practice using algebra to work with formulas in the following exercises.

EXERCISES

The formula for the area of a triangle is $A = \frac{1}{2}bh$ *where* b *is the base of the triangle and* h *is its height. Use this formula to answer the following questions.*

1. How does the triangle's area change when its base is doubled and its height remains the same?

2. How does the triangle's area change when its base and height are both doubled?

3. How does the triangle's area change when its base is doubled and its height is halved?

4. How does the triangle's area change when its base and height are both halved?

Solve each of the following problems.

5. If $n = 2r + s$, find n when $r = 14$ and $s = 31$.

6. If $a = \pi r^2$, find a when $\pi = 3.14$ and $r = 4$.

7. If $V = lwh$, find V when $l = 8$, $w = 5$, and $h = 6$.

8. If $x = \frac{1}{2}at^2$, find x when $a = -9.8$ and $t = 3$.

Write a formula that could be used to solve each of the following problems. Do not solve.

9. What is the total weight in pounds W of x objects weighing 7 pounds each?

10. What is the cost C in dollars of p slices of pizza and s sodas if a slice of pizza costs \$2.25 and a soda costs \$1.50?

11. A taxi ride costs g dollars for the first mile and h dollars for every additional mile. What is the cost C in dollars of a 5–mile taxi ride?

12. What is the average A of four scores a, b, c, and d?

4.2 SOLVING FOR SPECIFIC VARIABLES

Formulas can be rearranged, using the algebraic techniques you've learned, to produce equivalent statements. This can make your math easier. For example, the formula that relates Fahrenheit temperature to Celsius temperature is $F = \frac{9}{5}C + 32$, where C is the temperature in degrees Celsius, and F is the corresponding temperature in degrees Fahrenheit. This formula makes it easy to translate Celsius temperatures into Fahrenheit temperatures. To find the temperature on the Fahrenheit scale that corresponds to 35° C, you would simply replace C in the formula with the number 35, and solve:

$$F = \frac{9}{5}C + 32$$
$$F = \frac{9}{5}(35) + 32$$
$$F = 63 + 32$$
$$F = 95$$

The formula works neatly. But what if you want to convert Fahrenheit temperatures to Celsius temperatures? In that case, it would be helpful to have a formula that expresses C in terms of F. You can rearrange the formula $F = \frac{9}{5}C + 32$ to bring that about. Just isolate C.

$$F = \frac{9}{5}C + 32$$

Subtract 32 from both sides.

$$
\begin{array}{rl}
F & = \frac{9}{5}C + 32 \\
-32 & \quad -32 \\
\hline
F - 32 & = \frac{9}{5}C
\end{array}
$$

Then multiply both sides by $\frac{5}{9}$, the multiplicative inverse of $\frac{9}{5}$.

$$\frac{5}{9}(F - 32) = C$$

The resulting formula, $C = \frac{5}{9}(F - 32)$, is useful for finding Celsius temperatures when you know the Fahrenheit temperature. To produce this formula from the formula $F = \frac{9}{5}C + 32$, we *solved for C*. Solving for a specific variable can make formulas easier to use.

When a formula is solved for any one variable, the resulting formula is equivalent to the original. Rearranging a formula can make it easier to use.

EXERCISES

Solve each of the formulas below for the variable indicated.

1. $d = rt$, for t

2. $P = 2l + 2w$, for w

3. $A = \frac{1}{2}bh$, for h

4. $x \ \frac{1}{2}at^2$, for a

5. $p = mv$, for v

6. $A = \pi r^2$, for r

4.3 INEQUALITIES

Not all open sentences are equations. An *inequality* is an open sentence containing a symbol of inequality such as <, >, ≤, ≥, or ≠. Each of these symbols provides different information about the quantities in the open sentence.

Symbol	Meaning
<	is less than
>	is greater than
≤	is less than or equal to
≥	is greater than or equal to
≠	is not equal to

The definitions in the table above are the simplest explanations of the commonly used inequality signs. There are a number of ways to express inequality in English, however, and it's important to know how to represent these expressions algebraically. Here are some common English statements of inequality and their algebraic translations:

English Statement	Inequality
n is less than 5. n is lower than 5.	$n < 5$
n is less than or equal to 5. n is no greater than 5. n is at most 5. 5 is the maximum value of n. 5 is the greatest possible value of n.	$n \leq 5$
n is greater than 5. n is more than 5. n is higher than 5.	$n > 5$
n is greater than or equal to 5. n is no less than 5. n is at least 5. 5 is the minimum value of n. 5 is the least possible value of n.	$n \geq 5$
n is not equal to 5. n cannot equal 5.	$n \neq 5$

Unlike an equation, a simple inequality has a solution set that contains more than one value. The domain of an inequality is assumed to be the set of real numbers, as long as no other domain is specified. This means that there is an infinite number of replacement values that makes any simple inequality true. Take a look at the solution sets of these simple algebraic sentences:

Sentence	Solution Set
$x = 8$	{8}
$x \neq 8$	{all real numbers except 8}
$x < 8$	{all real numbers less than 8}
$x > 8$	{all real numbers greater than 8}
$x \leq 8$	{8, and all real number less than 8}
$x \geq 8$	{8, and all real numbers greater than 8}

GRAPHING INEQUALITIES

The solution set of a linear inequality can be graphed on a number line. The graph of an inequality generally takes the form of an open point or a closed point and a ray—an arrow extending forever in the positive or negative direction.

Examples

1. Graph the solution set of $g > 3$:
   The solution set of $g > 3$ contains all real numbers greater than 3.

   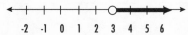

   -2 -1 0 1 2 3 4 5 6

   Notice that the point at 3 is open, because g cannot be equal to 3. The arrow extends in the positive direction to indicate all real numbers greater than 3.

2. Graph the solution set of $n \leq -5$:
   The solution set of $n \leq -5$ contains the number –5 and all real numbers less than –5.

   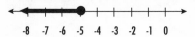

   -8 -7 -6 -5 -4 -3 -2 -1 0

   Notice that the point at –5 is closed, because n is equal

to –5. The arrow extends in the negative direction to include all real numbers less than –5.

3. Graph the solution set of $x \neq -1$:
   The solution set of $x \neq -1$ includes all real numbers except –1.

   -4 -3 -2 -1   0   1   2   3   4

Notice that the point at –1 is open, because x cannot equal –1. Two arrows extend in the positive and negative directions, to indicate all real numbers greater than –1 *or* less than –1.

Practice working with inequalities and their graphs in the following exercises.

EXERCISES

Write an inequality to match each of the following graphs.

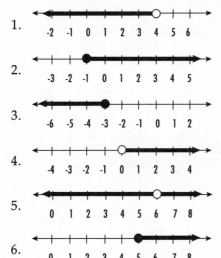

1.
   -2 -1   0   1   2   3   4   5   6

2.
   -3 -2 -1   0   1   2   3   4   5

3.
   -6 -5 -4 -3 -2 -1   0   1   2

4.
   -4 -3 -2 -1   0   1   2   3   4

5.
   0   1   2   3   4   5   6   7   8

6.
   0   1   2   3   4   5   6   7   8

For each of the following, define a variable and write the inequality that you would use to solve the problem. Do not solve.

7. Twice a number is greater than the number increased by five. State the possible values of the number.

8. Twelve more than three times a number is less than or equal to 20. State the possible values of the number.

9. The sum of two consecutive odd integers is greater than –11. State the possible values of the number.

10. Gerald's age decreased by seven is less than half Gerald's age. What is the oldest Gerald could be?

Graph the solution set of each inequality.

11. $n > -4$

12. $t < 1$

13. $a \neq -2$

14. $w \geq 5$

4.4 SOLVING INEQUALITIES

For the most part, inequalities can be solved just like equations. There's just one exception: When an inequality is multiplied or divided by a *negative number*, the inequality sign flips (from "less than" to "greater than," or *vice versa*). The addition property and multiplication property for equations can therefore be rewritten for inequalities, with a slight modification.

- *If the same number is added to (or subtracted from) both sides of an inequality, the resulting inequality will be equivalent to the original.*
- *If both sides of an inequality are multiplied or divided by the same positive number, the resulting inequality will be equivalent to the original.*
- *If both sides of an inequality are multiplied or divided by the same negative number, the resulting inequality will be equivalent to the original, provided that the sign of inequality is reversed.*

To solve an inequality, then, you can use all the tools you ordinarily use to solve equations. Just remember to flip the inequality sign if you multiply or divide by a negative.

Examples

Solve: $5 - n > 3$

Begin by subtracting 5 from both sides to get the variable alone.

$$
\begin{array}{rl}
5 - n > & 3 \\
\underline{-5 \quad\quad -5} & \\
-n > & -2
\end{array}
$$

To get rid of the negative sign on the n, multiply both sides by -1. This will require you to reverse the inequality sign.

$-1(-n) < -1(-2)$

$n < 2$

Solve: $-\dfrac{1}{5}x - 8 \le -11$

Begin by adding 8 to both sides to isolate the variable term.

$-\dfrac{1}{5}x - 8 \le -11$

$\underline{\phantom{-\dfrac{1}{5}x}\ +8\quad +8}$

$-\dfrac{1}{5}x\quad \le -3$

To isolate x, multiply both sides by –5, the multiplicative inverse of $-\dfrac{1}{5}$. This will require you to flip the inequality sign.

$-5\left(-\dfrac{1}{5}x\right) \ge -5(-3)$

$x \ge 15$

Practice solving inequalities in the following practice questions.

EXERCISES

Solve the following inequalities and graph their solution sets.

1. $n - 13 \ge 7$

2. $4x < -24$

3. $b + 3 > 4b - 12$

4. $6t - 4 \le 5t + 4$

5. $10w + 5 - 7w > -4$

6. $3(z + 4) > -12$

7. $\dfrac{3}{2}d + 2 < -1$

8. $\dfrac{1}{2}y \ge \dfrac{1}{3}y + 1$

Find the solution set for each of the following for the domain
$\{-3, -2, 0, 1, 3, 5\}$.

9. $3n + 5 \ge 2$

10. $3(t + 2) < 6$

11. $-3x + 2 \ge -1$

12. $-5x - 6 > 9$

4.5 COMPOUND INEQUALITIES

Remember the ideas of conjunction and disjunction from the study of logic? These connectives can be used to combine two inequalities into a single sentence called a *compound inequality*.

CONJUNCTIONS

We use compound inequalities in everyday conversation, when we say things like "lunch will cost between five and ten dollars." This statement is the conjunction of two inequalities: "the cost of lunch is greater than five dollars" and "the cost of lunch is less than ten dollars." Saying that a number is "between 5 and 10" is the same thing as saying that the number is "greater than 5 *and* less than 10." The word "and" indicates conjunction.

In algebraic terms, we could write the sentence this way:

Let l = the cost of lunch in dollars.

$(l > 5) \wedge (l < 10)$

This conjunction can also be written as a single open sentence:

$5 < l < 10$

To graph the solution set of a conjunction like this one, remember that the solution set of a conjunction is the set of all values that satisfy *both* statements. The solution set of $(l > 5) \wedge (l < 10)$ is the set of all value for which $5 < l$ *and* $l < 10$ are both true.

This is reflected when the solution set of a conjunction is graphed. Compare the graphs of $l > 5$ and $l < 10$ to the graph of the conjunction $(l > 5) \wedge (l < 10)$:

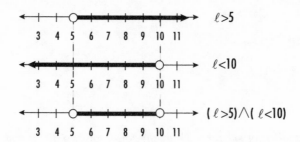

The graph of the solution set of $(l > 5) \wedge (l > 10)$ consists of all points common to both graphs—in other words, the overlap of the two individual graphs.

DISJUNCTIONS

Disjunctions can also be used to form compound inequalities. Consider the sentence, "Dennis will only buy a comic book if it's less than one year old or more than five years old." A book that Dennis buys will therefore be "less than one year old" *or* "more than five years old." Two inequalities are connected by the word *or* to form a disjunction. Suppose Dennis buys a comic book. The age of that comic book can be described with an algebraic sentence:

Let b = the age of the comic book in years

$(b < 1) \vee (b > 5)$

A disjunction *cannot* be written as a single open sentence. A disjunction must always consist of two distinct sentences separated by the symbol for disjunction or the word "or":

$b < 1$ or $b > 5$

The solution set of a disjunction is the set of all values that satisfy one or the other of its two statements, or both. The solution set of $(b < 1) \vee (b > 5)$, for example, is the set of all values for which $b < 1$ is true *and* the set of all points for which $b > 5$ is true.

This is reflected in the graph of the disjunction. Compare the graph of $(b < 1) \vee (b > 5)$ to the graph of $b < 1$ and the graph of $b > 5$:

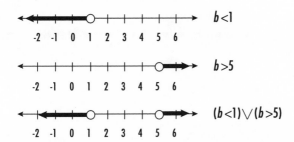

The graph of $(b < 1) \vee (b > 5)$ consists of all points that appear on *either* graph.

SOLVING COMPOUND INEQUALITIES

To solve a compound inequality, rewrite the inequality, if necessary, in the form of a conjunction or a disjunction. In this form, there are two separate inequalities separated by a logical connective ($\wedge$ or $\vee$). Solve each of these inequalities in the usual way, by isolating the variable. When you have found the solution sets of both inequalities, combine them into a compound inequality.

A compound inequality is considered solved when the variable is isolated in both inequalities.

Examples

Solve: $2 < x + 5 < 13$

Begin by rewriting the compound inequality as a conjunction:

$$(2 < x + 5) \land (x + 5 < 13)$$

Now, solve both inequalities separately.

$$\begin{array}{r} 2 < x + 5 \\ \underline{-5 \quad -5} \\ -3 < x \end{array}$$

$$\begin{array}{r} x + 5 < 13 \\ \underline{-5 \; -5} \\ x \quad < 8 \end{array}$$

Once both the equalities are solved, combine the solutions into one compound inequality.

$$-3 < x < 8$$

This is the solution set of $2 < x + 5 < 13$.

Solve: $(2a + 4 < 0) \lor (a + 6 \geq 9)$

The sentence is already written as a disjunction, so you don't have to rewrite it. Simply solve the two inequalities separately.

$$\begin{array}{r} 2a + 4 < \; 0 \\ \underline{-4 \; -4} \\ 2a \quad < -4 \end{array}$$

$$\frac{2a}{2} < \frac{-4}{2}$$

$$a < -2$$

$$\begin{array}{r} a + 6 \geq \; 9 \\ \underline{-6 \; -6} \\ a \quad \geq 3 \end{array}$$

$a \geq 3$

Once both inequalities are solved, combine the solutions into one statement:

$(a < -2) \vee (a \geq 3)$

This is the solution set of $(2a + 4 < 0) \vee (a + 6 \geq 9)$.

Practice working with compound inequalities in the following exercises.

EXERCISES

Write the compound inequalities represented by the following graphs.

1.

2.

3.

4.

Solve each of the following compound inequalities and graph the solution set.

5. $-3 \leq x - 3 < 1$

6. $(r + 6 > 2) \wedge (r - 4 < -5)$

7. $(s + 6 \leq 1) \vee (2s + 1 \geq 11)$

8. $(10 < 3t + 1) \wedge (t - 4 < 4)$

9. $\left(\dfrac{y}{3} + 2 < 3\right) \vee (y - 5 \geq 2)$

10. $(5 - n \le 1) \wedge (3n + 10 \le -2)$

4.6 INEQUALITIES IN WORD PROBLEMS

Many problems stated in English may be solved by using inequalities. Let's review the algebraic meanings of some common verbal phrases that relate to inequalities:

ENGLISH STATEMENT	INEQUALITY
n is less than 5. n is lower than 5.	$n < 5$
n is less than or equal to 5. n is no greater than 5. n is at most 5. 5 is the maximum value of n. 5 is the greatest possible value of n.	$n \le 5$
n is greater than 5. n is more than 5. n is higher than 5.	$n > 5$
n is greater than or equal to 5. n is no less than 5. n is at least 5. 5 is the minimum value of n. 5 is the least possible value of n.	$n \ge 5$
n is not equal to 5. n cannot equal 5.	$n \ne 5$

You can use this table to translate word problems into algebraic inequalities. Remember the four steps for solving word problems:

To Solve a Word Problem with an Inequality:

1. *Figure out what piece of information you must find. Use a variable to represent this information.*
2. *Write an inequality using this variable.*
3. *Solve the equation.*
4. *Check your solution.*

Examples

A rectangle's length is twice its width. If the perimeter of the rectangle must be at least 72, what are the possible values of the width of the rectangle?

Let w = the rectangle's width.

Then $2w$ = the rectangle's length.

The perimeter of a rectangle is given by the formula $p = 2w + 2l$, where w is the width and l is the length. You can use this formula to write an inequality.

The perimeter of the rectangle is at least 72.

The perimeter of the rectangle	is at least	72
$2w + 2(2w)$	$\geq$	72

$2w + 2(2w) \geq 72$

Simplify by multiplying and combining like terms.

$2w + 4w \geq 72$

$6w \geq 72$

Divide both sides by 6 to find the value of w.

$$\frac{6w}{6} \geq \frac{72}{6}$$

$w \geq 12$

The rectangle's width is at least 12.

The sum of two consecutive integers is not less than 3 times the lesser integer decreased by 13. What are the greatest possible integers for which this statement is true?

Let x = the smaller integer.

Then $x + 1$ = the larger integer.

Write an equation based on the statement in the question. Remember that the phrase "not less than" is equivalent to the phrase "greater than or equal to."

The sum of two consecutive integers	is not less than	three times	the lesser integer	decreased by 13
$x + (x+1)$	$\geq$	$3 \cdot$	x	-13

$x + (x + 1) \geq 3x - 13$

Simplify by combining like terms.

$2x + 1 \geq 3x - 13$

Subtract $2x$ from both sides.

$$\begin{array}{r} 2x + 1 \geq 3x - 13 \\ -2x \quad\quad -2x \\ \hline 1 \geq \quad x - 13 \end{array}$$

Add 13 to both sides to find the value of x.

$$\begin{array}{r} 1 \geq x - 13 \\ +13 \quad +13 \\ \hline 14 \geq x \end{array}$$

You find that which $14 \geq x$ can also be written $x \leq 14$. The greatest possible value of the smaller integer is 14. The greatest possible value of the larger integer $(x + 1)$ is therefore 15.

EXERCISES

For each of the following questions, assign a variable, write and solve an inequality, and clearly state the answer.

1. The sum of two integers is at least 52. One integer is three times the other. Find the smallest possible integer.

2. Three consecutive multiples of 4 add up to no more than 48. What are the greatest possible values of the numbers?

3. The length of a rectangle is five times the width. If the perimeter of the rectangle is not more than 36, what is the greatest possible width of the rectangle?

4. Vance has two more quarters than dimes and four more nickels than dimes. If the total value of these coins is at most $1.90, what is the greatest number of coins Vance could have?

5. Find the greatest integer that may be added to both the numerator and the denominator of the fraction $\dfrac{8}{47}$ so that the value of the resulting fraction is not greater than $\dfrac{1}{4}$?

6. A triangle is to have sides whose lengths are consecutive integers. If the perimeter of the triangle is less than 42, what is the greatest possible length of the triangle's longest side?

7. The maximum load of a freight elevator is 1,000 pounds. A cart weighing 180 pounds is filled with parcels weighing 40 pounds each. If this cart is to be lifted by the elevator, what is the greatest number of parcels that may be loaded?

8. Find the greatest integer that may be added to both the numerator and the denominator of the fraction $\frac{5}{14}$ so that the value of the resulting fraction is not greater than $\frac{1}{2}$?

SUMMARY

- It's possible to determine the value of any quantity in a formula if you know the values of the other quantities.

- When a formula is solved for any one variable, the resulting formula is equivalent to the original. Rearranging a formula can make it easier to use.

Symbol	Meaning
<	is less than
>	is greater than
≤	is less than or equal to
≥	is greater than or equal to
≠	is not equal to

- If the same number is added to (or subtracted from) both sides of an inequality, the resulting inequality will be equivalent to the original.
  If both sides of an equality are multiplied or divided by the same *positive* number, the resulting inequality will be equivalent to the original.
  If both sides of an equality are multiplied or divided by the same *negative* number, the resulting inequality will be equivalent to the original, provided that the sign of inequality is reversed.

- To solve a compound inequality, solve the two statements separately, and combine the two solution sets into a single statement.

- **To Solve a Word Problem with an Inequality:**
  1. Figure out what piece of information you must find. Use a variable to represent this information.
  2. Write an inequality using this variable.
  3. Solve the equation.
  4. Check your solution.

CHAPTER 5

Polynomials

Polynomials, algebraic expressions with multiple terms, are the building blocks of complex algebra. The expressions $n + 2$, $5m + 6n$, and $7xy^2 + 5xy - 8xy^2$ are polynomials. This chapter will familiarize you with the basic rules governing operations with polynomials.

5.1 MONOMIALS

When a group of one or more numbers or variables are combined by multiplication, the group is called a monomial. A monomial cannot contain addition or subtraction. All of the following, for example, are monomials:

$$2, \quad x, \quad \frac{2}{3}, \quad 4x, \quad -3xy, \quad 12x3y^3$$

A monomial *cannot* contain square roots, variables raised to negative exponents, or variables in the denominators of fractions.

A monomial is a constant, a variable, or the product of a constant and one or more variables.

Monomials that contain the same variables raised to the same powers are called *like monomials*. For example, $-2a^2b$ and $4a^2b$ are like monomials, while $5a^2b$ and $5ab^2$ are *not* like monomials. This distinction is important, because it changes the way arithmetic operations apply to monomials.

Like monomials may be added or subtracted according to the distributive property. This is called *simplifying* or *combining like terms*. To combine like monomials by addition or subtraction, add or subtract the coefficients and leave the variables alone. An expression that cannot be simplified further is said to be in *simplest form*.

Examples

$5ab^2 \boxed{+} 4ab^2 = (5 + 4)ab^2 = 9ab^2$

$8xy - 6xy = (8 - 6)xy = 2xy$

Remember that a variable or product of variables that has no written coefficient has an implied coefficient of 1. This becomes important when combining like terms.

$4m^2n + m^2n = (4 + 1)m^2n = 5m^2n$

DEGREE OF A MONOMIAL

The *degree* of a monomial is the sum of the exponents in that monomial. Remember when calculating degree that a variable with no written exponent has an implied exponent of 1.

MONOMIAL	COEFFICIENT	VARIABLES	EXPONENTS	DEGREE
8	8	none	0	0
x	1	x	1	1
$-4ab$	-4	a, b	1, 1	$1 + 1 = 2$
$5n^3$	5	n	3	3
$-2r^3s^2$	-2	r, s	3, 2	$3 + 2 = 5$

Practice working with monomials in the following exercises.

State the degree of each of the following monomials.

1. -12

2. n

3. $7ab$

4. $5x^3$

5. r^2s

6. $-4x^2y^3z$

Express each of the following expressions in simplest form.

7. $13y - 5y$

8. $-21bc + 16bc$

9. $x^2 - 3x^2$

10. $4a - 4a + 4$

11. $-5n^5m^3 + 11n^5m^3 + 4$

12. $2ab - 5a^2b + 1b - a$

5.2 WORKING WITH MONOMIALS

You've seen that like monomials may be added or subtracted according to the distributive property. This is done by adding or subtracting coefficients. But what about multiplying and dividing monomials? This is slightly more complicated.

MULTIPLYING MONOMIALS

To multiply a monomial by a constant, multiply the coefficient of the monomial by that constant factor.

$$4x - 3rt = -12rt \qquad 5(2x^2y^2) = 10x^2y^2$$

To multiply a monomial by another monomial, work with the coefficients and variables separately. Multiply the coefficients together to find the coefficient of the product. Different powers of the same variable should be multiplied together; remember that the product of powers of the same base is found by adding exponents and leaving the base the same.

For example, the product $(3a2b)(2ab)$ is found by multiplying the coefficients together ($3 \times 2 = 6$), multiplying the powers of a together ($a2 \times a = a^{2+1} = a$), and multiplying the powers of b together

$(b \times b = b^{1+1} = b^2)$. Combine the results of these multiplications to form the complete product: $(3a^2b)(2ab) = 6a^3b^2$.

> • To multiply as monomial by a constant, multiply the numerical coefficient by the constant and leave the variables the same.
> • To multiply a monomial by a monomial, multiply the coefficients together and multiply powers of the same base by adding exponents.

Examples

$7(2g^2h) = (7 \times 2)g^2h = 14g^2h$

$(6rs^3)(10r) = (6 \times 10) \times r^{1+3} \times s^2 = 60r^4s^2$

$(2ab)(3a^2b) = (2 \times 3) \times a^{1+2} \times b^{1+1} = 6a^3b^2$

RAISING MONOMIALS TO POWERS

To raise a monomial to a power, apply the exponent to the coefficient and each variable separately. Remember that when an exponential term is raised to a power, the exponents are multiplied. For example, to square the monomial $7xy^2$, square the coefficient ($7^2 = 49$), square x ($x^2 = x^2$), and square y^2 $\left(\left(y^2 \right)^2 = y^{2 \times 2} = y^4 \right)$. Combine the result of these exponential operations to find the complete result: $(7xy^2)^2 = 49x^2y^4$.

> To raise a monomial to a power, apply the exponent to the numerical coefficient, and raise each variable to that power by multiplying exponents.

Examples

$(2ab)^3 = 2^3 \times a^3 \times b^3 = 8a^3 \ b^3$

$(4m^2n^3)^2 = 4^2 \times (m^2)^2 \times (n^3)^2 = 16m^4n^6$

DIVIDING MONOMIALS

To divide a monomial by a constant, divide the monomial's numerical coefficient by that constant factor and leave the variables alone. For example, the monomial $10abc$ divided by 5 is $2abc$, because $10 \div 5 = 2$.

To divide a monomial by another monomial, find the quotient of the numerical coefficients, and then find the quotient of powers of the same base. Remember that the quotient of powers of the same base is found by subtracting exponents. Once you have found each of these quotients, combine them by multiplication to produce the complete quotient. For example, to divide the monomial $8x^5y^3$ by $4x^2y$, find the quotient of the coefficients $(8 \div 4 = 2)$, the quotient of the powers of x $(x^5 \div x^2 = x^{5-2} = x^3)$, and the quotient of the powers of y $(y^3 \div y = y^{3-1} = y^2)$. Combine these results to form the complete quotient: $8x^5y^3 \div 4x^2y = 2x^3y^2$

- To divide a monomial by a constant, divide the coefficient by that constant.
- To divide one monomial by another, divide the coefficients normally, and divide powers of the same bases by subtracting exponents.

Examples

1. $12a^6b^3 \div 4ab^2 = (12 \div 4) \times a^{6-1} \times b^{3-2} = 3a^5$

2. $\dfrac{5m^8n^3}{2m^4n} = \dfrac{5}{2} \times m^{8-4} \times n^{3-1} = \dfrac{5m^4n^2}{2}$

3. $\dfrac{14xy^5}{7x^3y^2} = \dfrac{14}{7} \times x^{1-3} \times y^{5-2} = 2x^{-2}y^3 = \dfrac{2y^3}{x^2}$

As you see in Example 3, dividing monomials can sometimes produce negative exponents. Remember that a negative exponent indicates the reciprocal of quantity indicated by the opposite, positive exponent: $x^{-2} = \dfrac{1}{x^2}$. When dividing monomials, it's conventional to write the quotient without negative exponents; in other words, to express quantities in fractional form, with positive exponents in the denominator, as in Example 3.

EXERCISES

Express each of the following products in simplest form.

1. $x^3 \cdot x^5$

2. $(3n)(n^2)$

3. $(-5)(3y^3)$

4. $(2ab)(ab^2)$

5. $(2xy)(3xy)(x^2y^3)$

6. $\sqrt{5c^2d} \cdot \sqrt{7cd}$

Simplify each of the following expressions.

7. $(g^2)^3$

8. $(ab)^2$

9. $(-3x^2y)^3$

10. $2n(4n)^2$

11. $(-2r^3s^5)^2$

12. $(-x^4)(-x)^4$

Express each of the following quotients as a monomial in simplest form.

13. $\dfrac{15b^6}{3b^2}$

14. $\dfrac{xy^2}{y}$

15. $\dfrac{x^4}{x^6}$

16. $\dfrac{4n^3m^2}{3n^2}$

17. $\dfrac{3a^2b^5c}{12a^4bc^2}$

18. $\dfrac{-18r^4st^6}{-6r^2t^3}$

5.3 POLYNOMIALS

Monomials are members of a larger category, the *polynomials*. A polynomial is a monomial, or a group of two or more monomials combined by addition or subtraction. Each monomial in a polynomial is called a *e*. A monomial is a polynomial with a single term. A polynomial with two unlike terms is called a *binomial*, and a polynomial with three unlike terms is called a *trinomial*.

A polynomial *in one variable* is one that contains only one variable, though it may contain different powers of that variable. For example, $2x^2 - 5x + 4$ is a polynomial in one variable. The degree of a polynomial is equal to the highest degree of any monomial within that polynomial. In a polynomial in one variable, the degree of the polynomial is equal to the polynomial's greatest exponent. The degree of the trinomial $2x^2 - 5x + 4$, for example, is 2.

A polynomial in one variable is said to be in *standard form* when its exponents are arranged in descending order. The polynomial $2x^2 - 5x + 4$ is in standard form, while the polynomial $m^3 + 3m^2 - 5 + 2m$ is not.

SIMPLIFYING POLYNOMIALS

If a polynomial contains like terms, then it may be *simplified*. To simplify a polynomial, combine its like terms by addition or subtraction, according to the operation signs within the polynomial. When the polynomial has no more like terms, it is said to be in *simplest form*.

Examples

1. *Simplify:* $3t^2 - 4t + 6 + t$

   The terms $-4t$ and t are like terms. Combine them into a single term to simplify the polynomial: $-4t + t = -3t$.

   $3t^2 - 4t + 6 + t = 3t^2 - 3t + 6$

2. *Simplify:* $a^2 - 5a + 3a^2 + 2a - 6$

   The terms a^2 and $3a^2$ are like terms, as are the terms $-5a$ and $2a$. Combine these terms to simplify the polynomial: $a^2 + 3a^2 = 4a^2$, and $-5a + 2a = -3a$.

   $a^2 - 5a + 3a^2 + 2a - 6 = 4a^2 - 3a - 6$

Practice working with polynomials in the following exercises.

EXERCISES

State the degree of each of the following polynomials.

1. $3n - 1$

2. $-8x^3$

3. $7a^2b - 3a + b$

4. $4x^3y^5z^4 - xyz$

Identify each of the following as a monomial, binomial, or trinomial.

5. $7r - 1$

6. $x^2 - 7x + 12$

7. $-4xyz$

8. $n + m + 2$

Simplify each of the following polynomials and express in standard form.

9. $8 + p - 7p$

10. $9x + 13 - 4x - 9$

11. $5w - 8 + 3w^3 - 7$

12. $y^2 - 3y^3 + 5y^2 + 7y^3$

13. $4(n^2 + 3) - 5(n^2 - 3n)$

14. $2(4c + 2c^2) + 3(-2c - c^2)$

5.4 ADDING AND SUBTRACTING POLYNOMIALS

ADDING POLYNOMIALS

To add two or more polynomials, combine their terms into a single polynomial. Then rearrange the new polynomial so that like terms appear in groups, and combine like terms. The resulting polynomial is the sum of the original polynomials.

Example

$$\left(x^2 + 5x - 4\right) + \left(3x^2 - 2x + 7\right) = x^2 + 5x - 4 + 3x^2 - 2x + 7$$
$$= \left(x^2 + 3x^2\right) + (5x - 2x) + (-4 + 7)$$
$$= 4x^2 + 3x + 3$$

It is sometimes convenient to write the addition of polynomials vertically, so that like terms line up in columns.

Example

$$x^2 + 5x - 4$$
$$+ \quad 3x^2 - 2x + 7$$
$$4x^2 + 3x + 3$$

Like terms are combined in each column, and the solution is found quickly. Sometimes the terms in one polynomial will not correspond perfectly to those in the other. In this case, use zero as a placeholder to keep like terms lined up vertically. Suppose, for example, you wanted to add the polynomials $c^2 - 7c + 10$ and $3c^2 - 2$. To express this addition vertically, you'll need a placeholder:

$$c^2 - 7c + 10$$
$$+ \quad 3c^2 + 0 - 2$$
$$4c^2 - 7c + 8$$

In this addition, the zero in the second polynomial lines up with the term $-7c$ in the first polynomial, which has no like term in the second.

SUBTRACTING POLYNOMIALS

To subtract one polynomial from another, flip the signs on the polynomial that is being subtracted and then add the two polynomials together. In other words, instead of subtracting each term, add the opposite of each term. For example, subtract the polynomial $d^2 - 3d + 13$ from $3d^2 + 8d + 28$.

Arrange the binomials vertically, with the polynomial being subtracted on the bottom. Then flip the signs on the subtracted polynomial, and add.

Original Equations

$$3d^2 + 8d + 28$$
$$-\left(d^2 - 3d + 13\right)$$

Signs Flipped

$$3d^2 + 8d + 28$$
$$+ \quad -d^2 + 3d - 13$$
$$2d^2 + 11d + 15$$

Once the subtraction problem has been converted to an addition problem, the math is relatively easy. The difference of $3d^2 + 8d + 28$ and $d^2 - 3d + 13$ is $2d^2 + 11d + 15$.

To add polynomials, combine like terms.

To subtract polynomials, flip the signs on the polynomial being subtracted, and then combine like terms.

EXERCISES

Add.

1. $(3d - 6) + (d + 2) =$

2. $(x^2 - 4x) + (5x - 3) =$

3. $(5t - 2t^2 + 4) + (-t^2 - 2t + 5) =$

4. $(-2x^2 + 7) + (5x - 4) + (5x^2 - 3x) =$

5. $\begin{array}{r} 3x - 4y + 11z \\ + \quad 4x + 7y - \ 3z \\ \hline \end{array}$

6. $\begin{array}{r} b^2 - 7b + 12 \\ + \quad -3b^2 + \ 0 - \ 7 \\ \hline \end{array}$

Subtract.

7. $(11t - 8) - (6t + 3) =$

8. $(a + 6b) - (5a + 7b) =$

9. $(4x^2y - 2xy + 3xy^2) - (3x^2y + 4xy - 2xy^2) =$

10. $(6s^2 - 3s + 5) - (7s^2 - 7s - 3) =$

11. $(9y - 11) - (-2y^2 + 4y - 6) =$

12. $(2x^3 + 5x^2 - 7x + 8) - (x^3 + 5x^2 - 3x + 5) =$

5.5 MULTIPLYING POLYNOMIALS

MULTIPLYING A POLYNOMIAL BY A MONOMIAL

To multiply a binomial by a monomial, use the distributive property. Multiply each term of the polynomial by the monomial separately. Add up these products to find the complete product of the monomial and polynomial. For example, to multiply $2n + 3$ by $5n$, begin by using the distributive property:

$$5n(2n + 3) = 5n(2n) + 5n(3)$$
$$= \quad 10n^2 + 15n$$

The resulting polynomial, $10n^2 + 15n$, is the product.

To multiply a polynomial by a monomial, multiply each term in the polynomial by the monomial.

Example

$4x^2(5x^2 - 7x - 3) =$

Distribute the multiplying term, $4x^2$, through the parentheses.

$4x^2(5x^2) + 4x^2(-7x) + 4x^2(-3) =$

$20x^4 + (-28x^3) + (-12x^2) =$

$20x^4 - 28x^3 - 12x^2$

The same distributive property is also used to multiply binomials and other polynomials together.

MULTIPLYING BINOMIALS

Consider the product $(x + 6)(x - 5)$. The distributive property must be used to multiply these binomials:

$(x + 6)(x - 5) = x(x - 5) + 6(x - 5)$

Then, use the distributing property a second time, to distribute through the parentheses.

$x(x - 5) + 6(x - 5) = x^2 - 5x + 6x - 30$

Finally, combine like terms to simplify the product.

$x2 - 5x + 6x - 30 = x^2 + x - 30$

This process of distribution and multiplication must be used whenever two binomials are multiplied. Because this procedure is so consistent, a shortcut can be used to find the product of two binomials. To multiply two binomials, multiply the first terms of each binomial; multiply the "outside" terms of the binomials; multiply the "inside" terms of the binomials; and multiply the last terms of each binomial.

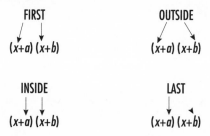

Finally, combine like terms to form the product of the two binomials.

To multiply two binomials, use the FOIL method:

F *Multiply the first terms*
O *Multiply the outside terms*
I *Multiply the inside terms*
L *Multiply the last terms*
Combine like terms to simplify the product.

MULTIPLYING POLYNOMIALS

The distributive property is used to multiply polynomials with more than two terms as well. When two polynomials are multiplied, every term of one polynomial must be multiplied by every term in the other polynomial.

Examples

1. $(x - 5)(x^2 + 3x - 10) =$
   $x(x^2 + 3x - 10) - 5(x^2 + 3x - 10) =$
   $x^3 + 3x^2 - 10x - 5x^2 - 15x + 50 =$
   $x^3 - 2x^2 - 25x + 50$

2. $(2x^2 + 5)(3x^3 + 7x - 3) =$
   $2x^2(3x^3 + 7x - 3) + 5(3x^3 + 7x - 3) =$
   $6x^5 + 14x^3 - 6x^2 + 15x^3 + 35x - 15 =$
   $6x^5 + 29x^3 - 6x^2 + 35x - 15$

To multiply any two polynomials, use the distributive property to multiply each term in one polynomial by every term in the other. Combine like terms to simplify the product.

EXERCISES

Multiply.

1. $y(y^2 - 3y + 4)$

2. $2d(4ad^2 - 7a^2d)$

3. $-3mn(4m^2n - mn + 5mn^2)$

4. $x^3y^2z(5x - 7y + 2z)$

Express each of the following products in simplest form.

5. $(x + 3)(x - 1)$

6. $(h - 6)(h + 7)$

7. $(2a - 3b)(a + 4b)$

8. $(p - 5)^2$

9. $(r - 7)(r + 7)$

10. $\left(t + \sqrt{5}\right)\left(t - \sqrt{5}\right)$

11. $(x + 3)(2x^2 - 4x + 1)$

12. $(3n^2 - 7n + 6)(2n^2 - 1)$

13. $(a - 1)(a^4 + a^3 + a^2 + a + 1)$

14. $(z + 2)^3$

5.6 DIVIDING POLYNOMIALS

DIVIDING A POLYNOMIAL BY A MONOMIAL

The distributive property governs the division of polynomials as well. Each term of the polynomial must be divided in turn by the monomial. Divide coefficients, and divide powers of the same bases by subtracting exponents.

To divide a polynomial by a monomial, divide each term in the polynomial by the monomial.

Examples

1. $\dfrac{4d^4 + 6d^3 - 2d^2}{2d} =$

$\dfrac{4d^4}{2d} + \dfrac{6d^3}{2d} - \dfrac{2d^2}{2d} =$

$2d^3 + 3d^2 - d$

2. $\dfrac{3a^2b^4 + 5a^3b^3 - 4a^4b^2}{7ab} =$

$\dfrac{3a^2b^4}{7ab} + \dfrac{5a^3b^3}{7ab} - \dfrac{4a^4b^2}{7ab} =$

$\dfrac{3ab^3}{7} + \dfrac{5a^2b^2}{7} - \dfrac{4a^3b}{7}$

RATIONAL EXPRESSIONS

A fraction whose numerator and denominator are polynomials is called a *rational expression,* or an *algebraic fraction.* The denominator of a fraction cannot equal zero, because a fraction represents division, and it is meaningless to divide by zero.

A fraction with a denominator of zero is said to be undefined.

The domain of a rational expression can therefore not contain any value that would make the denominator equal zero. Any value that makes the denominator equal zero must be excluded from the domain.

The domain of the expression $\dfrac{6}{n}$, for example, cannot include $n = 0$.

The domain of the expression $\dfrac{y-7}{y+2}$ cannot include $y = -2$.

EXERCISES

Express each of the following quotients in simplest form.

1. $\dfrac{4c - 6}{2}$

2. $\dfrac{5x^3 - 2x^2}{x}$

3. $\dfrac{32cd^2 - 8d}{4d}$

4. $\dfrac{18x^3y^2 - 3x^2y^2 + 21x^2y^3}{3xy}$

5. $\dfrac{s^6 - s^5 + s^4 - s^3}{s^3}$

6. $\dfrac{28n^4m^3 - 63n^3m^2}{7n^2}$

7. $\dfrac{4f^3g^2 - f^2g^3 + 5f^3g^3}{f^2g^2}$

8. $\dfrac{(s-k)^2 + (s-k)}{s-k}$

For each algebraic expression below, list the values of the variables that make the expression undefined.

9. $\dfrac{5}{x}$

10. $\dfrac{a^2}{a(a-3)}$

11. $\dfrac{r^2s^3}{3s-8}$

12. $\dfrac{23fg}{f^3(2g+3)}$

SUMMARY

- A monomial is a constant, a variable, or the product of a constant and one or more variables. The *degree* of a monomial is the sum of the exponents in that monomial.

- To multiply a monomial by a constant, multiply the numerical coefficient by the constant and leave the variables the same.

- To multiply a monomial by a monomial, multiply the coefficients together and multiply powers of the same base by adding exponents.

- To raise a monomial to a power, apply the exponent to the numerical coefficient, and raise each variable to that power by multiplying exponents.

- To add polynomials, combine like terms.

- To subtract polynomials, flip the signs on the polynomial being subtracted, and then combine like terms.

- To multiply a polynomial by a monomial, multiply each term in the polynomial by the monomial.

- To multiply two binomials, use the FOIL method:

  F Multiply the first terms.

  O Multiply the outside terms.

  I Multiply the inside terms.

  L Multiply the last terms.

  Combine like terms to simplify the product.

- To multiply any two polynomials, use the distributive property to multiply each term in one polynomial by every term in the other. Combine like terms to simplify the product.

- To divide a polynomial by a monomial, divide each term in the polynomial by the monomial.

- A fraction with a denominator of zero is said to be *undefined*.

6

Factoring

Factoring is the process of separating quantities joined in multiplication. In a very real sense, factoring is the opposite of multiplication. Factoring techniques will round out your bag of tricks for manipulating polynomials.

6.1 FACTORING POLYNOMIALS

FACTORING

The number 60 can be factored in a number of ways:

$$60 = \quad 4 \cdot 15$$

$$60 = \quad 2 \cdot 2 \cdot 15$$

$$60 = 2 \cdot 2 \cdot 3 \cdot 5$$

Each of these expressions represents a factored form of 60. The final expression, $2 \cdot 2 \cdot 3 \cdot 5$, cannot be factored any further. Each of the factors in this expression is a *prime number*, and cannot be factored further. The expression $2 \cdot 2 \cdot 3 \cdot 5$ is therefore called the *prime factorization* of 60.

A monomial can be factored much as a number can. The monomial $12x^2$ can be factored this way: $12x^2 = 2 \cdot 2 \cdot 3 \cdot x \cdot x$. This is a complete factorization of $12x^2$, in which no factor can be divided further.

FACTORING POLYNOMIALS

The terms of a polynomial may have factors in common. When this is the case, the common factor can be pulled out. This is called *factoring* the polynomial. In the binomial $10n^2 - 15n$, the two terms have a couple of factors in common; both terms are multiples of n, and both are multiples of 5. Either one of these factors can be factored out of the binomial:

$$10n^2 - 15n = n(10n - 15) \quad 10n^2 - 15n = 5(2n^2 - 3n)$$

Just as factoring a monomial is the opposite of multiplication, factoring a polynomial is the opposite of *distribution*. To reverse the factoring process shown above, you would distribute the factor through the parentheses.

To factor a polynomial completely, you must factor out the largest factor that is common to all of the terms in the polynomial. This largest factor is called the *greatest common factor*, and it is found by multiplying the largest numerical factor common to all of the terms by the highest power of each variable common to all of the terms.

The greatest common factor (GCF) of two or more monomials is the product of the greatest numerical factor and the variables that the monomials have in common.

The greatest common factor in the binomial $10n^2 - 15n$ is $5n$. To factor this binomial completely, you must remove the factor $5n$ from both terms:

$$10n^2 - 15n = 5n(2n - 3)$$

This is the polynomial in its completely factored form.

To factor a polynomial:
1. Identify the GCF.
2. Divide each term of the polynomial by the GCF, and write the quotient in parentheses.
3. Write the polynomial as the product of the GCF and the quantity in parentheses.

Examples

1. *Factor completely:* $12x^2 - 15x$

   The GCF of the two terms is $3x$. Divide each term by $3x$, and write the quotient in parentheses:

   $$\frac{12x^2}{3x} - \frac{15x}{3x} = (4x - 5)$$

   Write the polynomial as the product of the GCF and the quantity in parentheses:

   $$3x(4x - 5)$$

   This is the polynomial in completely factored form. You can check this result by distributing $3x$ through the parentheses. If the factorization is correct, distributing will restore the polynomial to its original form.

   $$3x(4x - 5) = 3x(4x) - 3x(5) = 12x^2 - 15x$$

   The factorization is correct.

2. *Factor completely:* $14x^3y^4 + 105x^2yz$

   The GCF of the two terms is $7x^2y$. Divide each term by $7x^2y$, and write the quotient in parentheses:

   $$\frac{14x^3y^4}{7x^2y} + \frac{105x^2yz}{7x^2y} = (2xy^3 + 15z)$$

   Write the polynomial as the product of the GCF and the quantity in parentheses:

   $$7x^2y(2xy^3 + 15z)$$

   This is the binomial in factored form. Check the factorization by distributing through the parentheses.

   $$7x^2y(2xy^3 + 15z) = 7x^2y(2xy^3) + 7x^2y(15z)$$
   $$= 14x^3y^4 + 105x^2yz$$

   The factorization is correct.

EXERCISES

State the GCF of each of the following pairs of monomials.

1. 14 and 105

2. $33a$ and $55a^3$

3. $3xy$ and $24z^2$

4. $20n^2m^3$ and $32n^3m$

Write each polynomial in factored form so that the GCF appears as a factor.

5. $5x - 5y$

6. $2cd + 2c$

7. $27c^2 - 18$

8. $3n^2 + 6n^5$

9. $g^2h + g^3h$

10. $rs + st + us$

11. $10x^2 - 15x + 55$

12. $12t^4 - 16t^3 + 4t^2$

6.2 SPECIAL CASES IN FACTORING

Sometimes a polynomial can be factored even when its terms have no factors in common. Examples of such polynomials include the *difference of two squares* and the *square of a binomial*.

THE DIFFERENCE OF TWO SQUARES

Observe the pattern produced by multiplying the following binomials:

$$(x + 2)(x - 2) = x^2 - 2x + 2x - 4 = x^2 - 4$$

$$(2b + 7)(2b - 7) = 4b^2 - 14b + 14b - 49 = 4b^2 - 49$$

$$(a + b)(a - b) = a^2 - ab + ab - b^2 = a^2 - b^2$$

In each case, the binomials on the left represent the sum and the difference of the same two quantities. When the sum $x + 2$ is multiplied by the difference $x - 2$, the result is the product $x^2 - 4$. Notice that x^2 is the square of x, and that 4 is the square of 2. The product $x^2 - 4$ is therefore called the *difference of two squares*.

The Difference of Two Squares
For any two numbers a *and* b,
$$(a + b)(a - b) = a^2 - b^2$$
$$a^2 - b^2 = (a + b)(a - b)$$

This pattern always holds. Memorizing it will allow you to multiply the sum and difference of two quantities easily $[(a+b)(a-b)=a^2-b^2]$, or to factor any binomial that takes the form of the difference of two squares $a^2-b^2=(a+b)(a-b)$.

THE SQUARE OF A BINOMIAL

Observe the pattern formed by the multiplication of these binomials:

$$(x+5)(x+5)=x^2+5x+5x+25=x^2+10x+25$$

$$(2n+3)(2n+3)=4n^2+6n+6n+9=4n^2+12n+9$$

$$(a+b)(a+b)=a^2+ab+ab+b^2=a^2+2ab+b^2$$

In each case, the two binomials on the left are identical. In other words, the product of the two binomials represents the *square* of a binomial. The product $(x+5)(x+5)$ can also be written $(x+5)^2$. The results of squaring these binomials follow a predictable pattern: the resulting trinomial is the sum of the square of the binomial's first term, twice the product of the two terms, and the square of the second term.

The Square of a Sum

For any two numbers a and b,

$$(a+b)^2=a^2+2ab+b^2$$

$$a^2+2ab+b^2=(a+b)(a+b)$$

This pattern, too, always holds. Knowing it will allow you to square a binomial quickly, or easily factor a trinomial of the form $a^2+2ab+b^2$.

The square of a binomial takes a slightly different form when the binomial represents a difference rather than a sum. Take a look at this pattern:

$$(y-6)(y-6)=y^2-6y-6y+36=y^2-12y+36$$

$$(3d-1)(3d-1)=9d^2-3d-3d+1=9d^2-6d+1$$

$$(a-b)(a-b)=a^2-ab-ab+b^2=a^2-2ab+b^2$$

Once again, the left side of each equation represents the square of a binomial, but this time each binomial is the difference of two quantities. The products on the right all take the same form: a trinomial formed by the square of the binomial's first term minus twice the product of the two terms, plus the square of the second term.

The Square of a Difference
For any two numbers a and b,
$$(a-b)^2 = a^2 - 2ab + b^2$$
$$a^2 - 2ab + b^2 = (a-b)(a-b)$$

Knowing this pattern will allow you to square a difference easily, or quickly factor a trinomial of the form $a^2 - 2ab + b^2$.

EXERCISES

Find each of the following products.

1. $(x - 6)(x + 6)$
2. $(b + 3)^2$
3. $(3n + 4)(3n - 4)$
4. $(a + b)(a - b)$
5. $(t^2 + 9)(a - 9)$
6. $(5 + 12p)(5 - 12p)$

Factor each of the following expressions.

7. $d^2 - 16$
8. $n^2 - m^2$
9. $9f^2 - 100$
10. $121 - 4y^2$
11. $24x^2 - 54$
12. $b^3 - 9b$
13. $x^4 - y^4$
14. $-16 + r^4$

6.3 FACTORING QUADRATIC TRINOMIALS

You've seen that trinomials of the form $a^2 + 2ab + b^2$ or $a^2 - 2ab + b^2$ can be factored into two binomials. Each of these trinomial expressions represents the square of some binomial.

The expressions $a^2 + 8a + 16$ and $a^2 - 8a + 16$ are examples of *quadratic polynomials*. A quadratic polynomial is a polynomial in a single variable that has a degree of 2. The binomial $a^2 - 9$ is also a quadratic polynomial. In a quadratic trinomial, the term of degree 2 is called the *quadratic term*. The term of degree 1 is known as the *linear term*; and the term of degree 0—the numerical term—is called the *constant term*.

Quadratic Polynomial	Quadratic Term	Linear Term	Constant Term
$5x^2$	$5x^2$	0	0
$-2n^2 + 4n$	$-2n^2$	$4n$	0
$a^2 - 9$	a^2	0	-9
$t^2 - 5t + 6$	t^2	$-5t$	6

The squares of binomials and the difference of two squares are not the only quadratic polynomials that can be factored. Many polynomials of this form can be factored into a pair of binomial factors. To do this, remember how two binomials are multiplied using the FOIL method:

Let a and b represent constants in the binomials $x + a$ and $x + b$. Watch what happens when these two binomials are multiplied using FOIL.

$$\begin{array}{cccc} \textbf{F} & \textbf{O} & \textbf{I} & \textbf{L} \end{array}$$
$$(x + a)(x + b) = x^2 + bx + ax + ab$$
$$= x^2 + (a + b)x + ab$$

The coefficient of the middle term is the sum of the two constant terms, and the third term is the product of the constants. This will be the case whenever the linear terms of both binomials have coefficients of 1. You can use this pattern to factor a quadratic polynomial—essentially doing FOIL in reverse.

Factoring $ax^2 + bx + c$ when $a = 1$

Suppose you wanted to factor the quadratic trinomial $x^2 + 7x + 12$. The quadratic term, x^2, has a coefficient of 1, which means that the reverse FOIL pattern applies. The trinomial will factor into the form $(x + ?)(x + ?)$, where the unknown terms are factors of 12 that add up to 7. To find the unknown constants, list the factors of 12:

12 and 1

6 and 2

4 and 3

−1 and −12

−2 and −6

−3 and −4

The only pair of factors that adds up to 7 is 3 and 4. Plug these factors into the two binomials to create the factored form of the trinomial.

$$x^2 + 7x + 12 = (x + 3)(x + 4)$$

This is the factorization of the trinomial. To check the factorization, you can multiply the binomials using FOIL. If the factorization is correct, then the product will be equal to the original expression.

F   O   I   L

$$(x + 3)(x + 4) = x^2 + 4x + 3x + 12 = x^2 + 7x + 12$$

The factorization is correct.

FACTORING $ax^2 + bx + c$ WHEN $a \neq 1$

Factoring a quadratic polynomial is a little different when the coefficient of the quadratic term is not 1. Suppose you wanted to factor the polynomial $3n^2 + 8n + 5$. The trinomial will factor into the form $(3n + ?)(n +)$, where the missing terms are factors of 5. When considering the middle term of the trinomial, however, you must remember that the coefficient of the middle term is the sum of the products of the "first" and "outside" terms.

To factor the polynomial, list and check the possible factors of $3n^2 + 8n + 5$:

Possible Factors	Outer + Inner Products
$(3n + 1)(n + 5)$	$15n + 1n = 16n$
$(3n + 5)(n + 1)$	$3n + 5n = 8n$
$(3n - 1)(n - 5)$	$-1n - 15n = -16n$
$(3n - 5)(n - 1)$	$-3n - 5n = -8n$

The second set of possible factors is correct:

$$3n^2 + 8n + 5 = (3n + 5)(n + 1)$$

Check the factorization by multiplying the binomials:

F   O   I   L

$$(3n + 5)(n + 1) = 3n^2 + 3n + 5n + 5 = 3n^2 + 8n + 5$$

The factorization is correct.

EXERCISES

Factor each of the following.

1. $x^2 + 5x + 6$
2. $a^2 - 7a + 12$
3. $n^2 - n - 20$
4. $d^2 + 2d - 15$
5. $y^2 - 4y + 4$
6. $3q^2 - 27q + 60$
7. $r^4 + 8r^2 + 15$
8. $2g^2 - 8g - 24$
9. $a^2 + 5ab + 6b^2$
10. $2t^2 - 3t - 20$
11. $4n^2 - n - 3$
12. $3y^2 - 4yz + z^2$

6.4 FACTORING COMPLETELY

A polynomial is said to be *factored completely* when none of its factors can be factored further. It is sometimes necessary to use several factoring techniques to factor a polynomial completely. When attempting to factor a polynomial, consider the following steps:

To Factor a Polynomial Completely:

1. Factor out the GCF, if possible.
2. Determine whether any binomial may be factored as the difference of two squares.
3. Determine whether any trinomial may be factored into two binomial factors.

Examples

1. *Factor completely:* $4n^2 - 36$

   Factor out the GCF, which is 4. Then factor the binomial as the difference of two squares:

   $$4n^2 - 36 = 4\left(n^2 - 9\right)$$
   $$= 4(n - 3)(n + 3)$$

2. *Factor completely:* $x^4 - x^3 - 20x^2$

   Factor out the GCF, which is x^2. Then factor into binomials:

   $$x^4 - x^3 - 20x^2 = x^2\left(x^2 - x - 20\right)$$
   $$= x^2(x - 5)(x + 4)$$

3. *Factor completely:* $a^4 - 2a^2b^2 + b^4$

   Factor into binomials. Then factor as the difference of two squares:

   $$a^4 - 2a^2b^2 + b^4 = \left(a^2 - b^2\right)^2$$
   $$= \left(a^2 - b^2\right)\left(a^2 - b^2\right)$$
   $$= (a - b)(a + b)(a - b)(a + b)$$

   Practice factoring polynomials in the following exercises.

EXERCISES

Factor each of the following polynomials completely.

1. $3x^2 - 48$

2. $n^3 + 12n^2 + 27n$

3. $6d^2 - 36d + 54$

4. $2t^2 - 28t + 98$

5. $\dfrac{1}{3}p^2 - \dfrac{4}{3}$

6. $3s^2 - s - 14$

7. $4m^2 - 40m + 100$

8. $2a - 8 + 10a^2$

9. $x^2y + xy^2 - 12y^3$

10. $-3n^2 + 3$

11. $z^4 - 1$

12. $t^4 - t^2 - 12$

6.5 SOLVING QUADRATIC EQUATIONS BY FACTORING

An equation in one variable in which the greatest exponent is 2 is called a quadratic equation. When such an equation is written as $ax^2 + bx + c = 0$, where a, b, and c are constants, the quadratic equation is said to be in *standard form*.

If the left side of a quadratic equation in standard form can be factored, this factorization can be used to solve the equation. This is done by using the *zero product property*, which states that a product can equal zero only if one or more of its factors equals zero.

For example, to solve the equation $x^2 + 3x - 10 = 0$, you could begin by factoring the left side of the equation. This produces the new equation $(x + 5)(x - 2) = 0$. Since a product can only equal zero if one or more of its factors equals zero, the equation $(x + 5)(x - 2) = 0$ is true only if $x + 5 = 0$ or $x - 2 = 0$. To find the possible values of x, solve both of these simple equations.

$$
\begin{array}{ll}
x + 5 = 0 & x - 2 = 0 \\
\underline{-5\ -5} & \underline{+2\ +2} \\
x = -5 & x = 2
\end{array}
$$

The solution set is {-5, 2}. To check this solution, replace the variable in the equation $x^2 + 3x - 10 = 0$ with each solution. Both replacement values should make the equation true.

To Solve a Quadratic Equation by Factoring
1. *Write the equation in standard form.*
2. *Factor the quadratic trinomial.*
3. *Set each binomial factor equal to zero, and solve.*
4. *State the solution set.*

Notice that every quadratic equation has two solutions, or *roots*. These roots may be numerically identical.

EXERCISES

Solve each of the following equations by factoring. List the complete solution set.

1. $d(d + 3) = 0$
2. $(b + 6)(b - 8) = 0$
3. $x^2 - 3x = 10$
4. $n^2 - 9n = 0$
5. $g^2 + g = 12$
6. $3s^2 - 4s + 1 = 0$
7. $m^2 + 4m - 5 = 0$
8. $p^3 - 4p = 0$
9. $6c^2 + 27c + 12 = 0$
10. $x^2 = 16$
11. $(t - 2)(t + 3) = 14$
12. $r^2 - 1 = 0$

6.6 WORD PROBLEMS

Many problems expressed verbally can be solved by using factoring techniques. The most common types of word problems to involve factoring are problems about relationships between numbers and problems about geometrical figures.

Examples

1. The square of a negative number is six more than the number. What is the number?

   Write an equation:

   Let x = the number.

   $$x^2 = x + 6$$

   Put the equation into standard form:

   $$x^2 - x - 6 = 0$$

Factor:

$$(x-3)(x+2)=0$$

Remember that a product can only equal zero if one of its factors equals zero. Set each factor equal to zero and solve to find the value of x.

$x - 3 = 0$ $x + 2 = 0$

$x = 3$ $x = -2$

discard

The solution set of the equation is $\{-2, 3\}$. The question specifies that the number is negative, so you can throw out the positive solution. The number is -2.

To check this solution, plug the number $x = -2$ into the original equation.

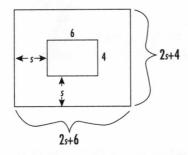

2. A rectangular garden with a length of 6 feet and a width of 4 feet is surrounded by a sidewalk s feet wide. If the area of the sidewalk is 96 square feet, what is the value of s?

Write an equation for the area of the sidewalk. Note that the area of the sidewalk is found by subtracting the area of the garden $(4 \times 6 = 24)$ from the area of the whole rectangle $(2s + 6) \times (2s + 4)$:

Let s = the width of the sidewalk.

$$(2s + 6)(2s + 4) - 24 = 96$$

Add 24 to both sides:

$$
\begin{array}{l}
(2s+6)(2s+4)-24 = 96 \\
\underline{ +24+24} \\
(2s+6)(2s+4) \quad\ = 120
\end{array}
$$

Use FOIL to multiply the two binomials:

$$\mathbf{F} \quad \mathbf{O} \quad \mathbf{I} \quad \mathbf{L}$$

$$(2s + 6)(2s + 4) = 4s^2 + 8s + 12s + 24 = 120$$

$$= 4s^2 + 20s + 24 = 120$$

Subtract 120 from both sides to put the equation in standard form:

$$4s^2 + 20s + 24 = 120$$
$$\underline{\quad\quad\quad -120 \quad -120}$$
$$4s^2 + 20s - 96 = 0$$

Factor:

$$4s^2 + 20s - 96 = 0$$

$$4\left(s^2 + 5s - 24\right) = 0$$

$$4(s - 3)(s + 8) = 0$$

Remember that a product can only equal zero if one of its factors equals zero. Set each factor equal to zero and solve to find the value of s.

$$s - 3 = 0 \qquad\qquad s + 8 = 0$$
$$s = 3 \qquad\qquad\quad s = -8$$
$$\qquad\qquad\qquad\qquad\quad \textit{discard}$$

The solution set of the equation is {–8, 3}. A length cannot be negative, so you can throw out the negative solution. The value of s is 3, which means that the width of the sidewalk is 3 feet.

To check this solution, plug the value $s = 3$ into the original equation.

Solve each of the following word problems algebraically, and check your answer.

1. When four times a number is subtracted from the square of that number, the result is 5. Find the number.

2. The length of a rectangle is equal to its width increased by 5. The area of the rectangle is 36. Find its dimensions.

3. A positive integer is 30 less than its square. Find the integer.

4. Find a number such that the product of the number decreased by 1 and the number increased by 6 is 18.

5. The sum of a negative number and its square is 56. Find the number.

6. The sum of the squares of two consecutive positive integers is 61. Find the integers.

7. One negative number is seven less than another. Their product is 18. Find the numbers.

8. The sum of the squares of two consecutive positive integers is 221. Find the numbers.

SUMMARY

- The *greatest common factor* (GCF) of two or more monomials is the product of the greatest numerical factor and the variables that the monomials have in common.

- **To factor a polynomial:**
    1. Identify the GCF.
    2. Divide each term of the polynomial by the GCF, and write the quotient in parentheses.
    3. Write the polynomial as the product of the GCF and the quantity in parentheses.

- **The Difference of Two Squares**
  For any two numbers a and b,

  $$(a+b)(a-b) = a^2 - b^2$$

  $$a^2 - b^2 = (a+b)(a-b)$$

- **The Square of a Sum**

  For any two numbers a and b,

  $$(a+b)^2 = a^2 + 2ab + b^2$$

  $$a^2 + 2ab + b^2 = (a+b)(a+b)$$

- **The Square of a Difference**

  For any two numbers a and b,

  $$(a-b)^2 = a^2 - 2ab + b^2$$

  $$a^2 - 2ab + b^2 = (a-b)(a-b)$$

- **To Factor a Polynomial Completely:**
  1. Factor out the GCF, if possible.
  2. Determine whether any binomial may be factored as the difference of two squares.
  3. Determine whether any trinomial may be factored into two binomial factors.

- **To Solve a Quadratic Equation by Factoring:**
  1. Write the equation in standard form.
  2. Factor the quadratic trinomial.
  3. Set each binomial factor equal to zero, and solve.
  4. State the solution set.

7

Irrational Numbers

An irrational number is a quantity that cannot be expressed as the ratio of two integers. The most common examples of irrational numbers are certain square roots, like $\sqrt{2}$. This chapter will review the definition of irrational numbers and the rules for working with them.

7.1 RATIONAL NUMBERS AND DECIMALS

A *rational number* is any number that can be expressed as the ratio of two integers. Most of the numbers you work with in everyday math are rational. These rational numbers can take a variety of forms.

All integers are rational numbers:

$$-365, \quad -1, \quad 0, \quad 5, \quad 56, \quad 3{,}575{,}0000$$

All fractions are rational numbers, as long as their numerators and denominators are integers:

$$-\frac{322}{11}, \quad -\frac{5}{6}, \quad \frac{1}{7}, \quad \frac{100}{101}, \quad \frac{17}{2}, \quad \frac{2{,}750}{3}$$

All *terminating decimals* (numbers that don't continue forever) are rational numbers:

$$-498.3, \quad -0.95, \quad 0.00003, \quad 2.4, \quad 36.125, \quad 2{,}868.00000487$$

These are the most common forms taken by rational numbers, the ones you've worked with often in the past. In addition, there are a few unusual forms that rational numbers can take.

REPEATING DECIMALS

A *repeating decimal* is a decimal number in which a digit or group of digits to the right of the decimal point repeat infinitely. A repeating decimal cannot be written down exactly in decimal form, because writing its exact value would require you to go on writing forever. Instead, a horizontal bar is used to indicate the repetition of a digit or group of digits.

The repeating decimal 0.33333..., for example, is written as $0.3\overline{3}$. The repeating decimal 0.125125125125125... is written as $0.\overline{125}$.

Despite their strange appearance, all repeating decimals are rational. In other words, every repeating decimal can be expressed as the ratio of two integers. Here's a simple method for converting a simple repeating decimal into a fraction whose numerator and denominator are integers: Write the smallest repeating group in the decimal as the numerator of a fraction. Count the number of decimal places in the repeating group. Then write that many nines in the denominator. The resulting fraction is equivalent in value to the original repeating decimal.

Examples

1. Express $0.3\overline{3}$ as the ratio of two integers.

   The smallest repeating group is the single digit 3. Place this number in the numerator. The denominator of the fraction will be 9, because there is one digit in the numerator.

   $$0.3\overline{3} = \frac{3}{9}$$

   Reduce.

   $$0.3\overline{3} = \frac{3}{9} = \frac{1}{3}$$

2. Express $0.\overline{125}$ as the ratio of two integers.

   The smallest repeating group is the three-digit group 125. Place this group in the numerator. The denominator of the fraction will be 999, because there is one digit in the numerator.

$$0.\overline{125} = \frac{125}{999}$$

The fraction cannot be reduced.

3. Express $1.6\overline{6}$ as the ratio of two integers.

In this case, not all of the number's digits repeat. Think of the number as the sum of a terminating decimal and a repeating decimal, and evaluate the two numbers separately:

$$1.6\overline{6} = 1.0 + 0.6\overline{6}$$

The smallest repeating group in the repeating decimal is the single digit 6. Place this number in the numerator. The denominator of the fraction will be 9, because there is one digit in the numerator.

$$0.6\overline{6} = \frac{6}{9}$$

Reduce.

$$0.6\overline{6} = \frac{6}{9} = \frac{2}{3}$$

To express the entire number as a fraction, add the two parts of the number together again.

$$1.6\overline{6} = 1.0 + 0.6\overline{6} = 1 + \frac{2}{3} = \frac{3}{3} + \frac{2}{3} = \frac{5}{3}$$

To express a repeating decimal as a fraction:
1. *Find the smallest repeating group in the decimal number.*
2. *Write this group in the numerator.*
3. *Count the decimal places in the numerator.*
4. *Write that many nines in the denominator.*
5. *Reduce.*

SQUARE ROOTS OF PERFECT SQUARES

Any square root whose radicand (the number under the square root sign) is a perfect square is a rational number:

$$\sqrt{1} = 1 \quad \sqrt{16} = 4 \quad \sqrt{81} = 9 \quad \sqrt{169} = 13$$

Test your knowledge of rational numbers with the following exercises.

EXERCISES

Express each of the following numbers as the ratio of two integers in simplest form.

1. 3

2. –6

3. 0.5

4. 1.25

5. $-8.\overline{3}$

6. 0.375

7. 0.16

8. $\sqrt{144}$

9. $\sqrt{400}$

10. $0.6\overline{6}$

7.2 REAL NUMBERS

Every real number is either rational or irrational. Every rational number can be expressed as a terminating decimal or a repeating decimal. In fact, every terminating decimal or repeating decimal is a rational number. Therefore no irrational number can take the form of a terminating or repeating decimal.

How, then, does an irrational number appear in decimal form? The answer is simple. An irrational number takes the form of a nonterminating, nonrepeating decimal. Take a look at these numbers:

0.12345678910111213141516 17...

0.01001000100001000001000 0001...

These numbers continue forever, and in both of these numbers you can discern a pattern. These are not repeating decimals, however, because neither number contains a digit or group of digits that is repeated consistently. These are nonterminating, nonrepeating decimals. In other words, they're irrational numbers.

Irrational forms can be written in nondecimal forms. Here are some commonly occurring irrational numbers:

$\sqrt{3} = 1.73205080...$

$\sqrt{7} = 2.64575131...$

$\pi = 3.141592654...$

Any square root whose radicand (the number under the square root sign) is *not* a perfect square is an irrational number. The value of π, which is the ratio of a circle's circumference to its diameter, is also irrational.

EXERCISES

State whether each of the following real numbers is rational or irrational. If the number is rational, rewrite it as the ratio of two integers in reduced form.

1. 0.3737373737373737373737...

2. 0.25225222522225222225...

3. $1.8\overline{8}$

4. $\dfrac{\pi}{4}$

5. 5π

6. $\sqrt{4}$

7. $\sqrt{13}$

8. $\sqrt{24}$

9. $\sqrt{289}$

10. $\sqrt{\dfrac{1}{100}}$

11. $\sqrt{\dfrac{9}{25}}$

12. $\sqrt{\dfrac{68}{17}}$

7.3 SQUARE ROOTS

The principal square root of a number is the positive factor that must be squared to produce that number. When there is no indication to the contrary, you should assume that the square root sign indicates the primary, or positive, square root. For example, the positive factor that must be squared to produce 25 is 5: $5^2 = 25$. Therefore $\sqrt{25} = 5$. Similarly, the positive factor that must be squared to produce 64 is 8, so $\sqrt{64} = 8$.

> *The principal square root of a number is the positive factor that must be squared to produce that number.*

Every positive number also has a *negative square root*. The negative square root of a number is the *negative* factor that must be squared to produce that number. The negative square root of 25, for example, is -5, because $(-5)^2 = 25$. The negative square root of 64 is -8.

A square root is denoted by a symbol called the *radical sign*, or simply the *radical*. The number under the radical sign (the number you're finding the square root of) is called the *radicand*.

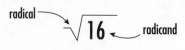

The radical sign alone generally indicates the primary square root:

$\sqrt{16} = 4$

The radical sign with a minus sign indicates the negative square root:

$-\sqrt{16} = -4$

The radical sign with a plus-or-minus sign indicates both the positive and negative square roots:

$\pm\sqrt{16} = 4, -4$

PERFECT SQUARES

A number is called a *perfect square* if its square root is a rational number. The numbers 25 and 64 are perfect squares, because their square roots (5 and 8, respectively) are integers. There is an infinite number of square roots, since the square of every nonzero integer is a perfect square:

$$1^2 = 1 \qquad \sqrt{1} = 1$$
$$2^2 = 4 \qquad \sqrt{4} = 2$$
$$3^2 = 9 \qquad \sqrt{9} = 3$$
$$4^2 = 16 \qquad \sqrt{16} = 4$$
$$5^2 = 25 \qquad \sqrt{25} = 5$$
$$6^2 = 36 \qquad \sqrt{36} = 6$$
$$7^2 = 49 \qquad \sqrt{49} = 7$$
$$8^2 = 64 \qquad \sqrt{64} = 8$$
$$9^2 = 81 \qquad \sqrt{81} = 9$$
$$10^2 = 100 \qquad \sqrt{100} = 10$$

And so on.

Not all perfect squares are integers. The number $\frac{4}{9}$ is a perfect square, because its square root is $\frac{2}{3}$, a rational number. The following examples are non-integer perfect squares.

$$\left(\frac{1}{2}\right)^2 = \frac{1}{4} \qquad\qquad \sqrt{\frac{1}{4}} = \frac{1}{2}$$

$$\left(\frac{3}{4}\right)^2 = \frac{9}{16} \qquad\qquad \sqrt{\frac{9}{16}} = \frac{3}{4}$$

$$\left(\frac{5}{8}\right)^2 = \frac{25}{64} \qquad\qquad \sqrt{\frac{25}{64}} = \frac{5}{8}$$

NEGATIVE RADICANDS

A negative radicand cannot be evaluated. The product of two negative numbers is positive; the product of two positive numbers is also positive. Therefore there is no real number that can be squared to produce a negative number. The square root of a negative number is said to be *imaginary*.

Test your understanding of square roots with the following exercises.

EXERCISES

Evaluate the following square roots.

1. $\sqrt{1600}$

2. $\sqrt{169}$

3. $-\sqrt{81}$

4. $\pm\sqrt{17^2}$

5. $\sqrt{36}$

6. $-\sqrt{121}$

7. $\pm\sqrt{64}$

8. $\sqrt{\frac{4}{25}}$

9. $\sqrt{\frac{49}{9}}$

10. $\sqrt{\dfrac{36}{400}}$

11. $\pm\sqrt{\dfrac{1}{169}}$

12. $-\sqrt{\dfrac{25}{196}}$

7.4 SIMPLIFYING RADICALS

A square root whose radicand is not a perfect square can often be simplified. The expression $\sqrt{12}$ can be simplified like this:

$$\sqrt{12} = \sqrt{2 \cdot 2 \cdot 3}$$
$$= \sqrt{2^2 \cdot 3}$$
$$= \sqrt{2^2} \cdot \sqrt{3}$$
$$= 2\sqrt{3}$$

The simplified form of $\sqrt{12}$ is $2\sqrt{3}$. The expression $2\sqrt{3}$ is said to be in *simplest form*, because the radicand is not divisible by any perfect square.

This simplification is made possible by the *product property of square roots*.

For any positive numbers a and b, $\sqrt{ab} = \sqrt{a} \cdot \sqrt{b}$.

Examples

1. *Simplify:* $\sqrt{20}$

    $$\sqrt{20} = \sqrt{4 \cdot 5} = \sqrt{4} \cdot \sqrt{5} = 2\sqrt{5}$$

2. *Simplify:* $6\sqrt{45}$

    $$6\sqrt{45} = 6\sqrt{9 \cdot 5} = 6 \cdot \sqrt{9} \cdot \sqrt{5} = 6 \cdot 3 \cdot \sqrt{5} = 18\sqrt{5}$$

3. *Simplify:* $\dfrac{2}{3}\sqrt{108}$

    $$\frac{2}{3}\sqrt{108} = \frac{2}{3}\sqrt{36 \cdot 3} = \frac{2}{3} \cdot \sqrt{36} \cdot \sqrt{3} = \frac{2}{3} \cdot 6 \cdot \sqrt{3} = 4\sqrt{3}$$

Practice simplifying radicals in the following exercises.

EXERCISES

Simplify each of the following radicals.

1. $\sqrt{32}$

2. $\sqrt{300}$

3. $\sqrt{126}$

4. $-\sqrt{90}$

5. $\sqrt{x^4}$

6. $\sqrt{n^7}$

7. $\sqrt{a^3b^2}$

8. $5\sqrt{72}$

9. $\frac{1}{3}\sqrt{117}$

10. $\sqrt{44f^3}$

11. $\sqrt{180x^2y^3z}$

12. $3\sqrt{8v^4w^5}$

7.5 OPERATIONS WITH RADICALS

There are simple rules governing operations with square roots.

ADDING AND SUBTRACTING RADICALS

Radicals can be combined by addition or subtraction only when they have the same radicand. When the radicands are the same, radicals can be added much like variables, by adding coefficients and leaving the radicals the same.

Examples

1. $3\sqrt{5} + 4\sqrt{5} = (3+4)\sqrt{5} = 7\sqrt{5}$

2. $\sqrt{15} + 7\sqrt{15} = (1+7)\sqrt{15} = 8\sqrt{15}$

3. $6\sqrt{3} - 2\sqrt{3} = (6-2)\sqrt{3} = 4\sqrt{3}$

To add or subtract radicals:

- *The radicands must be the same.*
- *Add or subtract coefficients, leaving the radicands unchanged.*

Adding or subtracting radicals that have the same radicand within an expression is called *combining like radicals*.

MULTIPLYING RADICALS

When radicals are multiplied, their radicands **do** change. To multiply two square roots, multiply the radicands, keeping the product under the radical.

$$\sqrt{2} \cdot \sqrt{5} = \sqrt{2 \cdot 5} = \sqrt{10}$$

$$\sqrt{7} \cdot \sqrt{6} = \sqrt{7 \cdot 6} = \sqrt{42}$$

Remember to simplify the radical produced by multiplication. It may simplify further than either of its factors.

$$\sqrt{24} \cdot \sqrt{6} = \sqrt{24 \cdot 6} = \sqrt{144} = 12$$

$$\sqrt{10} \cdot \sqrt{14} = \sqrt{10 \cdot 14} = \sqrt{140} = \sqrt{4 \cdot 35} = \sqrt{4} \cdot \sqrt{35} = 2\sqrt{35}$$

When the radicals have coefficients, the multiplication must be done in two steps. Multiply the numerical coefficients normally, and multiply the radicals by multiplying the radicands.

$$2\sqrt{3} \cdot 4\sqrt{5} = (2 \cdot 4)\sqrt{3 \cdot 5} = 8\sqrt{15}$$

$$8\sqrt{6} \cdot 7\sqrt{11} = (8 \cdot 7)\sqrt{6 \cdot 11} = 56\sqrt{66}$$

To multiply radicals:

- *Multiply numerical coefficients normally.*
- *Multiply radicals by multiplying radicands, keeping the product under the radical.*

DIVIDING RADICALS

The division of radicals follows rules very similar to those for multiplication. To divide one square root by another, divide the radicands and keep the quotient under the radical.

$$\sqrt{30} \div \sqrt{6} = \sqrt{30 \div 6} = \sqrt{5}$$

$$\frac{\sqrt{42}}{\sqrt{14}} = \sqrt{\frac{42}{14}} = \sqrt{3}$$

When dividing radicals with coefficients, divide the coefficients normally and find the quotient of the radicals by dividing radicands under the radical.

$$6\sqrt{3} \div 2\sqrt{3} = (6 \div 2)(\sqrt{3} \div \sqrt{3}) = 3(1) = 3$$

$$12\sqrt{15} \div 4\sqrt{3} = (12 \div 4)(\sqrt{15} \div \sqrt{3}) = 3\sqrt{5}$$

$$\frac{10\sqrt{26}}{2\sqrt{2}} = \left(\frac{10}{2}\right)\left(\frac{\sqrt{26}}{\sqrt{2}}\right) = 5\sqrt{\frac{26}{2}} = 5\sqrt{13}$$

To divide radicals:
- *Divide numerical coefficients normally.*
- *Divide radicals by dividing radicands and keeping the quotient under the radical.*

Practice performing operations on radicals in the following exercises.

EXERCISES

Rewrite each of the following expressions in the simplest possible form.

1. $5\sqrt{3} - \sqrt{3}$

2. $12\sqrt{7} + 4\sqrt{7}$

3. $3\sqrt{14} - 2\sqrt{7} + 4\sqrt{14}$

4. $-4\sqrt{6} + 2\sqrt{36} + 11\sqrt{6}$

5. $\sqrt{7} \times \sqrt{5}$

6. $-\sqrt{3} \times \sqrt{12}$

7. $\left(5\sqrt{5}\right)\left(8\sqrt{4}\right)$

8. $7\sqrt{11}\left(4\sqrt{2} - 3\sqrt{3}\right)$

9. $\sqrt{10} \div \sqrt{2}$

10. $\dfrac{\sqrt{24}}{\sqrt{6}}$

11. $\dfrac{9\sqrt{20}}{3\sqrt{2}}$

12. $\dfrac{14\sqrt{12} - 5\sqrt{12}}{-4\sqrt{6} + 7\sqrt{6}}$

7.6 THE PYTHAGOREAN THEOREM

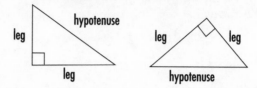

A *right triangle* is a triangle that contains a 90° angle. The side opposite the right angle in a right triangle is called the *hypotenuse*. The hypotenuse is always the triangle's longest side. The other two sides are called the *legs*.

The right triangle is important in geometry, because the lengths of a right triangle's sides are always related according to a certain formula. Specifically, the square of the length of the hypotenuse is equal to the sum of the squares of the lengths of the legs. This relationship is described by the *Pythagorean theorem*.

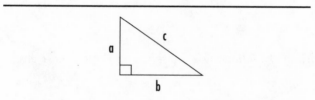

In any right triangle with legs a and b and hypotenuse c,
$a^2 + b^2 = c^2$.

All right triangles obey the Pythagorean theorem. This means that if you know the lengths of any two sides of a right triangle, you can find the length of the third side by using the formula $a^2 + b^2 = c^2$.

Examples

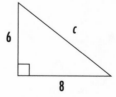

1. What is the length of the hypotenuse of a right triangle with legs of lengths 6 and 8?

Plug the values you know into the Pythagorean theorem:

$$c^2 = a^2 + b^2$$
$$c^2 = (6)^2 + (8)^2 \; a$$
$$c^2 = 36 + 64$$
$$c^2 = 100$$

Take the square root of both sides to find the value of c.

$$\sqrt{c^2} = \sqrt{100}$$

$$c = 10$$

Note that since a length cannot be negative, it is only necessary to consider the positive root of 100. The length of the hypotenuse is 10.

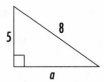

2. A right triangle has a hypotenuse of length 8 and a leg of length 5. What is the length of the other leg?

Plug the values you know into the Pythagorean theorem:

$$a^2 + b^2 = c^2$$

$$a^2 + (5)^2 = (8)^2$$

$$a^2 + 25 = 64$$

Subtract 25 from both sides.

$$a^2 + 25 = 64$$
$$\underline{\quad -25 \quad -25}$$
$$a^2 \quad\quad = 39$$

Take the square root of both sides to find the value of a.

$$\sqrt{a^2} = \sqrt{39}$$

$$a = \sqrt{39}$$

The length of the other leg is $\sqrt{39}$. This number has no precise decimal value, but a calculator could produce a decimal approximation.

As you will see, many right triangles include sides that have irrational lengths, like $\sqrt{39}$.

PYTHAGOREAN TRIPLES

A set of positive integers that satisfies the Pythagorean relationship is called a *Pythagorean triple*. These triples are fairly rare. Learning to recognize the most common triples can save you time when you work with a right triangle whose sides all have integer lengths.

The sets {3, 4, 5}, {5, 12, 13}, {8, 15, 17}, and {7, 24, 25} are some common Pythagorean triples. Each of these sets will satisfy the Pythagorean theorem:

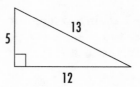

$$3^2 + 4^2 = 5^2 \leftrightarrow 9 + 16 = 25 \qquad 5^2 + 12^2 = 13^2 \leftrightarrow 25 + 144 = 169$$

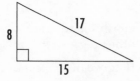
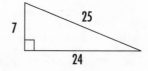

$$8^2 + 15^2 = 17^2 \leftrightarrow 64 + 225 = 289 \qquad 7^2 + 24^2 = 25^2 \leftrightarrow 49 + 576 = 625$$

Any whole-number multiple of a Pythagorean triple is also a Pythagorean triple. For example, multiplying each number in the set {3, 4, 5} by 2 produces the set {6, 8, 10}. This new set is also a Pythagorean triple:

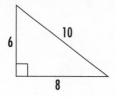

$$6^2 + 8^2 = 10^2 \leftrightarrow 36 + 64 = 100$$

Practice working with right triangles and the Pythagorean theorem in the following exercises.

Exercises

For each of the following figures, find the value of x.

1.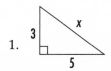

2.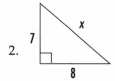

3.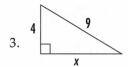

4.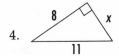

5. A right triangle has a hypotenuse of length 7 and a leg of length 5. What is the length of the remaining leg?

6. How long is the hypotenuse of a right triangle with legs that are 5 inches long?

7. A rectangle has a length of 12 and a width of 6. What is the length of a diagonal of the rectangle?

8. A right triangle has legs of lengths 8 and 15. What is the length of its hypotenuse?

9. A straight ladder 25 feet in length is leaned against a vertical wall so that its base is 15 feet from the wall. At what height does the ladder touch the wall?

10. If a square has sides 1 meter in length, what is the distance in meters from a corner of the square to the center of the square?

11. Which of the following could NOT be the lengths of the sides of a right triangle?
    (a) 9, 12, 15
    (b) 10, 12, 17
    (c) 8, 15, 17
    (d) 14, 48, 50

12. Which of the following could NOT be the lengths of the sides of a right triangle?
    (a) 1, $\sqrt{3}$, 2
    (b) 2, $\sqrt{5}$, 3
    (c) 4, $2\sqrt{5}$, 6
    (d) 5, $2\sqrt{6}$, 8

SUMMARY

- All terminating and repeating decimals are rational.

- Irrational numbers appear as nonterminating, nonrepeating decimals.

- The principal square root of a number is the positive factor that must be squared to produce that number.

- A number is called a *perfect square* if its square root is a rational number.

- A negative radicand cannot be evaluated. The square root of a negative number is said to be *imaginary*.

- For any positive numbers a and b, $\sqrt{ab} = \sqrt{a} \cdot \sqrt{b}$.

- **To add or subtract radicals:**
  The radicands must be the same.
  Add or subtract coefficients, leaving the radicands unchanged.

- **To multiply radicals:**
  Multiply numerical coefficients normally.
  Multiply radicals by multiplying radicands, keeping the product under the radical.

- **To divide radicals:**
  Divide numerical coefficients normally.
  Divide radicals by dividing radicands and keeping the quotient under the radical.

- **The Pythagorean theorem:**
  In any right triangle with legs a and b and hypotenuse c, $a^2 + b^2 = c^2$.

8

Geometry Basics

The following pages will provide you an introduction to the fundamental concepts of geometry, from the most basic elements of geometry (called *undefined terms*) to more complicated elements. Some basic rules and formulas of plane geometry will also be reviewed.

8.1 POINTS, LINES, AND PLANES

There are a few basic ideas in geometry that are easy to understand and so simple that they can't really be defined in terms of simpler things. Instead, these basic ideas are simply described, and used as the basis for definitions of more complex ideas. These simple ideas are called *undefined terms*. The *point*, the *line*, and the *plane* are the undefined terms of geometry.

UNDEFINED TERMS

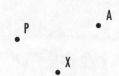

A *point* is an exact location. It has no size. Points are represented by dots, and named with capital letters.

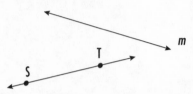

A *line* is a perfectly straight path that goes on forever in both directions. It has infinite length and no thickness. Lines are represented by sketched lines with arrows at both ends, and named by lowercase letters. A line can also be named for two points that lie on the line. Points that lie along a straight line are called *collinear points*.

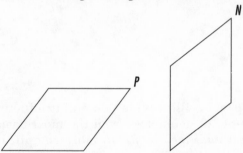

A *plane* is a perfectly flat surface that extends forever in all directions and has no thickness. Planes are represented by parallelograms and named by capital letters.

Using these undefined terms, other terms can be defined.

DEFINED TERMS

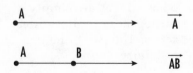

A *line segment* is a piece of a line with a finite length. It's defined as a pair of endpoints on a line and the set of all points between them. A line segment is generally named by its two endpoints.

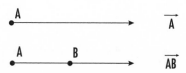

A *ray* is also part of a line. It's a straight path that goes on forever in *one* direction. A ray is defined as an endpoint on a line and all of the points on one side of that endpoint. A ray is named by its endpoint, or by its endpoint and another point on the ray.

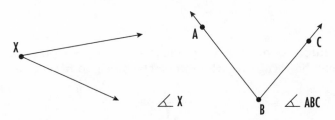

An *angle* is a figure formed by two distinct rays with the same endpoint. This endpoint is called the angle's *vertex*. The rays themselves are called the angle's *sides*. An angle is named for its vertex, or for three points: its vertex and one point on each ray.

SOME SIMPLE RULES

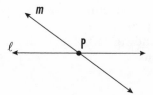

The intersection of two lines is a point. Two lines cannot meet in more than one point.

Two distinct points cannot lie on more than one line. In other words, two points are sufficient to define a line.

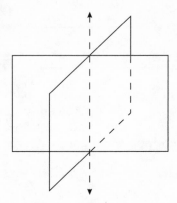

The intersection of two planes is a line. No other geometric shape can be formed by the intersection of two planes.

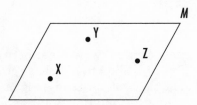

Three distinct points that do not lie in a straight line may not lie in more than one plane. There is only one plane that contains any group of three noncollinear points. In other words, three points are sufficient to define a plane.

Test your understanding of these geometric terms by answering the following questions.

EXERCISES

State whether each of the following statements is true or false.

1. No more than two lines may intersect at one point.

2. Parallel planes do not intersect.

3. A line may not lie in more than one plane.

4. Two distinct points may not lie on more than one line.

5. A line segment is a subset of a line.

6. Three collinear points can lie in more than one plane.

Refer to the figure at right to respond to each of the following.

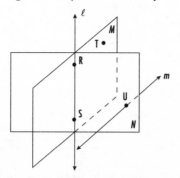

7. Name a point in plane *M* not in plane *N*.

8. Name three points in plane *M*.

9. Name all points common to line *m* and plane *N*.

10. Name the set of all points common to plane *M* and plane *N*.

11. Name a line segment common to plane *M* and plane *N*.

12. Name all points common to line *l* and line *m*.

8.2 ANGLES

An angle is formed by the union of two different rays that share a single endpoint. An angle is named by its vertex or by three points including its vertex and one point on each ray. When three points are used to name an angle, the vertex is always listed in the middle.

The space between the sides of an angle is called the angle's *interior*. The interior includes every point that could be included in a line segment drawn from one side of the angle to the other. Every point that is not in the interior or on the angle itself lies in the angle's *exterior*.

DEGREE MEASURE

The *measure* of an angle can be thought of as the amount of rotation required to move from one side of an angle to the other, using the vertex as the point of rotation. The unit in which this rotation is commonly measured is the *degree*. One complete rotation (a full circle) is a rotation of 360 degrees. A single degree is equal to $\frac{1}{360}$ of a complete rotation.

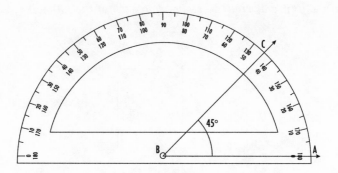

A protractor is sometimes used to find the measure of an angle in degrees. To measure an angle with a protractor, place the center point of the protractor at the vertex of the angle. A protractor usually has two scales numbered in opposite directions, allowing you to measure an angle from either side. Align one side of the angle with the number 0 on one of the protractor's scales. The number at which the other side of the angle falls on the same scale is the measure of the angle.

CLASSIFICATION OF ANGLES

Any angle can be assigned to one of five different types, according to its degree measure.

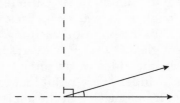

An *acute angle* is one whose measure is less than 90 degrees.

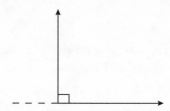

A *right angle* is one that measures exactly 90 degrees.

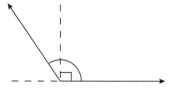

An *obtuse angle* is one whose measure is between 90 degrees and 180 degrees.

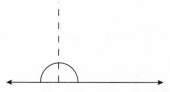

A *straight angle* is one that measures exactly 180 degrees. The angle's two rays then form a straight line.

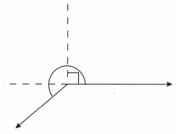

A *reflex angle* is one that measures more than 180°.

EXERCISES

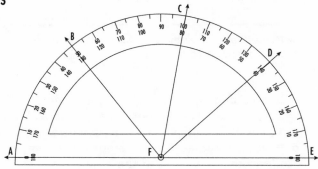

Referring to the figure above, characterize each of the following angles as an acute, right, obtuse, or straight angle, and state the measure of the angle.

1. ∠AFB
2. ∠AFC

3. ∠BFD

4. ∠CFE

5. ∠BFE

6. ∠AFE

7. ∠AFD

8. ∠DFE

8.3 SPECIAL PAIRS OF ANGLES

SUPPLEMENTARY AND COMPLEMENTARY ANGLES

When two angles add up to a straight line, they are said to be
supplementary. Whenever angles are created by a line's intersection
with another line or ray, supplementary angles are formed. Angles
do not have to be adjacent to be considered supplementary; any two
angles whose degree measures add up to 180 are supplementary
angles. If two angles are supplementary, then each is called the
supplement of the other.

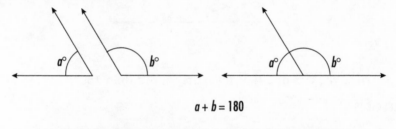

$$a + b = 180$$

---

*Two angles are supplementary when the sum of their
degree measures is 180.*

When two angles add up to a right angle, they are said to be
complementary. Again, angles do not have to be adjacent to be
complementary; any two angles whose degree measures add up to
90 are complementary angles. If two angles are complementary,
then each is called the *complement* of the other.

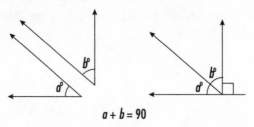

$$a + b = 90$$

> *Two angles are complementary when the sum of their degree measures is 90.*

Vertical Angles

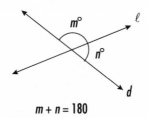

$$m + n = 180$$

When two lines intersect, four angles are formed. Two angles that have a side in common are called *adjacent angles*. Adjacent angles formed by the intersection of two lines are supplementary.

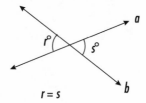

$$r = s$$

Any two nonadjacent angles formed by two intersecting lines are called *vertical angles*. Vertical angles may also be called *opposite angles*.

> *Vertical angles are equal in measure.*

Exercises

For each of the following figures, state the value of x.

1.

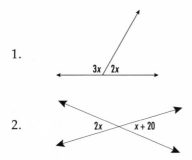

2.

3.

4.

5.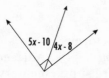

6.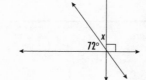

7.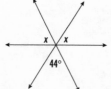

8.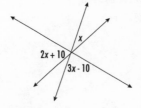

9. An angle is five times its supplement. Find the measure of the angle.

10. Find the measure of an angle if the angle is half of its complement.

11. Two angles are complementary. One angle is twelve less than twice the other. Find the measure of the smaller angle.

12. If $3x - 16$ is the measure of an angle in degrees, state the degree measure of the angle's supplement.

8.4 PARALLEL LINES

PARALLEL LINES AND TRANSVERSALS

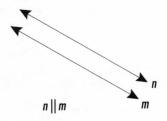

$n \parallel m$

Parallel lines are lines that lie in the same plane and do not intersect. The lines must run in exactly the same direction, so that they do not converge at any point along their lengths. The minimum distance between two parallel lines is constant.

When a third line crosses two other lines, this third line is called a *transversal*. A number of special relationships are created when a transversal crosses two parallel lines.

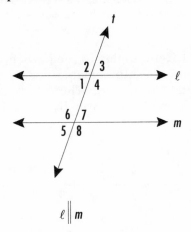

$\ell \parallel m$

Alternate interior angles are angles on opposite sides of the transversal and between the parallel lines. In the figure above, $\angle 1$ and $\angle 7$ are alternate interior angles; so are $\angle 4$ and $\angle 6$.

Alternate exterior angles are angles on opposite sides of the transversal and outside the parallel lines. In the figure above, $\angle 2$ and $\angle 8$ are alternate exterior angles; so are $\angle 3$ and $\angle 5$.

Corresponding angles are angles in analogous positions around the two points of intersection. For example, in the figure above, the following pairs of angles are corresponding angles:

$\angle 1$ and $\angle 5$

$\angle 2$ and $\angle 6$

$\angle 3$ and $\angle 7$

$\angle 4$ and $\angle 8$

Any two adjacent angles formed when a transversal intersects two parallel lines are supplementary. Any two vertical angles are, as always, equal in measure. The information provided by these rules can be summed up informally like this:

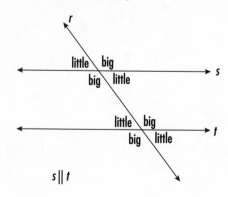

> When a transversal intersects two parallel lines, two kinds
> of angles are formed: big ones and little ones.
> - All of the big angles are equal.
> - All of the little angles are equal.
> - Any big angle and any little angle are supplementary.

PERPENDICULAR LINES

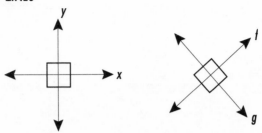

Two lines that intersect so as to form four right angles are said to be
perpendicular. Lines, line segments, and rays can all be perpendicular to other lines, line segments, or rays. It is possible for line
segments or rays to be perpendicular and lie in the same plane
without intersecting.

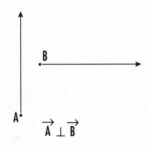

$$\overrightarrow{A} \perp \overrightarrow{B}$$

EXERCISES

*In each of the following figures, s and t are parallel. For each figure,
find the value of x.*

1.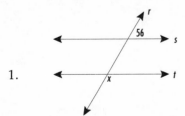

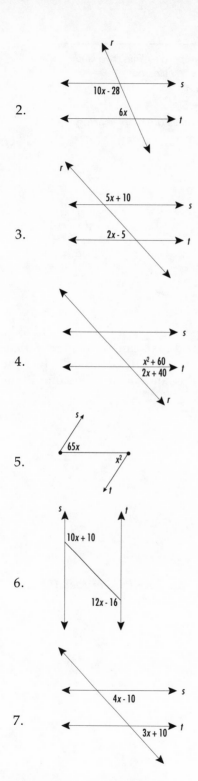

2.

3.

4.

5.

6.

7.

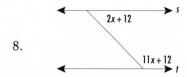

8.

In each of the following figures, determine whether lines l and m are parallel.

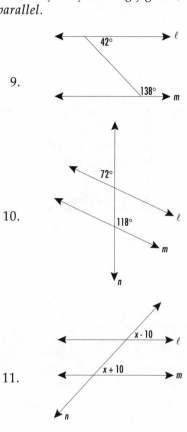

9.

10.

11.

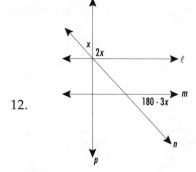

12.

8.5 POLYGONS

A *simple closed curve* is any continuous line that can be traced back to its starting point without crossing over itself. All of the following shapes are simple closed curves.

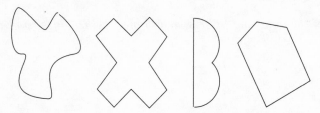

A *polygon* is a simple closed curve that is formed entirely by a series of line segments, which are called *sides*. There are two polygons among the figure above.

Polygons are generally classified by the number of their sides. The table at right gives the names of some common polygons.

Number of Sides	Name
3	triangle
4	quadrilateral
5	pentagon
6	hexagon
8	octagon
10	decagon

Polygons can take many different forms. They can have equal or unequal sides, acute or obtuse angles. Certain polygons have very uniform shapes, in which the sides are all of equal lengths and the interior angles of the polygon are all equal. These are called *regular* polygons.

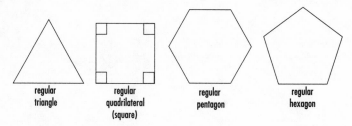

regular
triangle

regular
quadrilateral
(square)

regular
pentagon

regular
hexagon

> *A regular polygon has sides of equal length and angles of equal measure.*

The sum of the measures of a polygon's interior angles is constant for each type of polygon. All triangles have interior angle measures that add to the same sum; all quadrilaterals have angles that add to another sum; and so on. The sum of any polygon's angles can be found using a simple formula.

> *For any n-sided polygon:*
> *The sum of the interior angles in degrees = (n - 2)180*

A general polygon for the sake of discussion is sometimes referred to as an *n*-gon, where *n* is the number of the polygon's sides.

EXERCISES

1. Which of the following is *not* a polygon?

(a)

(b)

(c)

(d)

2. Which of the following is *not* a polygon?

(a)

(b)

(c)

(d)

3. Which of the following is a regular polygon?

(a)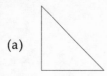

(b)

(c)

(d)

Find the degree measure of one interior angle of each of the following polygons.

4. A regular pentagon.

5. A regular hexagon.

6. A regular octagon.

7. A regular decagon.

8. Write a formula for the number of degrees in one interior angle of a regular n-gon. Let x = the measure of this interior angle.

8.6 TRIANGLES

Triangles are three-sided polygons, the simplest polygons that can be drawn. Any other polygon can be divided into triangles. Triangles occur commonly in real-world structures both artificial and natural. Understanding triangles is therefore one of the most important steps to understanding geometry.

By applying the formula for the sum of the angles of a polygon to a triangle, you can learn one of the most basic qualities of the triangle:

$$\text{The sum of the interior angles in degrees} = (n - 2)360$$
$$= (3 - 2)180$$
$$= 180$$

The formula states that the sum of the angle measures is 180°. This will prove true for any triangle.

$$a + b + c = 180$$

The measures of the three angles of a triangle always add up to 180 degrees.

TYPES OF TRIANGLES

Triangles can be assigned to different categories according to the equality or inequality of their measurements.

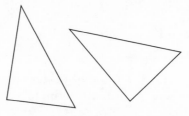

For example, a *scalene* triangle is one in which all three sides have different lengths and all three angles have different measurements

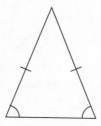

An *isosceles* triangle is one with two sides of equal length and two angles of equal measure. The two equal angles, which are called the *base angles,* are opposite the equal sides. The remaining angle, which is called the *vertex angle,* is formed by the two equal sides.

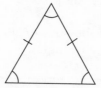

An *equilateral* triangle is one with three sides of equal length and three angles of equal measure. Since the measures of the three angles are equal and must add up to 180°, you can deduce that each angle in an equilateral triangle measures 60°.

Notice that when none of a triangle's sides are equal, none of its angles are equal; when two of its sides are equal, two of its angles are equal; and when all of its sides are equal, all of its angles are equal. This relationship is true for all triangles. When angles are equal, the opposite sides must be equal. When sides are equal, the opposite angles must also be equal.

Triangles may also be categorized according to the kinds of angles they contain.

For example, a triangle whose angles all measure less than 90° is called an *acute triangle*.

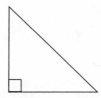

A triangle with one angle that measures 90° is called a *right triangle*.

A triangle with one angle that measures more than 90° is called an *obtuse triangle*.

RIGHT TRIANGLES

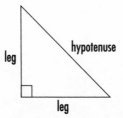

A right triangle has a right angle, which measures exactly 90°, and two smaller angles. The measures of the two smaller angles must add up to 90°, because the three angle measures must add up to 180°. The longest side of a right triangle is opposite the right angle, and is called the *hypotenuse*. The other two sides, which are perpendicular, are called the *legs* of the triangle.

Right triangles are of particular interest in the study of geometry because they appear frequently in buildings and everyday structures, and because the geometrical relationships within these triangles are strictly defined.

The most notable rule pertaining to right triangles is the Pythagorean theorem, which was reviewed in chapter 7. This theorem describes the relationship between the hypotenuse and legs of a right triangle.

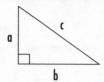

In any right triangle with legs a and b and hypotenuse c,
$a^2 + b^2 = c^2$.

Test your understanding of triangles in the following exercises.

EXERCISES

Determine whether each of the following statements is true or false

1. An equilateral triangle must be an acute triangle.

2. An isosceles triangle must be an obtuse triangle.

3. An isosceles triangle cannot be a right triangle.

4. A right triangle must be either a scalene triangle or an isosceles triangle.

For each of the following figures, find the value of x.

5.

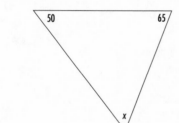

6.

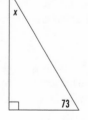

7.

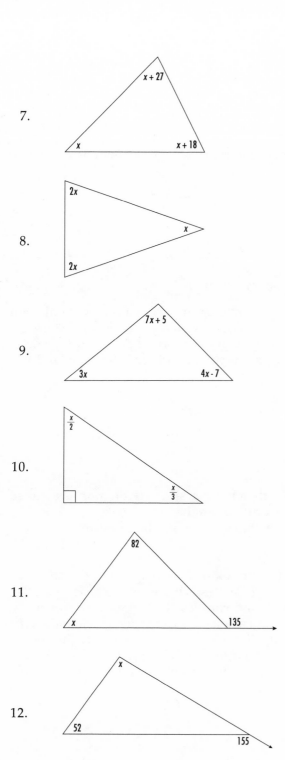

x + 27

x   x + 18

8.

2x

x

2x

9.

7x + 5

3x   4x - 7

10.

$\frac{x}{2}$

$\frac{x}{3}$

11.

82

x   135

12.

x

52

155

8.7 QUADRILATERALS

A quadrilateral is a four-sided polygon. The measures of the four angles of a quadrilateral add up to 360°. Quadrilaterals can be assigned to various categories depending on their characteristics.

PARALLELOGRAMS

A parallelogram is a quadrilateral in which each side is parallel to the opposite side.

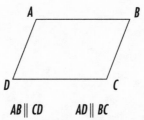

$$AB \parallel CD \qquad AD \parallel BC$$

Because the sides of a parallelogram are parallel, the rules for parallel lines and transversals apply here. Specifically, there are two types of angles created; big ones and small ones. The big angles are equal; the small angles are equal; and any big angle and any small angle are supplementary.

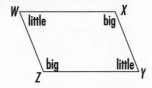

In a polygon, angles that have a side in common are called *consecutive angles*. Consecutive angles in a parallelogram are supplementary. Opposite angles are equal in measure.

RECTANGLES

A rectangle is a parallelogram that has four right angles. All parallelogram rules apply to rectangles: Opposite sides are parallel, opposite angles are equal, and consecutive angles are supplementary. A rectangle's two dimensions are called its *length* and *width*. The length is customarily the greater dimension, but this is not necessarily the case. Do not assume that the width of a rectangle is less than its length. A square, for example, is a rectangle whose length and width are equal.

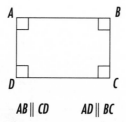

$$AB \parallel CD \qquad AD \parallel BC$$

There are a few rules that are true of rectangles that are not true of parallelograms. For example, a diagonal in a rectangle divides the rectangle into two right triangles. In each right triangle formed this way, the diagonal is the hypotenuse, and the length and width are the legs of the triangle. The diagonal's length can be found using the Pythagorean theorem when the rectangle's length and width are known.

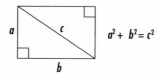

The diagonals of a rectangle are of equal length. These diagonals always *bisect* each other—that is, cut each other perfectly in half.

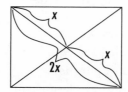

RHOMBUSES

A rhombus is a parallelogram with four sides of equal length. A square can be described as a rhombus with 90° angles. The diagonals of a rhombus are not generally equal in length, but they do always bisect each other perfectly. The diagonals of a rhombus are perpendicular.

TRAPEZOIDS

A trapezoid is *not* a parallelogram. A trapezoid has two parallel sides and two sides that are *not* parallel. The parallel sides are called *bases*, and the non-parallel sides are called *legs*. If the legs are of equal length, then the trapezoid is said to be isosceles.

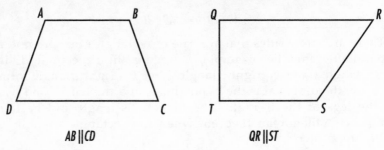

AB ∥ CD   QR ∥ ST

EXERCISES

1. Which of the following is *not* a parallelogram?
   (a) rhombus
   (b) rectangle
   (c) trapezoid
   (d) square

2. Which of the following statements is *not* true of a parallelogram?
   (a) Opposite angles are equal.
   (b) Consecutive angles are equal.
   (c) Opposite sides are parallel.
   (d) The sum of all four angle-measures is 360°.

For each of the following figures, find the value of x.

3.

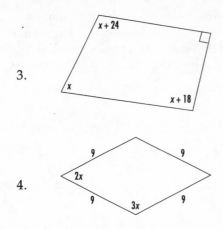

4.

5.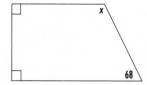

6.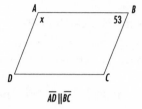

$\overline{AD} \parallel \overline{BC}$

7.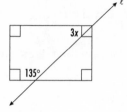

8.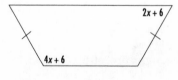

9.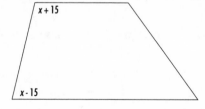

10.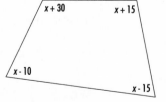

11. A rectangle has a length of 8 and a width of 6. Find the length of its diagonal.

12. A regular quadrilateral has a side of length 5. Find the length of the quadrilateral's diagonal.

SUMMARY

- An *acute angle* is one whose measure is less than 90 degrees.

  A *right angle* is one that measures exactly 90 degrees.

  An *obtuse angle* is one whose measure is between 90 degrees and 180 degrees.

  A *straight angle* is one that measures exactly 180 degrees. The angle's two rays then form a straight line.

  A *reflex angle* is one that measures more than 180°.

- Two angles are supplementary when the sum of their degree measures is 180.

- Two angles are complementary when the sum of their degree measures is 90.

- Vertical angles are equal in measure.

- When a transversal intersects two parallel lines, two kinds of angles are formed: big ones and little ones.

  All of the big angles are equal.

  All of the little angles are equal.

  Any big angle and any little angle are supplementary.

- A regular polygon has sides of equal length and angles of equal measure.

- For any *n*-sided polygon, the sum of the interior angles in degrees = (*n* - 2)180.

- The measures of the three angles of a triangle always add up to 180 degrees.

- A *scalene* triangle is one in which all three sides have different lengths and all three angles have different measures.

  An *isosceles* triangle is one with two sides of equal length and two angles of equal measure.

  An *equilateral* triangle is one with three sides of equal length and three angles of equal measure.

- A triangle whose angles all measure less than 90° is called an *acute triangle*.

  A triangle with one angle that measures 90° is called a *right triangle*.

  A triangle with one angle that measures more than 90° is called an *obtuse triangle*.

- A quadrilateral is a four-sided polygon. The measures of the four angles of a polygon add up to 360°.

- Because the sides of a parallelogram are parallel, the rules for parallel lines and transversals apply in parallelograms. Specifically, there are two types of angles created; big ones and small ones. The big angles are equal; the small angles are equal; and any big angle and any small angle are supplementary.

9

Proportion, Similarity, and Congruence

Proportion is a simple but powerful idea that has numerous applications in both algebra and geometry. The following pages will review the closely related ideas of ratio and proportion, and apply these ideas to similar and congruent figures in geometry.

9.1 RATIO

A ratio expresses the size of one quantity in terms of another quantity. For example, consider the ratio between the numbers 4 and 5. A ratio of 4 to 5 can be written in several different ways:

$$4 : 5 \quad \frac{4}{5} \quad 4 \div 5 \quad 0.8$$

These expressions are equivalent; each expresses the ratio, or quotient, of 4 and 5. The ratio of the two numbers says, essentially, that 4 is $\frac{4}{5}$ of 5. If expresses the size of the number 4 in terms of the number 5.

The ratio of 5 to 4 is a completely different quantity. This ratio too, of course, can be written in different ways:

$$5 : 4 \quad \frac{5}{4} \quad 5 \div 4 \quad 1.25$$

This ratio says, essentially, that 5 is $\frac{5}{4}$ of 4. Notice that the ratios 4 : 5 and 5 : 4 represent different relationships, and therefore have different numerical values.

Ratios can be reduced like ordinary fractions. This means that different ratios can have the same numerical values. Such ratios are called *equivalent ratios*. For example, a ratio of 40 to 50 could be written as a fraction, and then reduced:

$$\frac{40}{50} = \frac{10 \times 4}{10 \times 5} = \frac{10}{10} \times \frac{4}{5} = \frac{4}{5}$$

The ratio of 40 to 50 is equivalent to the ratio of 4 to 5. The ratio 4 : 5 cannot be reduced further, so this ratio is said to be in *simplest form*.

A ratio expresses the size of a quantity in terms of another quantity.

RATIOS VS. FRACTIONS

It's important to be aware that ratios are sometimes used differently from ordinary fractions. For example, imagine a garden divided into 9 equal parts. Suppose that 5 of these parts are planted with roses, and the remaining 4 parts with daffodils.

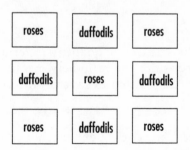

To discuss this garden using fractions in the usual way, you would relate parts of the garden to the whole garden. You might say, for example, that the garden is $\frac{5}{9}$ roses, or that daffodils make up $\frac{4}{9}$ of the garden. In each case, a part of the garden is related to the whole.

To discuss the garden using ratios, on the other hand, you might say instead that the ratio of roses to daffodils in the garden is 5 : 4, or that the ratio of daffodils to roses is $\frac{4}{5}$. In both of these cases, you are relating one part of the garden to another part.

You can find the size of one part of the ratio algebraically. When you know how big one part of the garden is, it becomes easy to say exactly how many roses there are, or exactly how many daffodils there are.

Examples

1. A garden consists of roses and daffodils in the ratio 5 : 4. If there are 108 flowers in the garden, how many daffodils does that garden contain?

   You know that the garden is five parts roses and four parts daffodils. To figure out how big one part of the ratio is, express the ratio algebraically:

   Let $5x$ = the number of roses,

   and $4x$ = the number of daffodils.

   Then, write an equation:

   $5x + 4x = 108$

   Combine like terms.

   $9x = 108$

   Divide both sides by 9 to find the value of x.

   $$\frac{9x}{9} = \frac{108}{9}$$

   $x = 12$

   Each part of the ratio is equivalent to 12 flowers. The number of daffodils is therefore 4(12), or 48. There are 48 daffodils in the garden.

2. The lengths of a triangle's sides are in the ratio 3 : 4 : 5. If the triangle has a perimeter of 84, what is the length of the triangle's shortest side?

   Express the ratio algebraically:

   Let $3x$ = the length of the shortest side,

   $4x$ = the length of the middle side,

   and $5x$ = the length of the longest side.

Write an equation:

$3x + 4x + 5x = 84$

Combine like terms.

$12x = 84$

Divide both sides by 12 to find the value of x:

$$\frac{12x}{12} = \frac{84}{12}$$

$x = 7$

The value of x is 7. The length of the triangle's shortest side, which is $3x$, is therefore equal to 3(7), or 21.

Test your understanding of ratios in the following exercises.

EXERCISES

Express each of the following ratios in simplest form.

1. 18 : 6

2. 5 : 40

3. 16 : 24

4. 32 : 200

Solve each of the following problems.

5. In a class of 20 students, boys and girls are in a ratio of 1 : 3. How many girls are there in the class?

6. A bag holds red, yellow, and green marbles in the ratio 1 : 4 : 7. If there are 28 green marbles in the bag, how many marbles does the bag hold altogether?

7. The length and width of a rectangle are in the ratio 5 : 3. If the perimeter of the rectangle is 64, what is the rectangle's area?

8. The ages of Tom, Dick, and Harry are in the ratio 6 : 7 : 8. If the sum of their ages is 63, how old is Dick?

9. The ratio of men to women in a club is 9 : 13. If there are 78 women in the club, what is the club's total membership?

10. The measures of the three angles of a triangle are in a ratio of 2 : 3 : 7. Find the measure of each angle.

11. In a student council meeting, a motion passed by a ratio of 5 : 2. If all 35 members of the council voted, how many voted against the motion?

12. Three numbers are in a ratio of 1 : 3 : 4, and the average of these numbers is 16. What are the numbers?

9.2 PROPORTION

A *proportion* is an equality of two ratios. Suppose, for example, that Jocelyn plays 5 tennis matches and wins 3. You can express the ratio of her wins to her total matches played as a fraction: $\frac{3}{5}$. Now, suppose that Sampson plays 15 tennis matches and wins 9. His ratio of wins to matches played can also be expressed as a fraction: $\frac{9}{15}$. These two ratios are equal.

$$\frac{3}{5} = \frac{9}{15}$$

Jocelyn's record of wins is *proportional* to Sampson's.

A proportion is an equation of two ratios, which takes the form $\frac{a}{b} = \frac{c}{d}$.

A proportion is written as an equation of two fractions, where the tops and bottoms of the two fractions represent the same quantities:

$$\frac{\text{matches won}}{\text{matches played}} = \frac{\text{matches won}}{\text{matches played}}$$

Remember that when two fractions are joined in an equation, cross-multiplying the fractions produced a new equation that is equivalent to the original. This technique can be used to solve a proportion that contains a variable, or to verify that two fractions are equal:

Compare the fractions $\frac{3}{5}$ and $\frac{9}{15}$ by cross-multiplication.

$$\frac{3}{5} = \frac{9}{15}$$

Cross-multiply to verify that the fractions are equal.

$$3 \times 15 = 5 \times 9$$
$$45 = 45$$

The fractions are equal, and the two records of matches won are proportional.

The Rule of Cross-Products

If two fractions are equal, then their cross-products are equal.

If $\frac{a}{b} = \frac{c}{d}$, then $ad = bc$.

Where $b \neq 0$ and $d \neq 0$.

Examples

1. Solve the proportion $\dfrac{x}{3} = \dfrac{56}{42}$.

$$\frac{x}{3} = \frac{56}{42}$$

Cross-multiply.

$42x = 3(56)$

$42x = 168$

Divide both sides by 42 to find the value of x.

$$\frac{42x}{42} = \frac{168}{42}$$

$x = 4$

The value of x is 4.

2. Solve the proportion $\dfrac{2}{x-1} = \dfrac{8}{3x+4}$.

$$\frac{2}{x-1} = \frac{8}{3x+4}$$

Cross-multiply.

$2(3x + 4) = 8(x - 1)$

Distribute.

$6x + 8 = 8x - 8$

Subtract $6x$ from both sides.

$$\begin{array}{r} 6x + 8 = 8x - 8 \\ \underline{-6x \qquad -6x \quad} \\ 8 = 2x - 8 \end{array}$$

Add 8 to both sides.

$$\begin{array}{r} 8 = 2x - 8 \\ \underline{+8 \qquad +8} \\ 16 = 2x \end{array}$$

Divide both sides by 2 to find the value of x.

$$\frac{16}{2} = \frac{2x}{2}$$

$8 = x$

The value of x is 8.

Practice working with ratios in the following exercises.

Solve each of the following proportions.

1. $\dfrac{3}{5} = \dfrac{x}{10}$

2. $\dfrac{x}{4} = \dfrac{45}{60}$

3. $\dfrac{13}{52} = \dfrac{5}{x}$

4. $\dfrac{63}{x} = \dfrac{7}{4}$

5. $\dfrac{x-2}{-2} = \dfrac{x-12}{3}$

6. $\dfrac{5}{x+8} = \dfrac{-3}{x}$

7. $\dfrac{2}{9} = \dfrac{x-3}{x+4}$

8. $\dfrac{x-6}{2x+12} = \dfrac{3}{2}$

9.3 SIMILARITY

When two figures have the same shape but not necessarily the same size, they are called *similar figures*. The polygons shown below, for example, are similar.

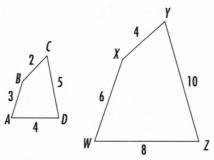

Because the two polygons are similar, you can see that for every part of polygon *ABCD*, there is a similar part of polygon *WXYZ*. These are called *corresponding parts*. For example, side *AD* corresponds to side *WZ*. Angle *BCD* corresponds to angle *XYZ*; and so on.

If you measure the angles in the two polygons, you will find that every angle in polygon *ABCD* has the same measure as the corresponding angle in polygon *WXYZ*. If this were not the case, the two polygons would not have the same shape, and would therefore not be similar.

Corresponding angles of similar polygons are equal in measure.

The corresponding *sides* in polygons *ABCD* and *WXYZ* are obviously not equal. If you compare the lengths of corresponding sides, you'll find that they are always in the same ratio:

$$\frac{WX}{AB} = \frac{6}{3} = \frac{2}{1} \qquad \frac{XY}{BC} = \frac{4}{2} = \frac{2}{1} \qquad \frac{YZ}{CD} = \frac{10}{5} = \frac{2}{1} \qquad \frac{WZ}{AD} = \frac{8}{4} = \frac{2}{1}$$

Each side of polygon *WXYZ* is twice as long as the corresponding side of polygon *ABCD*. This is always true of similar polygons; corresponding sides will always be related by a constant multiple. In other word, corresponding sides are proportional.

Corresponding sides of similar polygons are in proportion.

Examples

1. Polygons *LMNO* and *RSTU* are similar. Find the value of *x*.

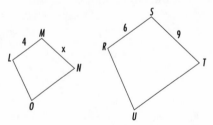

Sides *LM* corresponds to side *RS*, and side *MN* corresponds to *ST*. Write a proportion relating the lengths of these sides.

$$\frac{LM}{RS} = \frac{MN}{ST}$$

$$\frac{4}{6} = \frac{x}{9}$$

Cross-multiply.

$$4 \times 9 = 6x$$

$$36 = 6x$$

Divide both sides by 6 to find the value of x.

$$\frac{36}{6} = \frac{6x}{6}$$

$$6 = x$$

The value of x is 6.

2. Triangle ABC and triangle FGH are similar. The shortest side of $\triangle ABC$ is 2 cm long, and the shortest side of $\triangle FGH$ is 5 cm long. If the longest side of $\triangle ABC$ is 8 cm long, how long is the longest side of $\triangle FGH$?

Corresponding sides of similar polygons are proportional. The shortest side of $\triangle ABC$ corresponds to the shortest side of $\triangle FGH$. The longest side of $\triangle ABC$ corresponds to the longest side of $\triangle FGH$. Write a proportion relating these sides.

$$\frac{\text{shortest side of } \triangle ABC}{\text{shortest side of } \triangle FGH} = \frac{\text{longest side of } \triangle ABC}{\text{longest side of } \triangle FGH}$$

Let $x =$ the longest side of $\triangle FGH$.

$$\frac{2}{5} = \frac{8}{x}$$

Cross-multiply.

$$2x = 5(8)$$

$$2x = 40$$

$$x = 20$$

The longest side of $\triangle FGH$ has a length of 20 cm.

PROVING TRIANGLES SIMILAR

Two polygons are similar if all of their corresponding angles are equal in measure. To show that two triangles are similar, however, it's not necessary to show that all three pairs of corresponding angles are equal. Because the three angles of a triangle must add up to 180°, you know that if two pairs of angles are equal, the third pair of angles must be equal as well.

If two angles in one triangle are equal in measure to the corresponding angles in another triangle, the triangles are similar.

Practice working with similar polygons in the following exercises.

EXERCISES

The two figures in each of the following figures are similar. Find the value of the variable in each case.

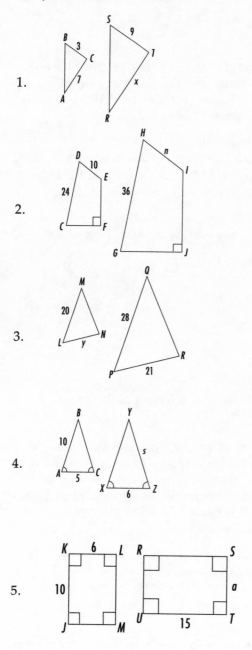

1.

2.

3.

4.

5.

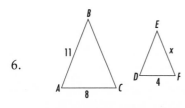

6.

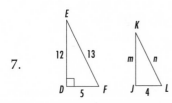

7.

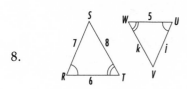

8.

Solve each of the following.

9. Triangles *ABC* and *DEF* are similar. Corresponding sides *AB* and *DE* are in the ratio 4 : 5. If *AC* = 12, what is the measure of corresponding side *DF*?

10. A tree 36 feet in height casts a shadow 32 feet long. At the same time, Willy casts a shadow four feet long. How tall is Willy?

11. A fencepost 4 feet tall casts a shadow 6 feet long. At the same moment, how long is the shadow of a flagpole 14 feet in height?

12. The heights of two similar triangles are in the ratio 5 : 8. If the smaller triangle has a perimeter of 35, what is the perimeter of the larger triangle?

9.4 CONGRUENCE

When two figures have the same shape and the same size—when, in other words, two figures are identical—they are called *congruent figures*. All of the following pairs of figures are congruent to one another:

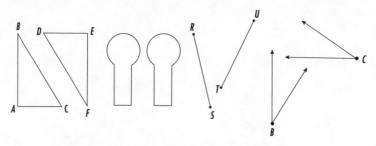

> **Corresponding angles** of congruent polygons are equal in measure.
> **Corresponding sides** of congruent polygons are equal in length.

PROVING TRIANGLES CONGRUENT

Two congruent polygons have six equal measurements: three angle measures and three lengths. To prove that two triangles are congruent, however, it is not necessary to prove that all six of these corresponding measurements are equal. In fact, you can prove two triangles congruent with as few as three measurements, as long as you've got the right ones.

1. **Side-Side-Side (SSS):** Two triangles must be congruent if three sides of one triangle are congruent to the corresponding sides of the other triangle.

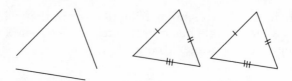

Only one triangle can be assembled from three sides of given lengths.

2. **Side-Angle-Side (SAS):** Two triangles must be congruent if two sides and the included angle of one triangle are congruent to the corresponding parts of the other triangle.

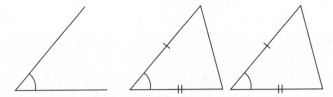

Only one triangle can be assembled including these sides and this angle; the third side must connect the endpoints of the existing two.

3. **Angle-Side-Angle (ASA):** Two triangles must be congruent if two angles and the side between them in one triangle are congruent to the corresponding parts of the other triangle.

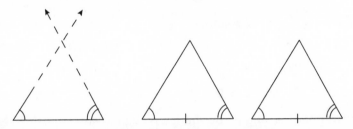

Only one triangle can be assembled including this side and these angles; the third vertex of the triangle must fall at the intersection of the angles' rays.

4. **Angle-Angle-Side (AAS):** Two triangles must be congruent if two angles and the side opposite one of the angles are congruent to the corresponding parts of the other triangle.

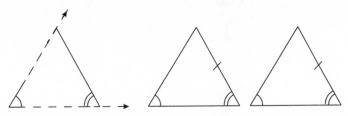

Only one triangle can be assembled including this side and these angles; there is only one position of the three vertices that will cause the angles' rays to meet both endpoints of the existing side.

Note: You *cannot* conclude that two triangles are congruent when:

- The three angles of one triangle are congruent to the corresponding angles of the other (AAA).
- Two sides and an angle opposite one of the sides of one triangle are congruent to the corresponding parts of the other (SSA).

SUMMARY

- A ratio expresses the size of a quantity in terms of another quantity.
- A proportion is an equation of two ratios, which takes the form $\frac{a}{b} = \frac{c}{d}$.
- **The Rule of Cross-Products**
  If two fractions are equal, then their cross-products are equal.
  If $\frac{a}{b} = \frac{c}{d}$, then $ad = bc$.
  Where $b \neq 0$ and $d \neq 0$.
- **Corresponding angles** of similar polygons are equal in measure.
- **Corresponding sides** of similar polygons are in proportion.
- If two angles in one triangle are equal in measure to the corresponding angles in another triangle, the triangles are similar.
- **Corresponding angles** of congruent polygons are equal in measure.
- **Corresponding sides** of congruent polygons are equal in length.
- Triangles may be proved congruent by the information represented by: **SSS, SAS, ASA,** or **AAS.**
- Triangles may *not* be proved congruent by the information represented by: **AAA,** or **SSA.**

10

Distance, Area, and Volume

Geometry includes considerations of all three dimensions. Length, or distance, is a one-dimensional quantity. Angle measure and area are two-dimensional quantities. Volume, a measure of enclosed space, is a three-dimensional quantity. This chapter will review the basic geometry of all three dimensions.

10.1 LENGTH, PERIMETER, AND AREA

PERIMETER

The *perimeter* of a polygon is the sum of the lengths of its sides.

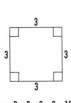

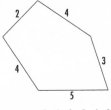

$p = 3 + 3 + 3 + 3 = 12$ $p = 2 + 4 + 3 + 5 + 4 = 18$ $p = 3 + 4 + 5 = 12$

When all of the linear measurements of a polygon are increased by the same factor, the perimeter is increased by the same factor. Look what happens when the length of each side of a square is doubled:

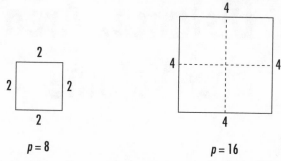

The larger square is *similar* to the original square–it's the same shape, but a different size. The perimeter of the larger square is twice the original perimeter, just as the length and width are twice the original length and width. This is true of any polygon.

When all of a polygon's linear measurements are increased or decreased by the same factor, the perimeter is also increased or decreased by that factor.

Because the relationships between the sides of some polygons are specifically defined, it's possible to write formulas for the perimeter of certain polygons.

Quadrilateral	Perimeter Formula
rectangle	$A = 2w + 2l$
square	$A = 4s$
rhombus	$A = 4s$

Area

The measure of the size of a flat surface is called *area*. Any simple closed curve has area. The measurement of area is not concerned with shape; all of the following figures, for example, have different shapes but equal areas.

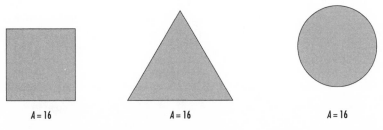

$A = 16$ $A = 16$ $A = 16$

Area is measured in *square units*. If a length is measured in centimeters, for example, then an area is measured in *square centimeters*. Area can be measured in square miles, square meters, square feet, and so on.

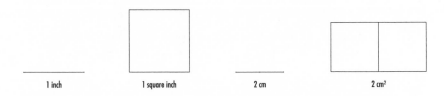

1 inch   1 square inch   2 cm   2 cm²

While perimeter varies directly as length in a polygon, area varies as the *square* of length in a polygon. What that means in everyday language is that if you increase every length in a polygon by a factor of 2, the perimeter will increase by a factor of 2, while the area will increase by a factor of 2^2, or 4. This can be clearly seen when the length and width of a square are doubled:

When the length and width of a square are increased by a factor of 3, the area is increased by a factor of 3^2, or 9.

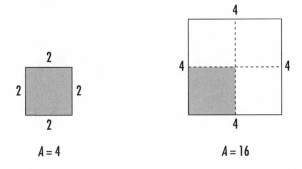

$A = 4$ $A = 16$

Note that the area increases as the square of the lengths in a polygon only when *all* lengths in the polygon are increased by the same factor, so that the new, larger shape is similar to the original polygon, but bigger. If only *one* dimension is doubled, the area is also doubled:

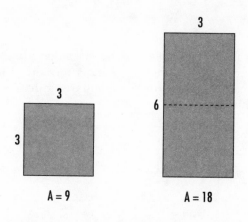

When all of a polygon's linear measurements are increased or decreased by the same factor, the area is increased or decreased by the square of that factor.

10.2 AREA

The areas of various polygons are calculated using different formulas.

TRIANGLES

The area of a triangle is equal to one-half the length of the triangle's base multiplied by the triangle's height. Any side of a triangle may be designated the triangle's base; the height of the triangle is the length of an altitude drawn perpendicularly to that side.

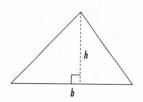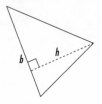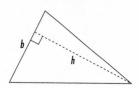

Because the legs of a right triangle are perpendicular, they may be considered the base and height of the triangle. This can make the area of right triangles particularly easy to calculate.

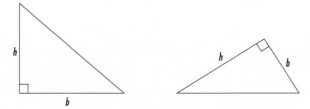

RECTANGLES

The area of a rectangle is found by multiplying its length by its width.

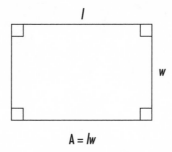

$$A = lw$$

A square is a regular rectangle, whose length and width are equal. The area of a square can therefore be found by squaring the length of one side.

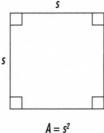

$$A = s^2$$

PARALLELOGRAMS

The area of a parallelogram is found by multiplying the base of the parallelogram by its height. The parallelogram's height is the length of an altitude drawn perpendicularly from the base to the opposite side.

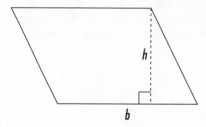

By mentally rearranging the parallelogram, you can see that this formula is essentially identical to the formula for the area of a rectangle.

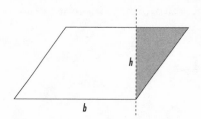

TRAPEZOIDS

The area of a trapezoid is found by multiplying the average of the lengths of its bases by its height. Remember that the bases of a trapezoid are its two parallel sides. To find their average length, add the lengths of the two bases together and divide by 2. The height of a trapezoid is the length of an altitude drawn perpendicularly from one base to the other.

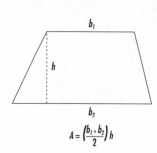

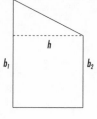

$$A = \left(\frac{b_1 + b_2}{2}\right) h$$

When the height of a trapezoid is not given but you know the length of the bases and one of the trapezoid's legs, it may be possible to find the height using the Pythagorean theorem. Just divide the trapezoid into a quadrilateral and a right triangle.

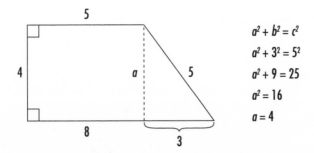

$$a^2 + b^2 = c^2$$
$$a^2 + 3^2 = 5^2$$
$$a^2 + 9 = 25$$
$$a^2 = 16$$
$$a = 4$$

SUMMARY OF AREA FORMULAS	
Polygon	**Area Formula**
triangle	$A = \dfrac{1}{2}bh$
rectangle	$A = lw$
square	$A = s^2$
parallelogram	$A = bh$
trapezoid	$A = \left(\dfrac{b_1 + b_2}{2}\right)h$

Examples

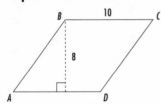

1. Find the area of parallelogram *ABCD*.

   The parallelogram's base has a length of 10, and its height is 8. The area of the parallelogram is the product of these measurements.

   $A = bh$

   $A = (10)(8)$

   $A = 80$

   The parallelogram has an area of 80.

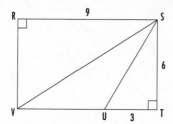

2. In the figure above, *RSTV* is a rectangle. If *RS* = 9, *ST* = 6, and *TU* = 3, find the area of triangle *SUV*.

Consider *VU* the base of Δ*SUV*. The length of *UV* can be found by subtracting the length of *TU* from the length of *TV*.

VU = *TV* – *TU*

VU = 9 – 3

VU = 6

The triangle has a base of 6. Next, you must find the height of Δ*SUV*. In this case, the altitude of Δ*SUV* actually lies outside the triangle. The altitude of a triangle is a perpendicular segment from the base to the opposite vertex. Segment *ST* is the altitude of Δ*SUV*; the height of Δ*SUV* is 6.

Once you know the base and height of the triangle, plug them into the formula for the area of a triangle.

$$A = \frac{1}{2}bh$$

$$A = \frac{1}{2}(6)(6)$$

$$A = 18$$

The area of Δ*SUV* is 18.

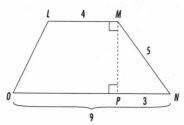

3. In the figure above, $\overline{LM}$ and $\overline{NO}$ are parallel. If $LM = 4$, $MN = 5$, $NP = 3$, $NO = 9$, and MP is perpendicular to NO, find the area of quadrilateral $LMNO$.

Because two sides of $LMNO$ are parallel and two are definitely not, the quadrilateral is a trapezoid. The parallel sides, $\overline{LM}$ and $\overline{NO}$, are the trapezoid's bases. Segment MP, which is perpendicular to both bases, is the altitude of the trapezoid. To find the length of $\overline{MP}$, apply the Pythagorean theorem to triangle MNP.

Let $a =$ the length of $\overline{MP}$.

$$a^2 + b^2 = c^2$$
$$a^2 + (3)^2 = (5)^2$$
$$a^2 + 9 = 25$$
$$a^2 = 16$$

Take the square root of both sides to find the value of a. Because a represents a length, consider only the positive root.

$$\sqrt{a^2} = \sqrt{16}$$
$$a = 4$$

Trapezoid $LMNO$ has an altitude of 4. Its bases have lengths of 4 and 9, respectively. Plug these numbers into the formula for the area of a trapezoid.

$$A = \left(\frac{b_1 + b_2}{2}\right)h$$
$$A = \left(\frac{4 + 9}{2}\right)4$$
$$A = (6.5)4$$
$$A = 26$$

The area of trapezoid $LMNO$ is 26.

Practice working with area in the following exercises.

EXERCISES

Find the area of each of the following polygons.

1.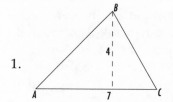

2.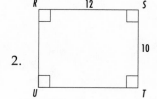

3.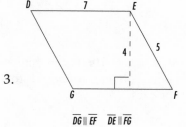

   $\overline{DG} \parallel \overline{EF}$ $\overline{DE} \parallel \overline{FG}$

4.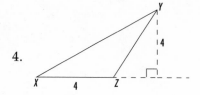

5.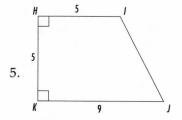

6.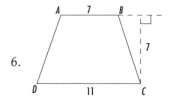

7.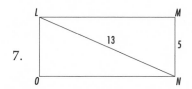

8.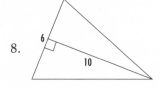

Solve the following problems. Remember that the Pythagorean theorem can be used to find the third side of a right triangle when two sides are known.

9. A triangle has an area of 12. If one side of the triangle has a length of 8, what is the length of an altitude drawn to that side?

10. A right triangle has a leg of length 8 and a hypotenuse of length 17. What is the area of this triangle?

11. The length of a rectangular garden is 5 feet greater than its width. If the garden has an area of 84 square feet, what are its dimensions?

12. A rectangle has a length of $x + 7$ and a width of $x - 7$. If the rectangle has an area of 72, what is the value of x?

13. The base of a parallelogram is 4 inches longer than the altitude drawn to that base. If the parallelogram has an area of 117 square inches, what is the length of the parallelogram's base in inches?

14. An isosceles trapezoid has a base of length 5 and a base of length 11. If a leg of the trapezoid has a length of 5, what is the trapezoid's area?

10.3 CIRCLES

A circle is defined as the set of points at a fixed distance from a given center point. That fixed distance is called the *radius* of the circle. A circle with a radius of 5 centimeters, for example, consists of all points at a distance of 5 cm from a center point.

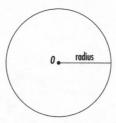

A line segment drawn from one point on a circle's edge to another is called a *chord*. Chords are usually named by their endpoints. The *diameter* of a circle is a chord that passes through the center of the circle. The diameter is equivalent to two radii of the circle. A diameter divides a circle into equal halves.

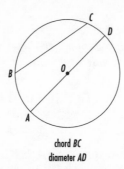

chord *BC*
diameter *AD*

A portion of a circle's edge is called an *arc*. An arc is named for its endpoints, or for its endpoints and a single point on the arc. When an arc is equal to exactly half of a circle, it is called a *semicircle*. A line segment connecting the endpoints of a semicircular arc is a diameter.

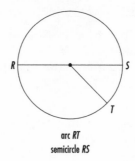

arc *RT*
semicircle *RS*

CIRCUMFERENCE

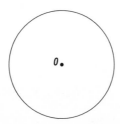

The length of a circle's edge is called the circle's *circumference*. The ratio of the circumference to the diameter is the same for every circle. Divide a circle's circumference by the length of its diameter, and you'll get a number slightly greater than 3. The number is 3.141592654.... You'll find that this number's value cannot be calculated exactly. It's an irrational number; in decimal form, the number goes on forever without repeating. The name given to this number is π.

Every scientific calculator has a fairly accurate decimal approximation of π programmed into it. If you don't have access to a calculator, it's common to use 3.14 or $\frac{22}{7}$ as approximations of π, although neither of these values represents its value exactly.

This means that the radius, diameter, and circumference of every circle are related in the same way. The diameter is twice the radius, and the circumference is equal to the diameter times π. If you know the radius or diameter of a circle, you can easily find the circumference.

Circumference of a Circle
For a circle of radius r and diameter d, C = 2πr or C = 2πd.

AREA

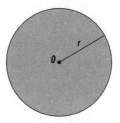

The area of a circle, like the circumference, is related to the circle's radius in a definite way. Once you know the radius of a circle, it's simple to find its area using the following formula.

Area of a Circle

For a circle of radius r, A = πr².

Examples

1. Circle O has a radius of 3 cm. What is the circle's area?

   You are given the radius of the circle: $r = 3$. Just plug this number into the formula for the area of a circle.

   $A = \pi r^2$

   $A = \pi(3)^2$

   Calculate the value of 3 squared.

   $A = 9\pi$

   The circle has an area of 9π cm^2

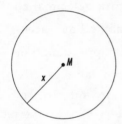

2. If circle M has an area of 25π, what is the value of x?

   You are given the area of the circle. Plug this value into the formula for the area of the circle and solve for the radius.

   $A = \pi r^2$

   $25\pi = \pi r^2$

   Divide both sides by π.

   $\dfrac{25\pi}{\pi} = \dfrac{\pi r^2}{\pi}$

   $25 = r^2$

   Take the square root of both sides. Because r represents a length, consider only the positive root.

   $\sqrt{25} = \sqrt{r^2}$

   $5 = r$

   The radius has a length of 5. Since $x =$ the length of the radius, the value of x is 5.

EXERCISES

1. If the radius of a circle is increased by a factor of 3, then the circumference is increased by what factor?

2. If the diameter of a circle is increased by a factor of 5, then the area is increased by what factor?

3. What is the area of a circle with a circumference of 8π?

4. What is the circumference of a circle with an area of 81π?

5. What is the diameter of circle with a circumference of 12?

6. What is the radius of a circle with an area of 25?

7. What is the area of a circle with a radius of $x - 3$?

8. A goat is tethered to a pole in the middle of a lawn. If the tether is 6 meters long, what is the area of the circular region in which the goat can graze?

9. A satellite in a perfectly circular path. If it travels $4,000,000\pi$ miles in one revolution, what is the radius of its orbit?

10. If a circle has a circumference c, what is the circle's area in terms of c?

Find the area of the shaded region in each of the following figures.

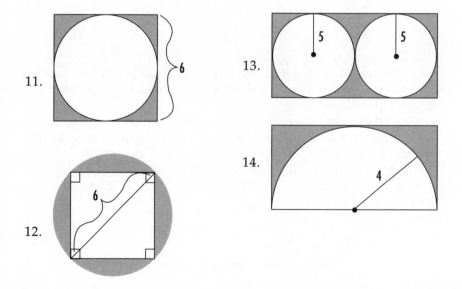

11.

12.

13.

14.

10.4 POLYHEDRONS

A *polyhedron* is a three-dimensional solid whose sides are polygons. Many familiar shapes, like cubes and pyramids, are polyhedrons.

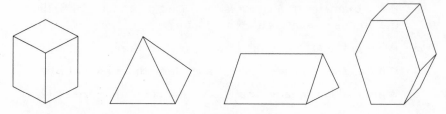

A solid has the attributes of length and area found in polygons; each edge has a length, and each side, or *face*, has an area. It is sometimes convenient to talk about the *surface area* of a polyhedron; this is the sum of the areas of the polyhedron's faces.

In addition to these familiar measurements, however, there is a new quantity that comes into play in solids. This is *volume*, the measure of the space enclosed by a solid.

PRISMS

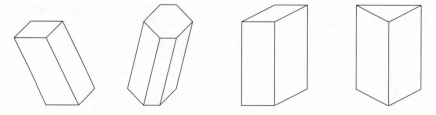

Prisms are a special set of polyhedrons. A prism has two parallel sides which are called *bases*. The other sides, which are called *lateral faces*, are parallelograms.

When the lateral faces of a prism are all perpendicular to the bases, the prism is called a *right prism*. In the figure above, two of the four prisms are right prisms.

The volume of a right prism is found by multiplying the area of its base by the prism's *height*. The height is the length of one of the prism's lateral edges.

Volume of a Right Prism

For a right prism with a base of area B and a height h,
$V = Bh.$

SPECIAL PRISMS

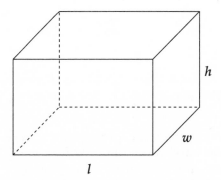

When the base of a right prism is a rectangle, the prism is called a *rectangular prism* or *rectangular solid*. A rectangular solid has six faces, each of which is a rectangle. The area of a rectangle is the product of its length and width; using this fact, a general formula for the volume of a rectangular solid can be written.

Volume of a Rectangular Solid

For any rectangular solid of length l, width w, and height h,
$V = lwh$.

When every face of a rectangular solid is a square, the solid is called a *cube*.

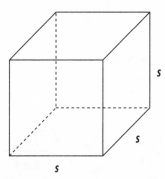

All of a cube's edges have equal length. In other words, the length, width, and height of a cube are all equal. A general formula for the volume of a cube can be written using this fact.

Volume of a Cube

For any cube with an edge of length s, $V = s^3$.

PYRAMIDS

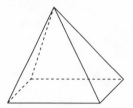 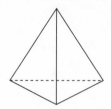 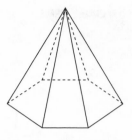

A pyramid is a solid formed by joining each vertex of a polygon to another point that is not in the plane of a polygon. The polygon is called the *base* of the pyramid, while the point is called the pyramid's *vertex*. The *altitude* of a pyramid is a line segment extending perpendicularly from the plane of the base to the vertex. The length of the altitude is the pyramid's *height*.

The volume of a pyramid is one-third the volume of a right prism with the same base and height.

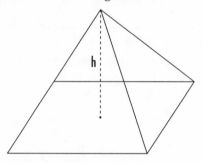

Volume of a Pyramid

For a pyramid with base of area B and a height h,

$V = \frac{1}{3}Bh.$

SUMMARY OF VOLUME FORMULAS	
Polyhedron	**Volume Formula**
right prism	$V = Bh$
rectangular solid	$V = lwh$
cube	$V = s^3$
pyramid	$V = \frac{1}{3}Bh$

EXERCISES

Find the volume of each of the following rectangular solids.

1.

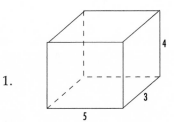

2.

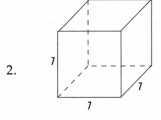

3.

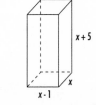

4.

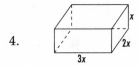

Find the volume of each of the following polyhedrons. Assume that prisms are right prisms and pyramids are right pyramids.

5.

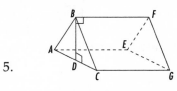

$AC = 8$ $AD = 4$ $BD = 5$ $BF = 8$

6.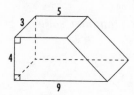

7.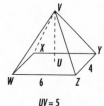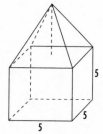

$UV = 5$

8.

Solve each of the following problems and state the solution clearly.

9. If each dimension of a cube is halved, then the cube's new volume will be what fraction of the cube's original volume?

10. A right prism has an octagonal base with an area of 0.5 square meters and a height of 3 meters. What is the prism's volume in square meters?

11. The rectangular base of a right pyramid has a length of 4 and a width of 3. If the pyramid has a volume of 20, what is the length of the pyramid's altitude?

12. A pyramid with height of 2 and a square base having an edge of length 2 is inscribed in a cube with an edge of length 2. What is the volume contained within the cube that is not contained within the pyramid?

10.5 CIRCULAR SOLIDS

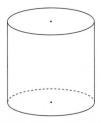 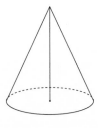 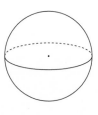

There is another set of common solids that does not fall within the set of polyhedrons. These are the circular solids. The basic circular solids are the *cylinder*, the *cone*, and the *sphere*.

CYLINDERS

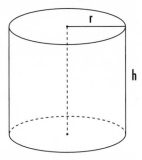

A cylinder has two parallel circular bases that are the same size. A right cylinder is one in which the lateral surface of the cylinder is perpendicular to its bases.

The volume of a right cylinder, like that of a right prism, is found by multiplying the area of the base by the height. Because the base of a cylinder is a circle, the area of the base can be expressed as a function of the radius ($A = \pi r^2$). This allows us to write a formula for the volume of a right cylinder in terms of its radius and height.

Volume of a Cylinder
For any cylinder of radius r and height h,
$V = pr^2h$

CONES

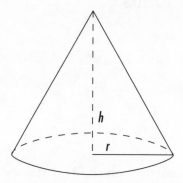

A cone is a solid similar to a pyramid, with a circular base and a vertex that does not lie in the plane of the base. The volume of a cone is one-third the volume of a cylinder with the same base and height.

Volume of a Cone

For a cone with a base of radius r and a height h,

$$V = \frac{1}{3}\pi r^2 h.$$

SPHERES

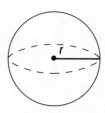

A sphere is a perfectly circular ball. It is defined as the set of all points in space at a given distance from a central point. The volume of a sphere can be found as a function of its radius.

Volume of a Sphere

For a sphere with radius r, $V = \frac{4}{3}\pi r^3$.

SUMMARY OF VOLUME FORMULAS	
Circular Solid	**Volume Formula**
cylinder	$V = \pi r^2 h$
cone	$V = \dfrac{1}{3}\pi r^2 h$
sphere	$V = \dfrac{4}{3}\pi r^3$

EXERCISES

Find the volume of each of the following circular solids.

1.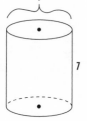

2.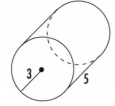

3.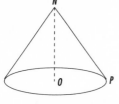

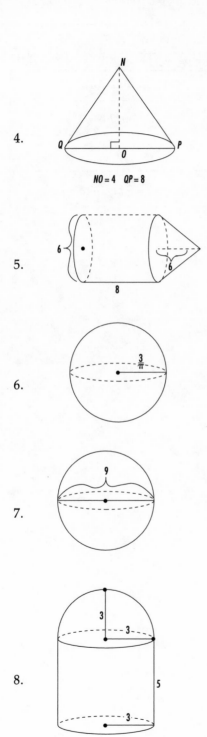

4. $NO = 4 \quad QP = 8$

5.

6.

7.

8.

Solve each of the following problems and state the solution clearly.

9. A cylinder's height is 2 more than its diameter. If the cylinder's volume is 160π, what is its radius?

10. A cone is inscribed in a cylinder with the same radius and height. What is the ratio of the volume within the cylinder that is contained within the cone to the volume within the cylinder that is **not** contained within the cone?

11. Find the volume of a sphere with a radius of π.

12. A cylinder's height is six times its radius. If the volume of the cylinder is 20.25π, what is its radius?

SUMMARY

- The *perimeter* of a polygon is the sum of the lengths of its sides.

SUMMARY OF AREA FORMULAS	
Polygon	**Area Formula**
triangle	$A = \frac{1}{2}bh$
rectangle	$A = lw$
square	$A = s^2$
parallelogram	$A = bh$
trapezoid	$A = \left(\dfrac{b_1 + b_2}{2}\right)h$

- Circumference of a Circle: $C = 2\pi r$ or $C = \pi d$

- Area of a Circle: $A = \pi r^2$

SUMMARY OF VOLUME FORMULAS	
Solid	**Volume Formula**
right prism	$V = Bh$
rectangular solid	$V = lwh$
cube	$V = s^3$
pyramid	$V = \frac{1}{3}Bh$
cylinder	$V = \pi r^2 h$
cone	$V = \frac{1}{3}\pi r^2 h$
sphere	$V = \frac{4}{3}\pi r^3$

11

Coordinate Geometry

Coordinate geometry is an area of geometry dealing with the position of points and sets of points in a plane. The fundamental ideas of coordinate geometry are very different from the ideas of plane geometry reviewed earlier in this book.

11.1 THE COORDINATE PLANE

The coordinate plane is formed by a vertical number line and a horizontal number line intersecting at their zero coordinates. The horizontal axis is called the *x-axis*, and the vertical axis is called the *y-axis*. The point at which the axes intersect is called the *origin,* and is generally labeled with an *O*. The four regions into which the plane is divided by the axes are called *quadrants*. The four quadrants are numbered counterclockwise from the upper right, as shown.

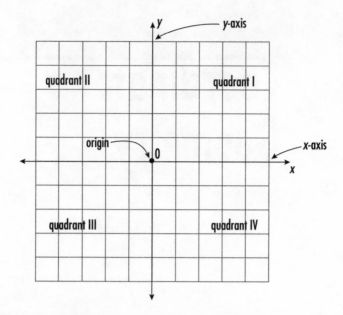

Within the coordinate plane, the location of any point can be denoted by naming the coordinate of the point on each axis. A point's coordinate on the x-axis is called its *x-coordinate*, or *abscissa*. Its coordinate on the y-axis is called its *y-coordinate*, or *ordinate*. Taken together, these coordinates are called an *ordered pair*. An ordered pair appears as a pair of numbers in parentheses, separated by a comma. By convention, the x-coordinate is listed first, followed by the y-coordinate.

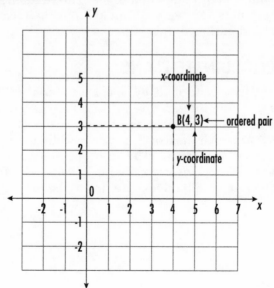

The process of plotting a point or a set of points (such as a line) on the coordinate plane is called *graphing*. To graph a point, find its *x*-coordinate on the *x*-axis and its *y*-coordinate on the *y*-axis; mark a point on the graph at the location that corresponds to these two coordinates.

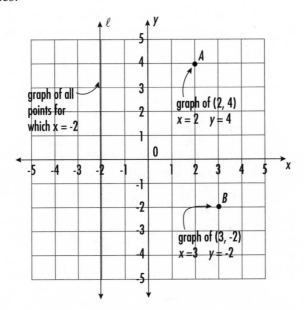

Remember that on the *x*-axis, the numbers to the right of the origin are positive and those to the left are negative. On the *y*-axis, the numbers above the origin are positive, and those below are negative.

EXERCISES

Name the ordered pair corresponding to each point on the graph at right.

1. A

2. B

3. C

4. D

5. E

6. F

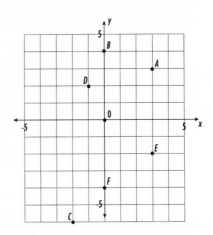

For each of the following ordered pairs, state the quadrant in which the point falls, or the axis on which the point falls if it is not within a quadrant (a point on an axis lies in no quadrant).

7. (6, –7)

8. (3, 1)

9. (–2, 7)

10. (0, –3)

11. (–1, –9)

12. (12, 0)

For each of the following, find the area of the triangle determined by the three ordered pairs given.

13. (0, 0), (0, 4), (3, 0)

14. (–5, –2), (3, 3), (4, –2)

15. (–3, 2), (7, –4), (7, 4)

16. (2, 5), (6, –1), (8, 5)

11.2 SLOPE

Slope is a measure of the steepness of a line. It's expressed as the ratio of vertical change to horizontal change in a line. For example, suppose you walked up a ramp, and noticed that after walking 32 feet horizontally, you have gained 3 feet in elevation. The vertical change in your position is 3 feet, and the horizontal change is 32 feet. The slope of the ramp is therefore $\frac{3}{32}$.

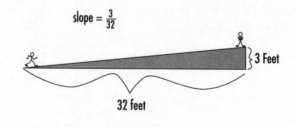

$$slope = \frac{vertical\ change}{horizontal\ change}$$

Sometimes, the formula for slope is given as $\text{slope} = \dfrac{\text{rise}}{\text{run}}$. It's a helpful way to remember the formula, and it means the same thing: "Rise" is vertical change, and "run" is horizontal change.

On the coordinate plane, the slope of a line can be found by comparing two points on the line. The simplest way to do this is simply to count units on the graph to find the ratio of vertical change to horizontal change.

Example

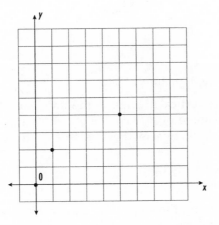

1. What is the slope of the line shown in the graph above?

   Select two points on the line, and count squares on the graph to find the vertical change and horizontal change between them. In this case, the vertical change is 2 and the horizontal change is 4. The slope of the line is therefore $\dfrac{2}{4}$, which reduces to $\dfrac{1}{2}$.

   Another way to find the vertical and horizontal change is by finding the difference between the coordinates of two points on a line.

Examples

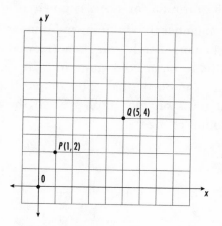

2. Find the slope of line PQ.

To find the vertical change in the line from P to Q, subtract the y-coordinate of P from the y-coordinate of Q: $4 - 2 = 2$. The vertical change in the line from P to Q is therefore 2 units.

To find the horizontal change, subtract the x-coordinates: $5 - 1 = 4$. The horizontal change is 4 units.

To find the find the slope, write the ratio of vertical change to horizontal change:

$$\frac{\text{rise}}{\text{run}} = \frac{2}{4} = \frac{1}{2}$$

The slope of the line is $\frac{1}{2}$.

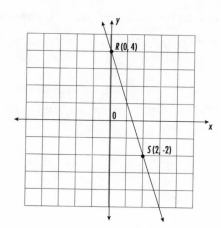

3. If the slope of line RS is m, what is the value of m?

Subtract the y-coordinates to find the vertical change:

$-2 - 4 = -6$.

Subtract the x-coordinates to find the horizontal change:

$2 - 0 = 2$.

Write the ratio of vertical change to horizontal change:

$$\frac{-6}{2} = \frac{-3}{1} = -3.$$

The value of m is -3.

The method of finding the difference of coordinates to calculate slope can be written as a formula.

The Slope Formula

For a line of slope m containing the points (x_1, y_1) and

(x_2, y_2), $m = \dfrac{y_2 - y_1}{x_2 - x_1}$.

It doesn't matter which point you start with when you're finding the difference; you'll get the same result either way. Just make sure to put the same point's coordinates first in both the horizontal and vertical calculations.

THE SIGN OF SLOPE

Reviewing examples 2 and 3 above, you may note that one line has a positive slope, while the other has a negative slope. While it may take calculation to determine the exact slope of a line, it is always possible to determine the sign of a line's slope just by glancing at its graph:

- If a line rises from left to right, it has positive slope.

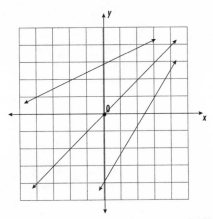

- If a line falls from left to right, is has negative slope.

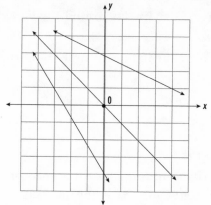

- If a line is horizontal, it has a slope of zero.

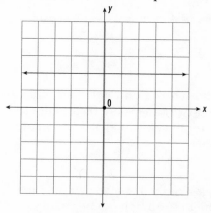

- If a line is vertical, it is said to have no slope, or its slope is said to be undefined. This is because its horizontal change, which forms the denominator of the slope fraction, is zero.

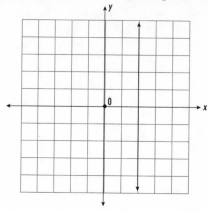

Parallel Lines

There are a few general rules regarding the slope of parallel lines.

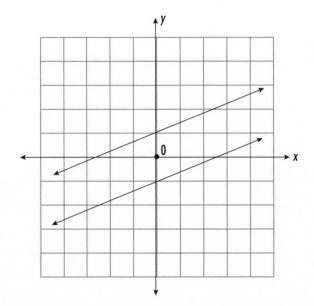

- Parallel lines have equal slope. If it is given that two lines are parallel, then the slope of one line must also be the slope of the other.

- Lines of equal slope are parallel. If you demonstrate that two lines have the same slope, you have proven that the lines are parallel.

Note: These rules do not apply to vertical lines, which have no slope.
Test your understanding of slope in the following exercises.

Exercises

Find the slope of a line passing through each of the following pairs of points and state it in simplest form. If the line has no slope, indicate that its slope is undefined.

1. (0, 0), (5, 5)
2. (0, 4), (4, 0)
3. (−1, −1), (3, 2)
4. (−2, −6), (−1, 7)
5. (−5, 0), (6, 1)

6. (–3, 4), (–2, 2)

7. (–4, 7), (8, –6)

8. (112, 89), (97, 94)

Solve the following problems and state your solution clearly.

9. A line passes through quadrant II and the origin. Its slope is
   (a) positive
   (b) zero
   (c) negative
   (d) undefined

10. A line lies parallel to the y-axis. Its slope is
    (a) positive
    (b) zero
    (c) negative
    (d) undefined

11. A line passes through quadrant I and the origin. Its slope is
    (a) positive
    (b) zero
    (c) negative
    (d) undefined

12. A line passes through the point (3, 0) and has a slope of 1. Through which of the following points must the line also pass?
    (a) (–1, –4)
    (b) (0, 3)
    (c) (6, 0)
    (d) (2, 5)

11.3 LINEAR EQUATIONS

A *linear equation* is an equation like $y = 2x + 3$, in which no variable is raised to a power higher than 1. Solutions for equations of this type can be expressed as ordered pairs of the form (x, y). To find a solution to the equation, substitute a value for x in the equation, and solve for y. Write the resulting values of x and y as an ordered pair.

While a great many linear equations are written in two variables, like $y = 2x + 3$, some linear equations contain only a single variable. The equations $y = 0$ and $x = 5$ are also linear equations.

A linear equation has an infinite number of solutions. The graph of the set of all solutions of a linear equations is a line.

Here are some solutions of the equation $y = 2x + 3$:

(0, 3), because $2(0) + 3 = 3$

(1, 5), because $2(1) + 3 = 5$

(–2, –1), because $2(–2) + 3 = –1$

(–1, 1), because $2(–1) + 3 = 1$

As you can see on the graph at right, the graphs of all of these solutions fall on a line. This line represents the complete solution set of $y = 2x + 3$. Every point on the line is a solution of the equation.

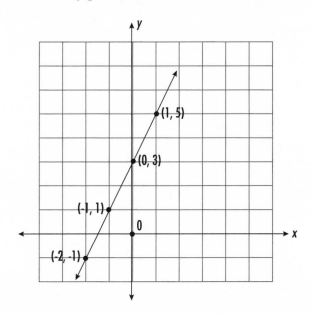

Notice that the slope of the line is 2, which is equal to the coefficient of x in the line's equation. The coordinate at which the line intersects the y-axis is $y = 3$. This coordinate is called the *y-intercept* of the line. The y-intercept, you may observe, is equal to the constant term of the equation $y = 2x + 3$.

THE SLOPE-INTERCEPT FORM

Any linear equation in two variables can be arranged in the form $y = mx + b$. Simply solve a linear equation for y, and the result will be an equation in this form. It's called the *slope-intercept form* of a linear equation, and it provides some useful information about the equation's graph.

Slope-Intercept Form of a Linear Equation

For any linear equation of the form $y = mx + b$, where m and b are constants, m is equal to the slope of the line, and b is equal to the y-intercept of the line.

Once you've put a linear equation in slope-intercept form, you can tell the slope and y-intercept of the line without graphing it. By the same token, if you know the slope and y-intercept of a line, you can easily write the equation of the line. Just plug the values of the slope and y-intercept into the equation $y = mx + b$.

Examples

1. What is the slope of the graph of $5y + 3x = -10$?

   Rearrange the equation so that it's in slope-intercept form. This is done by isolating y.

   Subtract $3x$ from both sides.

   $$\begin{array}{rl} 5y + 3x = & -10 \\ \underline{-3x \quad -3x} & \\ 5y \quad = & -3x - 10 \end{array}$$

   Divide both sides by 5.

   $$\frac{5y}{5} = \frac{-3x}{5} - \frac{10}{5}$$

   $$y = -\frac{3}{5}x - 2$$

   When the equation is in slope-intercept form, the coefficient of x is $-\frac{3}{5}$. The slope of the line is therefore $-\frac{3}{5}$.

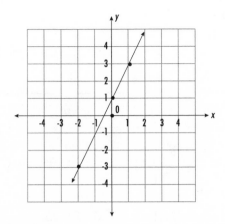

2. What is the equation of the line shown in the graph above?

Find the slope by counting the rise and run between two points on the line, or by using the slope formula. The slope of the line is 2.

The line crosses the y-axis at $y = 1$. The y-intercept of the line is therefore 1.

To write the equation of the line, substitute the values $m = 2$ and $y = 1$ into the equation $y = mx + b$:

$y = (2)x + (1)$

The equation of the line is $y = 2x + 1$.

GRAPHING LINEAR EQUATIONS

There are two common methods of graphing a linear equation.

Method 1

The simplest way to graph a linear equation is to make a *table of values* for the equation, plot three or four points, and graph the line determined by that group of points.

Example

3. Graph the equation $y = \dfrac{3}{2}x - 3$.

Begin by making a table of values:

x	$\dfrac{3}{2}x-3$	y	(x, y)
−2	$\dfrac{3}{2}(-2)-3$	−6	(−2, −6)
0	$\dfrac{3}{2}(0)-3$	−3	(0, −3)
2	$\dfrac{3}{2}(2)-3$	0	(2, 0)
4	$\dfrac{3}{2}(4)-3$	3	(4, 3)

Plug values for x into the equation, and see what values of y are produced. Record these ordered pairs, and plot them on a graph. Use a straight-edge to draw a line through the plotted points. This is the graph of $y=\dfrac{3}{2}x-3$.

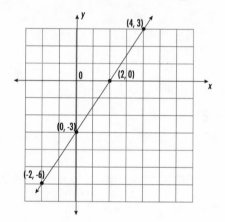

Method 2
The second way to graph a linear equation is a little more elegant. Begin by putting the equation in slope-intercept form, if it is not in that form already. Then plot the point where the graph intersects the y-axis; this is the point $(0, b)$. Finally, read the line's slope from the equation, and draw a line of that slope through the y-intercept. This is the graph of the equation.

Example

4. Graph the equation $2y + 6x - 5 = -3$.

First, rearrange the equation into slope-intercept form:

$2y + 6x - 5 = -3$

$2y = -6x + 2$

$y = -3x + 1$

The slope of the line is –3, and the y-intercept is 1. Plot the point $(0, 1)$. Then draw a line through this point with a slope of –3. Do this by counting down 3 and right 1, and plotting a point, and then repeating the process (think of the slope as $\frac{-3}{1}$, a fall of 3 for every run of 1). Connect these points with a line; this is the graph of $2y + 6x - 5 = -3$.

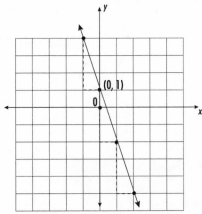

Practice working with linear equations in the following practice questions.

EXERCISES

1. Which of the following is the equation of the line in the graph at right?

   (a) $y = x - 2$

   (b) $y = -x - 2$

   (c) $y = 2x + 1$

   (d) $y = 2x - 1$

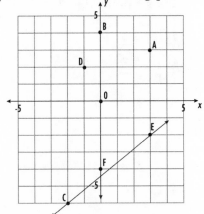

2. Which of the following is the equation of the line in the graph at right?
   (a) $y = -3x + 2$
   (b) $y = 3x - 2$
   (c) $y = 3x$
   (d) $y = -3x$

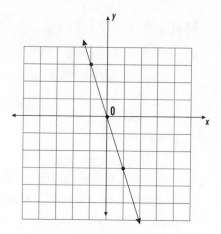

3. Which of the following is the equation of the line in the graph at right?
   (a) $y = -\frac{1}{2}x + 1$
   (b) $y = \frac{1}{2}x + 1$
   (c) $y = 2x + 1$
   (d) $y = -2x + 1$

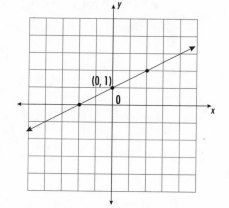

4. Which of the following is the equation of the line in the graph at right?
   (a) $y = -2$
   (b) $y = 2$
   (c) $x = -2$
   (d) $x = 2$

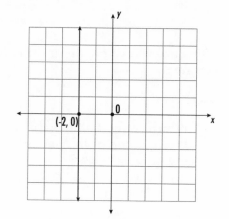

State whether the lines represented by each pair of equations are parallel or skew.

5. $y = 4$
   $y = -3$

6. $y = -4x + 7$
   $y = -2x + 7$

7. $3y - 2x = -12$
   $6y - 5 = 4x + 1$

8. $4y + 5 = 3(x + 1)$
   $3y + 5 = 4x + 5$

For each of the following, choose the point which falls on the graph of the equation given.

9. $3x = 12$
   (a) $(-4, 3)$
   (b) $(0, 0)$
   (c) $(2, 4)$
   (d) $(4, -6)$

10. $y = 5x - 2$
    (a) $(-2, 12)$
    (b) $(1, 7)$
    (c) $(2, 8)$
    (d) $(3, 0)$

11. $y = -\dfrac{5}{4}x + 9$
    (a) $(8, -1)$
    (b) $(4, -5)$
    (c) $(0, 5)$
    (d) $(-4, 4)$

12. $y - 1 = \dfrac{1}{4}(x + 8)$
    (a) $(-16, 2)$
    (b) $(-12, 0)$
    (c) $(-8, -1)$
    (d) $(0, -1)$

11.4 GRAPHING LINEAR INEQUALITIES

A linear inequality is identical to a linear equation, except that the equal sign is replaced by a sign of inequality. In the same way, the graph of a linear inequality is very similar to the graph of a linear equation. The main difference is that the graph of an inequality includes the region on one side of the line, and may or may not include the line itself. Take a look at these examples:

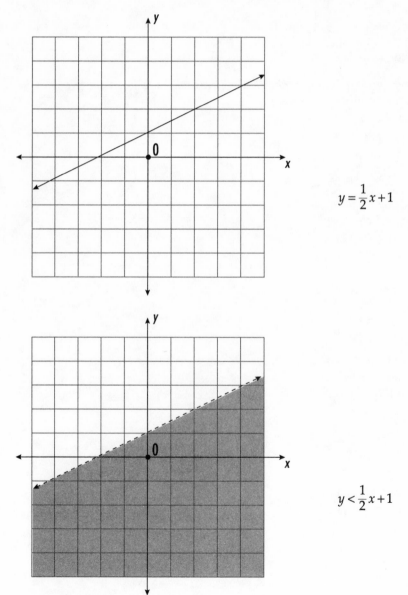

$$y = \frac{1}{2}x + 1$$

$$y < \frac{1}{2}x + 1$$

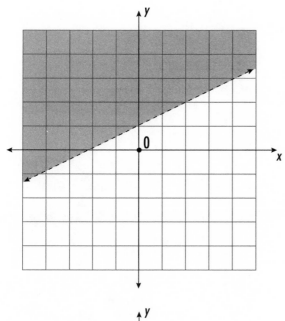

$$y > \frac{1}{2}x + 1$$

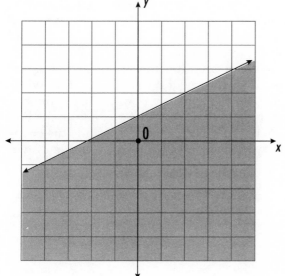

$$y \le \frac{1}{2}x + 1$$

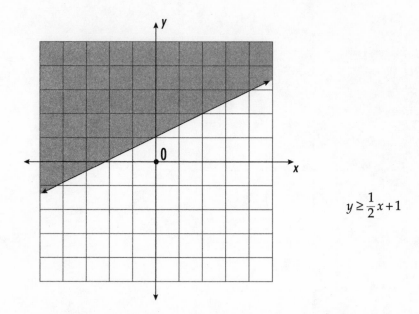

$$y \geq \frac{1}{2}x + 1$$

When an inequality indicates that y is **greater than** some expression, then the graph is shaded *above* the line of equality. When an inequality indicates that y is **less than** some expression, then the graph is shaded **below** the line of equality.

In the graph of any linear inequality, the graph of the corresponding equation forms the boundary of the shaded region. When the inequality does not include the equation (< or >), the boundary is not included in the graph. This is represented by making the line of equality a dotted line. When the inequality *does* include the equation ($\leq$ or $\geq$), the boundary *is* included in the graph, and is drawn as a solid line.

You can think of the graph of $y \leq \frac{1}{2}x + 1$ as the union of the graph of the inequality $y < \frac{1}{2}x + 1$ and the graph of the equation $y = \frac{1}{2}x + 1$.

Practice working with the graphs of linear inequalities in the following exercises.

Write the inequality that is graphed in each of the following.

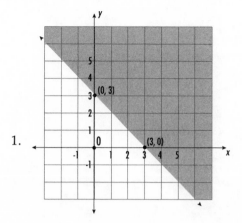

1.

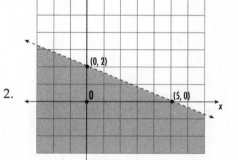

2.

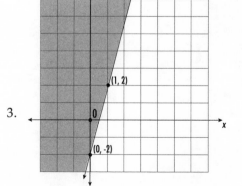

3.

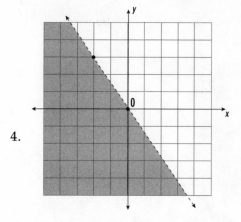

4.

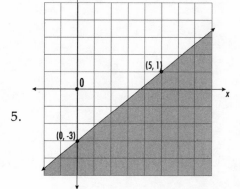

5.

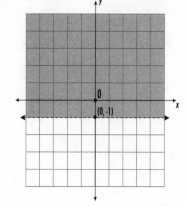

6.

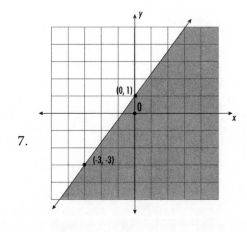

7.

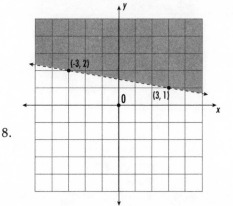

8.

Graph each of the following inequalities.

9. $y < 2$

10. $y \geq -2x - 3$

11. $y \leq -\dfrac{1}{2}x + 1$

12. $y > 2(x - 1)$

11.5 GRAPHING SYSTEMS

A system of equations or inequalities is a group of two or more statements that must be solved at the same time. To solve a system, you have to combine information from the different statements somehow. One way of doing this is by graphing the different statements on a single graph. The point or set of points where the graphs overlap is the solution of the system.

SYSTEMS OF LINEAR EQUATIONS

The solution of a system of linear equations is a single point–an ordered pair. For example, take a look at the graph of this system of equations:

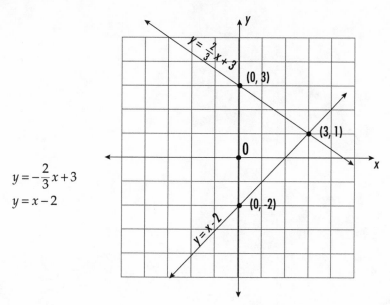

$$y = -\frac{2}{3}x + 3$$
$$y = x - 2$$

The graph of $y + 2 = -\frac{2}{3}x + 5$ and the graph of $y = x - 2$ intersect at the point (3, 1). This ordered pair is the only pair of values for which both equations are true. You can check this solution by plugging the values $x = 3$, $y = 1$ into both equations. If the values satisfy both equations, the solution is correct.

$$y = -\frac{2}{3}x + 3$$
$$1 = -\frac{2}{3}(3) + 3$$
$$1 = -2 + 3$$
$$1 = 1$$
$$y = x - 2$$
$$1 = 3 - 2$$
$$1 = 1$$

Both equations are satisfied, so the solution is correct.

It is possible for a system of linear equations to have no solution. For example, look at the graph of this system of equations:

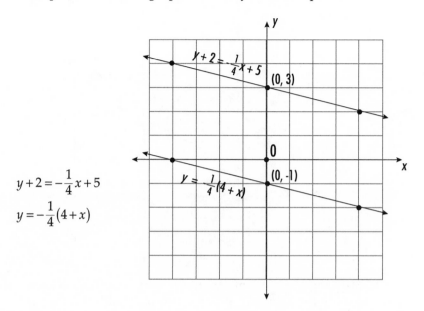

$$y+2=-\frac{1}{4}x+5$$

$$y=-\frac{1}{4}(4+x)$$

The graph of $y+2=-\frac{1}{4}x+5$ and the graph of $y=-\frac{1}{4}(4+x)$ are parallel lines. This can be shown by writing both equations in slope-intercept form: $y=-\frac{1}{4}x+3$ and $y=-\frac{1}{4}x-1$. The lines have equal slope, which means that they are parallel, and will never intersect. Because their graphs do not intersect, you can conclude that the two equations have no solutions in common. Consequently the system of equations has no solution; its solution set is the empty set, {}.

SYSTEMS OF LINEAR INEQUALITIES

A system of linear inequalities can also be solved graphically. The method used is almost identical to that used for systems of equations. The main difference is that while the solution set of a system of equations is a single point at which lines intersect, the solution set of a system of inequalities is the area in which shaded regions overlap. For example, take a look at this system of inequalities:

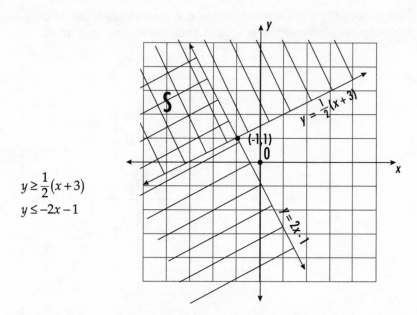

$$y \geq \frac{1}{2}(x+3)$$
$$y \leq -2x-1$$

When solving a system of inequalities by graphing, it's conventional to shade the shaded regions using parallel lines, to make the area of overlap easy to see. In this case, the solution set is in the upper left of the graph; it's marked with a bold letter "S."

A system of linear inequalities can also have no solution. This occurs when the shaded regions of the inequalities do not overlap at any point. Take a look at the graph of this system of inequalities:

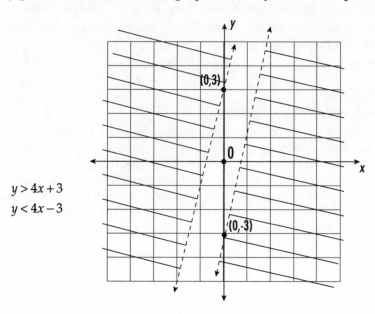

$$y > 4x+3$$
$$y < 4x-3$$

The boundary lines of the graphs are parallel, and the shaded regions do not overlap at any point. From this you can conclude that the two inequalities have no solutions in common, and the solution set of the system is the empty set, {}.

Practice working with the graphs of systems in the following exercises.

EXERCISES

Solve each of the following systems of equations graphically, and clearly state the solution set of the system.

1. $y = 1$
   $y = 2x - 3$

2. $y = x + 1$
   $y = 3(x - 1)$

3. $y = -\frac{1}{4}x + 3$

   $y = -\frac{3}{2}x - 2$

4. $y = -2(x + 1)$
   $y = -5x + 1$

5. $-\frac{1}{4}x + 4$

   $y = 4x - 13$

6. $y = -\frac{1}{3}x - 4$

   $y = \frac{7}{3}x + 4$

Graph the system of inequalities below, and mark the solution set clearly with the letter S. Then, state whether each of the points listed is within the system's solution set.

$y < 2(x - 3)$

$y \geq -\frac{1}{5}(x - 25)$

7. $(0, 0)$

8. $(1, 8)$

9. $(5, 4)$

10. $(7, 6)$

11.6 SOLVING SYSTEMS ALGEBRAICALLY

Sometimes, the graphical method of solving a system of linear equations is too difficult or unwieldy. When that's the case, the system can be solved algebraically instead. There are two basic methods of solving systems: the substitution method and the addition method. Both methods work by combining the equations in the system into a single equation in one variable that can be solved.

SUBSTITUTION

In the substitution method of solving systems, isolate a variable in one equation to produce a definition of one variable in terms of the other. Then, substitute that definition into the other equation to produce an equation in on variable, and solve.

Examples

1. Using the substitution method, solve the system of equations $x = -3y$ and $x - y = 4$.

   The first equation, $x = -3y$, defines x in terms of y. The variable x is already isolated, and you know that x is equal to $-3y$. Use this information to create an equation in one variable, by substituting $-3y$ for x in the second equation.

   $x - y = 4$

   $-3y - y = 4$

   $-4y = 4$

   Divide both sides by -4 to find the value of y.

   $$\frac{-4y}{-4} = \frac{4}{-4}$$

   $y = -1$

   The value of y is -1. To find x, plug the value $y = -1$ into one of the original equations and solve for x.

   $x = -3y$

   $x = -3(-1)$

   $x = 3$

   The value of x is 3.

   The solution of the system is $x = 3$, $y = -1$, which can be written as the ordered pair $(3, -1)$.

2. Using the substitution method, solve the system of equations $2x - y = 3$ and $3x - 2y = 1$.

Begin by isolating a variable in one equation. In the first equation, it's a simple matter to isolate y.

$2x - y = 3$

First, add y to both sides.

$$\begin{array}{rl} 2x - y = & 3 \\ +y & +y \\ \hline 2x = & y + 3 \end{array}$$

Then subtract 3 from both sides.

$$\begin{array}{rl} 2x & = y + 3 \\ -3 & -3 \\ \hline 2x - 3 & = y \end{array}$$

You're left with the equation $2x - 3 = y$, which defines y in terms of x. Now, substitute $2x - 3$ for y in the second equation, and solve for x.

$3x - 2y = 1$

$3x - 2(2x - 3) = 1$

Distribute.

$3x - 4x + 6 = 1$

Simplify by combining like terms.

$-x + 6 = 1$

Subtract 6 from both sides.

$-x = -5$

Multiply both sides by –1 to find the value of x.

$x = 5$.

The value of x is 5. To find y, plug $x = 5$ into one of the original equations and solve.

$2x - y = 3$

$2(5) - y = 3$

$10 - y = 3$

Subtract 10 from both sides.

$-y = -7$

Multiply both sides by −1 to find the value of y.

$y = 7$

The solution of the system is $x = 5$, $y = 7$, which can be expressed as the ordered pair (5, 7).

ADDITION

The addition method also works by eliminating one variable, leaving an equation in a single variable that can be solved normally. In this method, the two equations in a system are put into the same form and then added together so that one of the variables drops out.

Example

3. Using the addition method, solve the system of equations $2x + y = 7$ and $3x − y = 8$.

   The equations are already in the same form, so you don't have to manipulate them. Just arrange them vertically.

   $2x + y = 7$

   $3x − y = 8$

   As you can see, adding these two equations together will cause the variable y to drop out.

   $$\begin{array}{r} 2x + y = 7 \\ + \quad 3x − y = 8 \\ \hline 5x \quad\;\; = 15 \end{array}$$

   You're left with the equation $5x = 15$. Divide both sides by 5 to find the value of x.

   $$\frac{5x}{5} = \frac{15}{5}$$

   $x = 3$

   Substitute 3 for x in one of the original equations and solve to find the value of y.

   $2x + y = 7$

   $2(3) + y = 7$

   $6 + y = 7$

   $y = 1$

   The solution of the system is $x = 3$, $y = 1$, or (3, 1).

Sometimes, the equations in a system must be modified before one of the variables can be eliminated by addition. This is done by multiplying one or both equations by constants so that one of the variables has the same coefficient in both equations, with opposite signs.

Examples

4. Using the addition method, solve the system of equations $2x + y = 5$ and $9x + 3y = 21$.

$$2x + y = 5$$
$$9x + 3y = 21$$

As the equations are written, no variable will drop out if the equations are added together. This can be fixed by multiplying the first equation by -3.

$$-3(2x + y) = -3(5)$$
$$-6x - 3y = -15$$

Add the equations now, and y will drop out.

$$-6x - 3y = -15$$
$$9x + 3y = 21$$
$$3x = 6$$

You're left with the equation $3x = 6$. Divide both sides by 3 to find the value of x.

$$3x = 6$$
$$x = 2$$

Substitute 2 for x in one of the original equations and solve to find the value of y.

$$2x + y = 5$$
$$2(2) + y = 5$$
$$4 + y = 5$$
$$y = 1$$

The solution of the system is $x = 2$, $y = 1$, or $(2, 1)$.

5. Using the addition method, solve the system of equations $4x - 3y = 25$ and $5x + 4y = 8$.

$$4x - 3y = 25$$
$$5x + 4y = 8$$

As the equations are written, no variable will drop out when they are added together. To fix this, multiply the first equation by 4 and the second by 3.

$4(4x - 3y) = 4(25)$

$16x - 12y = 100$

$3(5x + 4y) = 3(8)$

$15x + 12y = 24$

Now, add the equations.

$$\begin{array}{r} 16x - 12y = 100 \\ 15x + 12y = 24 \\ \hline 31x = 124 \end{array}$$

You're left with the equation $31x = 124$. Divide both sides by 31 to find the value of x.

$$\frac{31x}{31} = \frac{124}{31}$$

$x = 4$

Substitute 4 for x in one of the original equations and solve to find the value of y.

$5x + 4y = 8$

$5(4) + 4y = 8$

$20 + 4y = 8$

$4y = -12$

$y = -3$

The solution of the system is $x = 4$, $y = -3$, or $(4, -3)$.

WORD PROBLEMS

Many kinds of mathematical problems can be solved using systems of equations.

Examples

6. The sum of two numbers is 27, and their difference is 18. What are the numbers?

   Write two equations based on the information in the question.

   "The sum of two numbers is 28"   "their difference is 16"

   $$a + b = 28 \qquad\qquad a - b = 16$$

Add the two equations together.

$a + b = 28$

$\underline{a - b = 16}$

$2a \quad = 44$

Divide both sides by 2 to find the value of a.

$$\frac{2a}{2} = \frac{44}{2}$$

$a = 22$

Substitute 22 for a in one of the original equations to find the value of b.

$a + b = 28$

$22 + b = 28$

$b = 6$

The two numbers are 6 and 22.

7. The length of a rectangle is 3 more than twice its width. If the perimeter of the rectangle is 30, what are its dimensions?

Write two equations based on the information in the question.

"The length of a rectangle is 3 more than twice its width"
$l = 2w + 3$

"the perimeter of the rectangle is 30"

$2l + 2w = 30$

Use the substitution method: Replace l in the second equation with the expression $2w + 3$.

$2l + 2w = 30$

$2(2w + 3) + 2w = 30$

Distribute.

$4w + 6 + 2w = 30$

Combine like terms.

$6w + 6 = 30$

Subtract 6 from both sides.

$6w = 24$

Divide both sides by 6.

$w = 4$

Substitute 4 for w in one of the original equations to find the value of l.

$l = 2w + 3$

$l = 2(4) + 3$

$l = 8 + 3$

$l = 11$

The rectangle has a width of 4 and a length of 11.

Practice solving systems of equations in the following exercises.

EXERCISES

Solve the following systems of linear equations using the substitution method.

1. $y = 3x + 1$
   $3x + 2y = 11$

2. $x = y + 4$
   $2x + y = 5$

3. $x - 10 = y$
   $2y - x = -6$

4. $x = 2y - 6$
   $5y - 3x = 11$

Solve the following systems of linear equations using the addition method.

5. $3x - 5y = -1$
   $-3x + 7y = 5$

6. $4x + 2y = 0$
   $3x - 2y = -14$

7. $2x - 5y = 1$
   $3x - 4y = -2$

8. $-2x + 5y = 3.25$
   $5x - 2y = 15.5$

For each of the following, write a system of equations in two variables, solve, and state the answer to the question clearly.

9. A bag contains 12 coins, all of which are nickels or dimes. If the total value of the coins is $0.85, how many coins of each kind does the bag contain?

10. At Manny's Joint, four burgers and two slush drinks cost $15.00. At the same prices, two burgers and three slush drinks cost $13.50. What is the unit price of each item?

11. A rectangle's length is 2 less than twice its width. If the perimeter of the rectangle is 38, what are its dimensions?

12. Manny's Joint sold 500 goopy drinks in a day. A small goopy drink sold for $2.50, and a large goopy drink sold for $3.50. If Manny's Joint made a total of $1,400.00 selling goopy drinks, how many goopy drinks of each size were sold that day?

SUMMARY

- slope = $\dfrac{\text{vertical change}}{\text{horizontal change}}$

- **The Slope Formula**

  For a line of slope m containing the points (x_1, y_1) and (x_2, y_2),

  $$m = \frac{y_2 - y_1}{x_2 - x_1}$$

- If a line rises from left to right, it has positive slope.
  If a line falls from left to right, is has negative slope.
  If a line is horizontal, it has a slope of zero.
  If a line is vertical, it is said to have no slope, or its slope is said to be undefined.

- Parallel lines have equal slope. If it is given that two lines are parallel, then the slope of one line must also be the slope of the other.

- **Definition of a Linear Equation**
  A linear equation is any equation that can be expressed in the form $Ax + By = C$, where A, B, and C are constants, and A and B are not both zero.

- **Slope-Intercept Form of a Linear Equation**

  For any linear equation of the form $y = mx + b$, where m and b are constants, m is equal to the slope of the line, and b is equal to the *y-intercept* of the line.

- When a system of statements is graphed, the point or set of points where the graphs overlap is the solution of the system.

- Systems of linear equations may be solved algebraically by either of two simple methods: the *substitution method* and the *addition method*.

12

Transformations and Symmetry

Transformation is the process of moving every point in a figure according to a certain rule. Every point in the new figure corresponds to a point in the original figure. The new figure is called the *image*; the original figure is sometimes called the *preimage*. There are four basic kinds of transformation: *reflection, rotation, translation,* and *dilation*. This chapter will review each of these, together with related types of symmetry.

12.1 LINE REFLECTION AND LINE SYMMETRY

Line reflection is a type of transformation in which each point in a figure is "flipped over" a line into a new position. In transformations, the image of a point P is often denoted by P', which is read as "P prime."

When a point is reflected in a line, its image lies on the other side of the line, at the same distance from the line as the original. This line is called the *line of reflection*. If a point lies *on* the line of reflection, then its image is itself.

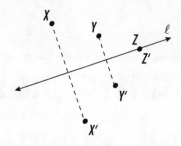

In the figure above, you can see that X and X' are at equal distances from line ℓ, and on opposite sides of the line. A segment connecting X and X' would be perpendicular to the line of reflection. The same is true of points Y and Y'. Because point Z lies on the line of reflection, Z and Z' have identical positions; they are the same point.

Entire figures can be reflected in a line. Take a look at how line reflection affects each of the following figures.

Line Symmetry

A figure is said to have *line symmetry* when a line can be drawn through the figure dividing it into equal halves, so that each half is the reflection of the other. Not all figures have line symmetry.

Figures that do have line symmetry may be symmetrical across more than one line of symmetry.

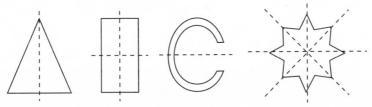

Test your understanding of line reflection and line symmetry with the following exercises.

EXERCISES

Name the image of each of the following for a reflection in line ℓ.

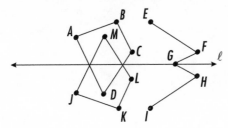

1. M

2. A

3. G

4. Angle CBA

5. Segment EF

6. Quadrilateral $JKLM$

State whether each of the following figures possesses line symmetry. If so, say how many distinct lines of symmetry can be drawn for the figure.

7.

8.

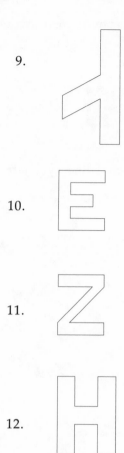

9.

10.

11.

12.

12.2 ROTATION AND ROTATIONAL SYMMETRY

Rotation is a type of transformation in which every point in a figure moves in a circular path around some fixed point of rotation called the *center*. The point of rotation may be either inside the figure or outside it.

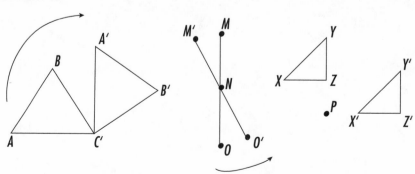

A rotation may turn a figure through any number of degrees, from angles smaller than 1° to angles greater than 360° (more than one rotation).

ROTATIONAL SYMMETRY

For some figures, the image produced by a rotation of less than 360° is identical to the original image. These figures are said to have *rotational symmetry*. The angle of rotation required to produced an identical image can vary from figure to figure. Each of the following figures has rotational symmetry.

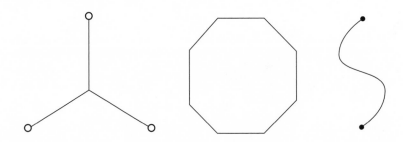

The first figure above produces an image identical to itself in rotations of 120° or 240°. The second figure produces an image identical to itself in any rotation of a multiple of 45°. The third figure produces an identical image in a rotation of 180°. A circle, rotated around its center point, produces an identical image for *any* rotation.

POINT SYMMETRY

Point symmetry is a specific sort of rotational symmetry. A figure is said to have point symmetry when the image produced by a rotation of 180° is identical to the original figure. Not all figures with rotational symmetry have point symmetry. There's a simple test: a figure with point symmetry looks the same when you turn it upside down.

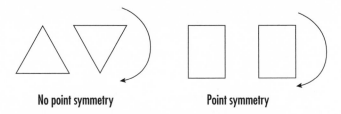

No point symmetry   Point symmetry

EXERCISES

State whether each of the following figures has rotational symmetry; if so, state the angles of rotation (between 0° and 360°) that will produce an identical image.

1.

2.

3.

4.

5.

6.

7.

8.

9. Which of the following has line symmetry but not point symmetry?

   (a) T

   (b) H

   (c) N

   (d) S

10. Which of the following has point symmetry but not line symmetry?

    (a) H

    (b) B

    (c) Z

    (d) A

11. Which of the following has both point and line symmetry?

(a) S

(b) N

(c) T

(d) I

12. Which of the following has neither point nor line symmetry?

(a) K

(b) Z

(c) P

(d) E

12.3 OTHER TRANSFORMATIONS

TRANSLATION

In *translation* a figure is displaced in some direction without rotating or changing in size. Translation is probably the simplest transformation to understand. It's simply the act of sliding a figure away from its original position without turning it. Here are some examples of translation:

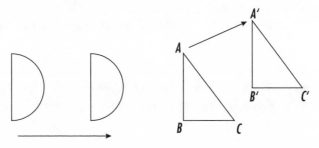

DILATION

In *dilation*, a figure is increased in size. Specifically, the distance between every point in the figure and a certain center point is increased by some factor. The center point of the dilation may be inside or outside the figure. Here are two examples of dilation:

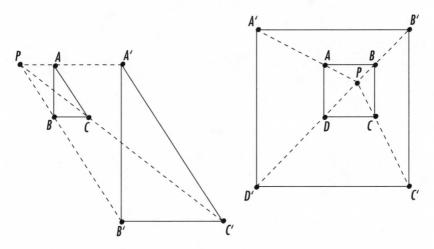

In some important respects, dilation is quite different from the other kinds of transformations reviewed here. This is because lengths within a figure change during dilation.

In reflection, rotation, and translation, the resulting image is the same size and shape as the original figure. In other words, the figure and its image are *congruent*. These transformations are sometimes called *isometries*, because the measurements of the figure are preserved during transformation.

In dilation, however, the lengths in a figure may change. Angle measures and proportions are conserved, meaning that the figure and its image are the same shape, although they are different in size. In other words, the figure and its image are *similar* but not *congruent*. Dilation is not an isometry.

Test your understanding of transformations with the following exercises.

EXERCISES

In each of the following, assume that the image is the result of a single transformation. Name the type of transformation pictured in each case.

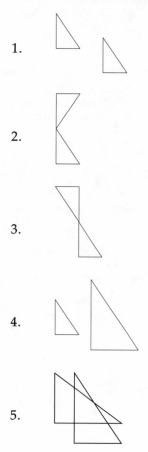

1.

2.

3.

4.

5.

6.

7.

8.

9. Angle measure is preserved in
   I. reflection
   II. rotation
   III. dilation
   (a) I only
   (b) II and III only
   (c) I and III only
   (d) I, II, and III

10. Distance is preserved in
    I. reflection
    II. rotation
    III. dilation
    (a) II only
    (b) I and II only
    (c) II and III only
    (d) I, II, and III

SUMMARY

- In reflection, a figure is "flipped" over a line of reflection. The image is congruent to the original figure.

- In rotation, a figure is turned around a point of rotation. The image is congruent to the original figure.

- In translation, the figure is slid without turning in a direction within the plane of the figure. The image is congruent to the original figure.

- In dilation, the distance between every point in the figure and a center point is changed by the same factor. The image is similar but not congruent to the original figure.

- A figure has line symmetry when it can be divided in half by a line so that each half is the reflection of the other.

- A figure has rotational symmetry when it can be rotated through some angle less than 360° to produce an image identical to the original.

- A figure has point symmetry when it can be rotated 180° to produce an image identical to the original.

13

Probability

When you flip a coin, you are uncertain of the outcome. When you enter a lottery, you are also uncertain of the outcome. Nevertheless, you consider your chances in the two events differently; you believe that you are more likely to win the coin toss than to win the lottery. You form this expectation by doing a simple calculation of probability. This chapter will review some more sophisticated ways of calculating probabilities.

13.1 PROBABILITY BASICS

For any random procedure, there is a number of possible outcomes. For very simple procedures, like the toss of a coin or the selection of a card from a deck, the number of possible outcomes can be determined exactly. For example, there are two possible outcomes of the toss of a coin: heads and tails. If a deck contains 52 cards, then there are 52 possible outcomes of a random card selection.

The *probability*, or *likeliness* of an event E is sometimes written as $P(E)$, where E is the event in question. For example, the probability that the flip of a coin will come up heads could be denoted by P(heads) or P(H).

The probability of an outcome is usually expressed as a fraction. An outcome that produces that result is called a *success*. The probability of a success is equal to the number of successful outcomes divided by the number of possible outcomes.

$$P(E) = \frac{successful\ outcomes}{total\ possible\ outcomes}$$

Examples

1. A fair die is tossed. What is the probability that the result will be a 4?

   A die, in case you're wondering, is one half of a pair of dice. It's sometimes called a "fair die" because it's made so that each of its six sides has an equal probability of turning up when the die is rolled.

   In this case, there are six possible outcomes, because the die has six sides. Only one of these sides has a "4" on it, so the probability of rolling a 4 is $\frac{1}{6}$.

2. A fair die is tossed. What is the probability that the result will be an odd number?

   Of the six numbers on the die, three are odd: 1, 3, and 5. The probability of rolling an odd number is therefore equal to $\frac{3}{6}$.

3. A card is drawn at random from a standard 52-card deck. What is the probability that the card drawn will be a queen?

   There are four queens in a standard deck. The probability of drawing a queen at random is therefore $\frac{4}{52}$.

You can sometimes calculate probabilities even when you have incomplete information about a situation.

Example

4. A bag contains red and green apples in the ratio 3 : 4. If an apple is chosen at random, what is the probability that the apple will be green?

Begin by treating this as an ordinary ratio problem, as reviewed in chapter 9. Let $3x$ = the number of red apples in the bag, and $4x$ = the number of green apples. The total number of apples in the bag is therefore $3x + 4x$, or $7x$.

Since there are $4x$ green apples in the bag out of a total of $7x$ apples, the probability of picking a green apple at random can be expressed as $\frac{4x}{7x}$. The x in the numerator and the x in the denominator cancel out, leaving you with a numerical fraction.

The probability of picking a green apple is $\frac{4}{7}$.

EXERCISES

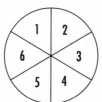

The six sections of the spinner shown are of equal size. Find the probability of getting each of the following results.

1. 6

2. an even number

3. a multiple of 3

4. a number greater than 5

5. a number greater than or equal to 2

6. a prime number

A card is picked at random from a standard 52-card deck. Find the probability of drawing each of the following.

7. an ace

8. a spade

9. a seven of hearts

10. a king of diamonds

11. a black jack

12. an even-numbered card

13. The ratio of boys to girls at a dance is 3 : 5. If a door prize is awarded randomly to one of the people at the dance, what is the probability that a boy will receive the prize?

14. A sack contains black and white marbles. There are 24 white marbles in the sack. If the probability that a marble drawn at random from the sack will be white is 30%, how many marbles are in the sack altogether?

13.2 IMPOSSIBILITY AND CERTAINTY

What is the probability of getting an 8 when you roll a standard die? But wait, you say; it can't be done. It is impossible to get an 8 when a single die is rolled. This can be expressed mathematically. The probability of an event is the number of successful outcomes divided by the total number of possible outcomes. Use this formula to evaluate the probability of this impossible event numerically.

There are six possible outcomes when a die is rolled. There are no outcomes that produce a result of 8; the number of successful outcomes is therefore zero. The probability of rolling an 8 is therefore $\frac{0}{6}$, or 0. The probability of an event cannot be less than 0.

The probability of an impossible event is zero.

What is the probability that the roll of a die will result in an integer? Again, the answer seems obvious. Every number on a die is an integer, so it's certain that the result when a die is rolled will be an integer. How is this expressed mathematically?

There are six possible outcomes when a die is rolled. Every outcome produces an integer, so there are six successful outcomes. The probability of rolling an integer is therefore $\frac{6}{6}$, or 1. The probability of an event cannot be greater than 1.

The probability of a certain event is 1.

THE PROBABILITY OF COMPLEMENTS

Suppose the probability that it will rain on a given day is $\frac{3}{5}$. What is the probability that it will *not* rain? These two events—raining and not raining—are called complements. One or the other *must* occur. If one does not occur, the other does. If one does occur, then the other does not.

When two events are complements, the probabilities of the two events add up to 1. In this case, $P(\text{rain})$ and $P(\text{not rain})$ must add up to 1. You can use this fact to find the probability that it will not rain, since you know the probability that it will.

$P(\text{rain}) + P(\text{not rain}) = 1$

$\frac{3}{5} + P(\text{not rain}) = 1$

$P(\text{not rain}) = 1 - \frac{3}{5} = \frac{2}{5}$

The probability that it will *not* rain on this day is $\frac{2}{5}$.

The probability that an event will occur and the probability that it will not occur add up to 1.
For any event E,
$P(\text{not } E) = 1 - P(E)$

Example

1. What is the probability that a card drawn at random from a standard deck will not be a jack?

   There are 4 jacks in a standard deck, out of a total of 52 cards. The probability that a randomly selected card will be a jack is therefore $\frac{4}{52}$.

   To calculate the probability that the card will *not* be a jack, subtract the probability that it will be a jack from 1.

   $P(\text{not jack}) = 1 - \frac{4}{52}$

   $P(\text{not jack}) = \frac{52}{52} - \frac{4}{52}$

   $P(\text{not jack}) = \frac{48}{52}$

   The probability that a randomly selected card will not be a jack is $\frac{48}{52}$.

Test your understanding of probability with the following exercises.

EXERCISES

One letter is to be selected at random from each of the following words. Find the probability that the selected letter will be an O.

1. POSTER

2. CARPOOL

3. ROBOT

4. COCOON

5. A letter is to be selected at random from each of the following words. For which of the words is the probability of selecting an I greatest?
   (a) OHIO
   (b) ILLINOIS
   (c) MICHIGAN
   (d) MISSISSIPPI

6. A letter is to be selected at random from each of the following words. For which of the words is the probability of selecting an A greatest?
   (a) KANSAS
   (b) ALASKA
   (c) ALABAMA
   (d) ARKANSAS

A bag contains 5 red marbles, 4 white marbles, and 3 blue marbles. Find the probability of selecting each of the following.

7. a white marble

8. a green marble

9. a white or blue marble

10. a blue or red marble

11. A card is to be drawn at random from a row of ten cards. If the probability that this card will *not* be a king is $\frac{4}{5}$, how many kings are in the row of cards?

12. A bag contains 24 candies that are lemon-, cherry-, or orange-flavored. If there are 8 lemon-flavored candies, what is the probability that a candy selected at random will be cherry- or orange-flavored?

13.3 ADDING PROBABILITIES

In order to calculate the probability of one event *or* another occurring, it's necessary to add probabilities. This is done in a couple of different ways, depending on the kinds of events you're considering.

WHEN OUTCOMES DON'T OVERLAP

Suppose that a card is drawn at random from a standard deck. What is the probability that a six *or* a seven will be drawn? These are outcomes that don't overlap; it's impossible to for a card to be both a six and a seven. When this is the case, the probability that one event *or* another will happen is equal to the sum of the probability of each event happening alone.

In this case, the probability of drawing a six is $\frac{4}{52}$, and the probability of drawing a seven is also $\frac{4}{52}$. In other words, $P(6) = \frac{4}{52}$ and $P(7) = \frac{4}{52}$. The probability of drawing a six *or* a seven is the sum of these probabilities:

$$P(6 \text{ or } 7) = P(6) + P(7)$$
$$P(6 \text{ or } 7) = \frac{4}{52} + \frac{4}{52} = \frac{8}{52}$$

When outcomes don't overlap,
$P(A \text{ or } B) = P(A) + P(B)$

WHEN OUTCOMES DO OVERLAP

Now, suppose that we reshuffle the deck and once again draw a card at random. What is the probability that the card will be a five or a diamond? This is a different question, because the outcomes do overlap.

There are 4 fives in the deck, so the probability of drawing a five is $\frac{4}{52}$. There are 13 diamonds in the deck, so the probability of drawing a diamond is $\frac{13}{52}$. There would seem to be 17 ways to get a five or a diamond, for a probability of $\frac{17}{52}$. In this case, however, it's possible for a card to be a five *and* a diamond. In adding the probabilities together, you would count the five of diamonds twice—once as a five and once as a diamond. You must subtract one of the successful outcomes to compensate for this card's being counted twice. The actual probability of drawing a five or a diamond is $\frac{16}{52}$.

When outcomes overlap, it's necessary to use a modified version of the formula for the probability of one event *or* another. Add the two individual probabilities together, and subtract the probability of getting an overlapping outcome.

$$P(A \text{ or } B) = P(A) + P(B) - P(A \text{ and } B)$$

Examples

1. What is the probability that the roll of a die will produce a 5 or an even number?

   In this case, the outcomes do not overlap. The probabilities can simply be added.

   The probability of getting a 5 is $\frac{1}{6}$, since one of the six possible outcomes yields a 5.

   The probability of getting an even number is $\frac{3}{6}$, since three of the six possible outcomes are even.

   The probability of getting a 5 or an even number is $\frac{1}{6} + \frac{3}{6}$, or $\frac{4}{6}$.

2. A letter is chosen at random from the alphabet. What is the probability that the letter occurs in STOP or TAN?

   In this case, the two outcomes overlap, because STOP and TAN have a letter in common.

   Because 4 of the 26 letters occur in STOP, the probability that the chosen letter occurs in STOP is $\frac{4}{26}$. In other terms, $P(\text{STOP}) = \frac{4}{26}$.

   Because 3 of the 26 letters occur in TAN, the probability that the chosen letter occurs in TAN is $\frac{3}{26}$. In other terms, $P(\text{TAN}) = \frac{3}{26}$.

There is one outcome that occurs in both STOP and TAN: the letter T. In other terms, $P(\text{STOP and TAN}) = \frac{1}{26}$.

To find the probability that the chosen letter will occur in one word or the other, use the formula:

$P(A \text{ or } B) = P(A) + P(B) - P(A \text{ and } B)$

$P(\text{STOP or TAN}) = P(\text{STOP}) + P(\text{TAN}) - P(\text{STOP and TAN})$

$P(\text{STOP or TAN}) = \frac{4}{26} + \frac{3}{26} - \frac{1}{26}$

$P(\text{STOP or TAN}) = \frac{6}{26}$

EXERCISES

Supposing that a single die is rolled, find the probability of each of the following.

1. a 2 or a 4

2. an even number or a 1

3. a prime number or an odd number

4. a number greater than 4 or an even number

5. an odd number or a multiple of 3

6. an even number or a multiple of 7

A letter is chosen at random from the word FACETIOUS. Find the probability of each of the following results.

7. the letter T or the letter U

8. a vowel or the letter A

9. a letter occurring after Q in the alphabet or a vowel

10. a vowel or a consonant

11. $P(A) = 0.4$, $P(B) = 0.35$, and $P(A \text{ and } B) = 0.14$. What is $P(A \text{ or } B)$?

12. A card is selected at random from a standard deck. Find the probability that the card is an ace or a spade.

13.4 MULTIPLE EVENTS

All of the rules reviewed so far have dealt with the outcome of a single event, like the toss of a coin or the selection of a marble from a bag. What about the outcome of a series of events? Suppose, for example, that **two** dice are rolled, or that a coin is flipped and a card is chosen from a deck. Each of these cases represents a simple series of events.

Probabilities for a series of events are calculated just like probabilities for a single event: by counting the number of successful outcomes and the number of possible outcomes, and dividing. The trick is counting the possible outcomes of a series of events, which can be difficult.

THE SAMPLE SPACE

Suppose that a pair of dice are rolled. For each die there are six possible outcomes, 1–6; but how many outcomes are possible for the two dice together? The possible outcomes can be arranged as a table:

Second Die						
1	(1, 1)	(2, 1)	(3, 1)	(4, 1)	(5, 1)	(6, 1)
2	(1, 2)	(2, 2)	(3, 2)	(4, 2)	(5, 2)	(6, 2)
3	(1, 3)	(2, 3)	(3, 3)	(4, 3)	(5, 3)	(6, 3)
4	(1, 4)	(2, 4)	(3, 4)	(4, 4)	(5, 4)	(6, 4)
5	(1, 5)	(2, 5)	(3, 5)	(4, 5)	(5, 5)	(6, 5)
6	(1, 6)	(2, 6)	(3, 6)	(4, 6)	(5, 6)	(6, 6)
	1	2	3	4	5	6
			First Die			

For each of the six possible results for the first die, there are six possible results for the second. That makes a total of 36 different outcomes for this series of two events. This is called the *outcome set* or *sample space* for the experiment. Because there are two events happening, each outcome can be expressed as an ordered pair.

You can use the sample space to compute probabilities. The probability or rolling two sixes, for example, is $\frac{1}{36}$, because only 1 of the 36 outcomes produces that result. The probability of getting two numbers whose sum is 5, on the other hand, is $\frac{4}{36}$, because 4 outcomes produce that result: (1, 4), (2, 3), (3, 2), and (4, 1). Notice that (2, 3) and (3, 2) are distinct results.

Suppose that a die is rolled and then a coin is flipped. The outcome space for this series of events could be diagrammed like this:

Coin Tossed						
Heads	(1, H)	(2, H)	(3, H)	(4, H)	(5, H)	(6, H)
Tails	(1, T)	(2, T)	(3, T)	(4, T)	(5, T)	(6, T)
	1	2	3	4	5	6
			Die Rolled			

In this case, there are twelve possible outcomes.

Finally, consider the case in which two coins are tossed. The outcome space for these two events looks like this:

Second Coin		
Heads	(H, H)	(T, H)
Tails	(H, T)	(T, T)
	Heads	Tails
	First Coin	

THE COUNTING PRINCIPLE

You may notice a pattern in these tables. The roll of a die has 6 possible outcomes, and when two dice are rolled, there are 6×6, or 36, possible outcomes. The toss of a coin has 2 possible outcomes, and when a coin is tossed and a die is rolled, there are 2×6, or 12, possible outcomes. This is the *counting principle* at work.

The Counting Principle

If one activity can happen in m different ways, and another activity can happen in n different ways, then the two activities together can happen in mn different ways.

LISTING OUTCOMES

There are two common ways of representing the possible outcomes of a pair of events: listings and tree diagrams.

A sample space listing is a simple expression of the possible outcomes as a series of ordered pairs. Often, these pairs are arranged as in the tables shown earlier in this section. A sample space listing for rolling a die and flipping a coin, for example, might look like this:

(1, H), (2, H), (3, H), (4, H), (5, H), (6, H)

(1, T), (2, T), (3, T), (4, T), (5, T), (6, T)

To calculate probabilities using a sample space listing, count the successful outcomes for a given result and compare them to the total number of outcomes.

A *tree diagram* represents outcomes as branching lines. The diagram is read from left to right, and a new set of branches is started for each event. Here is a tree diagram for flipping a coin and rolling a die:

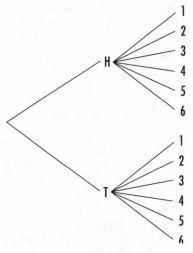

A *tree diagram* is a visual demonstration of the counting principle. The number of branches at the far right is the number of possible outcomes.

Exercises

1. Bob owns seven jackets and eight ties. How many jacket-and-tie combinations can he wear?

2. A restaurant offers 6 appetizers, 9 entrees, and 5 desserts. If a complete meal includes 1 appetizer, 1 entree, and 1 dessert, how many different meals can be ordered at the restaurant?

3. In an experiment, two coins are flipped and a standard die is rolled. How many possible outcomes does the experiment have?

4. In another experiment, a die is rolled three times. How many possible outcomes does this experiment have?

5. In the experiment in exercise #4, what is the probability that all three rolls produce sixes?

6. In the experiment in exercise #4, what is the probability that all three rolls produce the same number?

For each of the following, (a) list the sample space and (b) make a tree diagram showing all possibilities.

7. Two coins are tossed.

8. A die is rolled and a coin is flipped.

9. A letter is chosen randomly from COAT, and a letter is chosen randomly from HAT.

10. A letter is chosen randomly from MICE. One of the remaining letters is then chosen randomly.

13.5 MULTIPLYING PROBABILITIES

To calculate the probability of two events happening together, multiply the individual probabilities of the two events. There are two different ways of doing this, depending on the relationship between the two events.

If the outcome of one event does not affect the probability of the other event, the events are said to be *independent*. When one event's outcome *does* influence the probability of the other event, the events are said to be *dependent*.

INDEPENDENT EVENTS

When a die is rolled twice, the two events are independent. The result of the first roll does not affect the probability of the second roll.

Accordingly, to calculate the probability of rolling a 6 both times, you would simply multiply the probability of getting a 6 the first time by the probability of getting a 6 the second time: $\frac{1}{6} \times \frac{1}{6} = \frac{1}{36}$. The probability of rolling two sixes is therefore $\frac{1}{36}$. (This, by the way, is the same result you would get by making a chart of the sample space and counting outcomes, as in section 13.4.)

Probability of Independent Events
If the probability that one event will occur is *a*, and the probability that another event will occur is *b*, then the probability that both events will occur is *ab*.

Examples

1. A bag contains 4 white and 5 black marbles. One marble is selected at random, and its color is noted. The marble is then replaced, and a second marble is selected at random. What is the probability that both marbles will be black?

   These are independent events. Because the first marble is replaced before the second marble is chosen, the result of the first event doesn't affect the second. To find the probability that both marbles are black, multiply the probabilities that each marble will be black.

   $$P(\text{black}) = \frac{5}{9}$$

   The probability that the first marble will be black is $\frac{5}{9}$.

   The probability that the second marble is black is also $\frac{5}{9}$.

   The probability that both are black is therefore $\frac{5}{9} \times \frac{5}{9}$, or $\frac{25}{81}$.

2. There are seven girls and three boys in Mr. Jira's class, and there are five girls and six boys in Mrs. Kaminsky's class. If one student is chosen at random from each class, what the probability that both will be boys?

   These events are also independent, because the selection made in one classroom has no affect on the selection made in the other.

   $$P(\text{boy}) = \frac{3}{10}$$

   The probability that the student chosen from Mr. Jira's class is a boy is $\frac{3}{10}$.

   $$P(\text{boy}) = \frac{6}{11}$$

   The probability that the student chosen from Mrs. Kaminsky's class is a boy is $\frac{6}{11}$.

   The probability that both students are boys is $\frac{3}{10} \times \frac{6}{11}$, or $\frac{18}{110}$.

Dependent Events

Suppose that two cards are drawn at random from a standard deck without replacement. What is the probability that both cards will be kings?

The first and second drawings in this case are dependent events. The result of the first drawing affects the probability of the second. Here's how it works. When the first card is drawn, the deck holds 52 cards, 4 of which are kings. The probability of getting a king the first time is therefore $\frac{4}{52}$. When the second card is drawn, however, the situation has changed. One card—a king—is already missing from the deck. Now there are 51 cards in the deck, 3 of which are kings. The probability of getting a king the second time is therefore $\frac{3}{51}$.

The probability that *both* cards will be kings is the product $\frac{4}{52} \times \frac{3}{51}$, or $\frac{12}{2652}$. As you can see, drawing two kings from a deck of cards in two tries is not very likely.

Probability of Dependent Events
If the probability that one event will happen is *a*, and the probability that second event will happen after the first event is *b*, then the probability that both events will happen is *ab*.

Calculating the probability of dependent events is not very different from calculating the probability of independent events. In each case, you multiply the probabilities of the separate events together. The difference is that for dependent events, the calculation for the second event must take the first event into account.

Examples

3. A bowl contains 3 apples and 5 oranges. A piece of fruit is chosen at random and not replaced. A second piece of fruit is then chosen. What is the probability that both pieces of fruit are apples?

   These two events are dependent, because the result of the first choice affects what's left for the second choice.

   $P(\text{apple}) = \frac{3}{8}$

The probability that the first piece of fruit is an apple is $\frac{3}{8}$.

For the second drawing, there are 2 apples and 5 oranges left.

$P(\text{apple}) = \frac{2}{7}$ The probability that the second piece of fruit is an apple is $\frac{2}{7}$.

The probability that both pieces of fruit are apples is the product $\frac{3}{8} \times \frac{2}{7}$, or $\frac{6}{56}$.

4. A bag contains 4 red marbles and 6 blue marbles. If two marbles are chosen at random from the bag, what is the probability that the marbles will be the same color?

These events are dependent. There are two successful outcomes: (red, red) and (blue, blue). The probability that the two marbles will be the same color is the sum of $P(\text{red}, \text{red})$ and $P(\text{blue}, \text{blue})$.

The probability that both marbles are red is the product $\frac{4}{10} \times \frac{3}{9}$, or $\frac{12}{90}$.

The probability that both marbles are blue is the product $\frac{6}{10} \times \frac{5}{9}$, or $\frac{30}{90}$.

The probability that both marbles or blue or both marbles are red is the sum $\frac{12}{90} + \frac{30}{90}$, or $\frac{42}{90}$.

Test your understanding of probability with the following exercises.

EXERCISES

A bag contains three yellow marbles and four green marbles. A marble is chosen at random, its color is noted, and it is replaced. A second marble is then chosen at random. Find each of the following.

1. $P(\text{yellow, green})$
2. $P(\text{green, green})$
3. $P(\text{yellow, yellow})$
4. $P(\text{both the same color})$
5. $P(\text{not both green})$
6. $P(\text{both different colors})$

Two cards are selected at random from a standard deck without replacement. Find each of the following.

7. P(jack, jack)

8. P(spade, spade)

9. P(both the same suit)

10. P(five, six)

13.6 PERMUTATIONS

Consider the number of ways in which the letters A, B, C, and D can be arranged. You can use the counting principle to find the number of possible arrangements.

Imagine four empty positions for the letters to occupy. There are four letters that could be placed in the first position:

4

Once a letter is placed in the first position, there are three letters left that could be placed in the second position:

4	3

That leaves two letters for the third position and, finally, only one letter for the last position:

4	3	2	1

In other words, there are four ways to fill the first position, three ways to fill the second, two ways to fill the third, and one way to fill the fourth. Using the counting principle, multiply these numbers together to find the total number of possible outcomes.

$4 \times 3 \times 2 \times 1 = 24$

There are 24 possible arrangements of the letters A, B, C, and D. These arrangements can also be called *permutations*.

In counting permutations, a special numerical quantity called a *factorial* is often useful. The expression 4! is read "four factorial," and denotes the product $4 \times 3 \times 2 \times 1$. For any positive integer n, the quantity $n!$ is equal to the product of all integers between n and 1, inclusive.

A group of n objects in n positions can be arranged in n! different permutations.

ARRANGEMENTS OF N OBJECTS IN FEWER THAN N POSITIONS

Suppose you are asked how many three-letter arrangements can be made from the letters of the word BRAIN. You're being asked to arrange 5 letters in only 3 positions. That means that some letters will be left out of each arrangement. Once again, use the counting principle to find the number of permutations.

Sketch the three available positions:

5	4	3

There are five letters available for the first position. Once it's filled, there are four letters remaining to fill the second position, which leaves three letters available for the third position.

The total number of permutations is the product $5 \times 4 \times 3$, or 60.

The number of permutations of n objects in r positions is represented by the expression $_nP_r$. For example, the expression $_5P_3$ denotes the number of permutations of five objects in three spaces, as shown above. As we've just seen, $_5P_3 = 60$. In fact, the value of $_nP_r$ can be found for any meaningful values of n and r using a simple formula.

For n objects arranged in r positions,

$$n\,Pr = \frac{n!}{(n-r)!}$$

Example

1. How many four-digit numbers can be written using the digits 2, 3, 4, 5, 6, and 7 if no digit is used twice?

   The question is essentially asking you to count the permutations of 6 objects in 4 positions. You can use the permutations formula to find out how many there are.

   $$_nP_r = \frac{n!}{(n-r)!}$$

   $$_6P_4 = \frac{6!}{(6-4)!}$$

   $$_6P_4 = \frac{6!}{2!} = \frac{6 \times 5 \times 4 \times 3 \times 2 \times 1}{2 \times 1}$$

   $$_6P_4 = \frac{6 \times 5 \times 4 \times 3 \times 2 \times 1}{2 \times 1} = 6 \times 5 \times 4 \times 3$$

   $$_6P_4 = 360$$

   It's possible to form 360 different four-digit numbers using the digits 2, 3, 4, 5, 6, and 7.

Arrangements with Special Positions

Suppose you're asked how many four-letter arrangements ending in S can be made from the letters of the word SALMON. You're being asked to arrange 6 letters in only 4 positions, so that S is always the last letter. This may seem difficult, but it's easier than it looks. Just apply the counting principle.

Sketch the four available positions. Put a 1 in the fourth position, because this position can be filled in only one way—with the letter S:

			1

There are five ways to fill the first position (S is already taken). That leaves four ways to fill the second position, and three ways to fill the third. The fourth position is taken by the letter S.

5	4	3	1

The total number of permutations is $5 \times 4 \times 3 \times 1$, or 60. Sixty four-letter arrangements ending in S can me made from the letters of the word SALMON.

Even permutation questions with strange rules governing its positions can be solved. Just think the question through and use the counting principle.

Test your understanding of permutations with the following exercises.

Exercises

Provide numerical answers to each of the following.

1. In how many ways can 7 books be arranged on a shelf?

2. In how many arrangements can 5 friends sit in a row on a bench?

3. How many 6-digit numbers can be formed using the digits 3, 4, 5, 6, 7, and 8, if no digit is repeated?

4. How many 3-digit numbers can be formed using the digits 3, 4, 5, 6, 7, and 8, if no digit is repeated?

5. How many **odd** four-digit numbers can be formed using the digits 1, 4, 8, and 9, if no digit is repeated?

6. How many odd four-digit numbers can be formed using the digits 1, 4, 8, and 9, if digits **may** be repeated?

7. How many six-letter combinations can be formed from the letters of the word DIMPLE, if every combination begins with M and ends with D?

8. How many four-digit numbers greater than 2,000 can be formed using the digits 0, 1, 2, 3, 4, 5, and 6, if no digit is repeated?

Evaluate each of the following.

9. $_7P_4$

10. $_5P_5$

11. $_{12}P_4$

12. $_{11}P_3$

SUMMARY

- $P(E) = \dfrac{\text{successful outcomes}}{\text{total possible outcomes}}$

- The probability of an impossible event is zero.

- The probability of a certain event is 1.

- The probability that an event will occur and the probability that it will not occur add up to 1.
  For any event E,
  $P(\text{not } E) = 1 - P(E)$

- $P(A \text{ or } B) = P(A) + P(B) - P(A \text{ and } B)$

- **The Counting Principle**
  If one activity can happen in m different ways, and another activity can happen in n different ways, then the two activities together can happen in mn different ways.

- **Probability of Independent Events**
  If the probability that one event will occur is a, and the probability that another event will occur is b, then the probability that both events will occur is ab.

- **Probability of Dependent Events**
  If the probability that one event will happen is a, and the probability that second event will happen **after the first event** is b, then the probability that both events will happen is ab.

- A group of n objects in n positions can be arranged in $n!$ different permutations.

- For n objects arranged in r positions,
  $$_nP_r = \frac{n!}{(n-r)!}$$

14

Statistics

Statistics is the field of mathematics dealing with the collection, organization, and interpretation of data. This chapter will deal principally with the three *measures of central tendency* called the mean, median, and mode, and with the idea of *frequency*.

14.1 MEAN AND MEDIAN

THE MEAN

The *arithmetic mean* of a set of numbers is another term for the average of that set. To find the mean of a set of numbers, add the numbers together and divide the sum by the number of elements in the set.

$$mean = \frac{sum\ of\ values}{number\ of\ values}$$

The mean is called a *measure of central tendency* because its value lies between the extreme values of a set. If the values of a set are closely grouped, then the mean lies near the center of this group. When the values in a set are more widely scattered, the mean is less meaningful. As a measure of central tendency, the mean is most useful when working with closely grouped data sets.

Examples

1. What is the mean of 52, 53, 56, and 57?

   Add the numbers together and divide by 4.

   $$\text{mean} = \frac{52 + 53 + 56 + 57}{4} = \frac{218}{4} = 54.5$$

   The mean of the numbers is 54.5. Notice that since the numbers are closely grouped, the mean lies near the center of the group. In this case, the mean provides useful information about the numbers in the set.

2. What is the mean of 4, 10, 17, and 89?

   Add the numbers together and divide by 4.

   $$\text{mean} = \frac{4 + 10 + 17 + 89}{4} = \frac{120}{4} = 30$$

   The mean of these numbers is 30. Because these numbers are not closely grouped, the mean tells us less about the values in the set.

THE MEDIAN

The *median* is another commonly used measure of central tendency. While the mean is determined by averaging data values, the median is determined by arranging data values in order and selecting the center value or values.

The median of a set of numbers is the number in the middle when the numbers are arranged in order. If the set contains an even number of elements, so that no one number is in the middle, then the median is the average of the two middle values.

Examples

1. What is the median of 24, 29, 32, 27, and 34?

   Arrange the numbers in order: 24, 27, 29, 32, 34. The middle number is 29, so this set of numbers has a median of 29.

2. What is the median of 12, 15, 17, 22?

   This set of numbers has an even number of elements. When the numbers are arranged in order, 15 and 17 are in the middle. Take the average of these two numbers to find the median of the set.

   $$\text{median} = \frac{15+17}{2} = \frac{32}{2} = 16$$

   The set's median is 16.

QUARTILES

Just as the median is a number that divides a set of numbers into two halves containing the same number of values, *quartiles* are numbers that divide a set into quarters containing the same number of values.

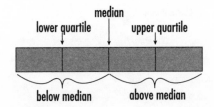

There are three quartiles in a set: the lower quartile, the middle quartile, and the upper quartile. The middle quartile of a set is the same thing as the median.
The lower quartile is the median of the numbers below the set's median. The upper quartile is the median of the numbers above the set's median.

Examples

3. Find the median, lower quartile, and upper quartile of the set {5, 9, 12, 16, 19, 23, 30}.

   Arrange the numbers in order.

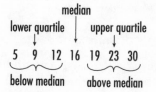

The middle number, 16, is the median of the set.

The numbers below the median are 5, 9, and 12 (16 is neither above nor below the median). The median of this group is 9, so the lower quartile is of the set 9.

The numbers above the median are 19, 23, and 30. The median of this group is 23 so the upper quartile of the set is 23.

4. Find the median, lower quartile, and upper quartile of the set {43, 49, 52, 55, 59, 64, 72, 81}.

Arrange the numbers in order.

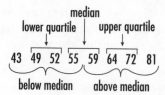

The set contains an even number of elements, so the median is the average of the two middle numbers, 55 and 59.

$$\text{median} = \frac{55 + 59}{2} = \frac{114}{2} = 57$$

The median of the set is 57.

The numbers below the median are 43, 49, 52, and 55. The lower quartile is the median of this group.

$$\text{median} = \frac{49 + 52}{2} = \frac{101}{2} = 50.5$$

The lower quartile is 50.5.

The numbers above the median are 59, 64, 72, and 81. The upper quartile is the median of this group.

$$\text{median} = \frac{64 + 72}{2} = \frac{136}{2} = 68$$

The upper quartile is 68.

PERCENTILES

Suppose that in a list of 20 scores, 16 scores are less than or equal to 42. Because those 16 scores represent 80% of the list of 20, the score of 42 represents the *80th percentile*. Similarly, the 40th percentile is the score which 40% of the scores fall at or below.

> The nth percentile is the value that n% of the values in a set fall at or below.

The median of a set is equivalent to the 50th percentile. The lower quartile is equivalent to the 25th percentile, and the upper quartile is equivalent to the 75th percentile.

Example

5. In the set of scores {3, 4, 5, 6, 7, 8, 9, 10, 11, 12}, a score of 9 represents what percentile?

   Seven of the scores are less than or equal to 9, and there's a total of 10 scores. In other words, 70% of the scores are less than or equal to 9. A score of 9 represents the 70th percentile.

EXERCISES

For each of the following sets of numbers, find (a) the mean and (b) the median.

1. 1, 2, 3, 4, 5

2. 0.5, 0.6, 1.0, 1.4, 1.9, 2.4

3. 1, 2, 3000

4. –7, –3, –1, 0, 5, 8, 14, 16

A class's test scores on an examination are 74, 94, 77, 89, 77, 87, 78, 86, 82, 85, 83, 84, 83. Find each of the following.

5. the median

6. the lower quartile

7. the upper quartile

8. the mean

Solve each of the following.

9. Julia's scores on four math tests are 83, 77, 89, and x. If her mean score on the four tests is 87, what is the value of x?

10. In a track event, two runners get times of 48 seconds, one runner gets a time of 45 seconds, and three runners get times of 44 seconds. What is the mean time for these runners in seconds?

11. On a test, 7 students in Mrs. Kukri's class scored above the 80th percentile. How many students scored at or below the 80th percentile?

12. A number is chosen randomly from the set 7, 8, 8, 9, 11, 11, 11, 16. Find the probability that the selected number is equal to the:
    (a) lower quartile
    (b) median
    (c) upper quartile

14.2 MODE AND FREQUENCY

In some data sets, certain data values occur more than once. A class's scores on a math test, for example, might include three scores of 92. If one value occurs more frequently than any other, this value is called the *mode* of the data set.

The mode of a set is the value that occurs most frequently.

In the set {1, 3, 5, 2, 6, 3, 6, 9, 7, 3}, for example, the mode is 3. No other value occurs as frequently.

If a few values occur with equal frequency, then the set may have more than one mode. In the set {15, 20, 20, 25, 35, 40, 40, 55}, for example, there are two modes: 20 and 40. Because it has two modes, this set is said to be *bimodal*.

If the values in a data set all occur with equal frequency, the set is said to have *no mode*. For example, the following two data sets have no mode:

{1, 2, 3, 4, 5, 6, 7, 8}

{3, 3, 6, 6, 9, 9, 12, 12, 15, 15}

Example

1. The table below shows the scores of 35 students in a talent competition. What is the mode of the scores?

Score	Frequency
4	3
5	5
6	0
7	12
8	8
9	4
10	3
Total:	35

The frequency column tells you how often each score occurs. The score of 7 occurs 12 times—more often than any other score. The mode of the set is 7.

2. What is the mode of the set $\{a, c, f, r, s, c, h, v, a, p\}$?

Most of the values in the set occur only one time, but two values occur twice: a and c. The set is bimodal, and the modes are a and c.

FREQUENCY

The number of times a data value occurs in a data set is called the *frequency* of that value. The mode of a set is simply the value with the greatest frequency. Frequency is commonly used in many kinds of statistical interpretation. Some of these are quite familiar; in many surveys, for example, people are asked a multiple-choice question, and the number of people choosing each answer is recorded. The surveyors are interested in the frequency with which each answer occurs.

Examples

3. The final averages of 24 students in a history class are 73, 84, 92, 88, 76, 96, 90, 84, 79, 87, 91, 99, 96, 71, 94, 73, 96, 76, 79, 80, 84, 99, 91, and 80. Construct a frequency table for these values.

First, write the averages in order: 71, 73, 73, 76, 76, 79, 79, 80, 80, 84, 84, 84, 87, 88, 90, 91, 91, 92, 94, 96, 96, 96, 99, 99.

Next, make a table with a column for the averages and a column for their frequencies. It may be helpful to make an additional column in the middle in which to tally up the frequencies.

Production: Add appropriate tally-marks in center column.

Average	Tally	Frequency
71	/	1
73	//	2
76	//	2
79	//	2
80	//	2
84	///	3
87	/	1
88	/	1
90	/	1
91	//	2
92	/	1
94	/	1
96	///	3
99	//	2
	Total:	24

There's a lot of information in this table, and it's spread very thinly, which limits the table's usefulness as a tool for interpretation. For this reason, frequency tables are often constructed for certain intervals, rather than individual data values. Take a look at the next example.

4. Using the data from example #3, construct a frequency table using the intervals 71–75, 76–80, 81–85, 86–90, 91–95, and 96–100.

Use the table from example #3 to help you. Construct a new table with a column for score intervals rather than individual scores.

Interval	Frequency
71–75	3
76–80	6
81–85	3
86–90	3
91–95	4
96–100	5
Total:	24

This is a typical frequency table, with frequencies reported for certain intervals.

CUMULATIVE FREQUENCY

Cumulative frequency is a alternative way of recording frequency. Where an ordinary frequency table shows the frequency with which scores occur in a certain interval, a cumulative frequency table shows the frequency with which scores occur *below* certain values.

Below, a frequency table and a cumulative frequency table have been constructed for the same 12 data values.

Interval	Frequency
1–10	2
11–20	2
21–30	2
31–40	2
41–50	2
51–60	2
Total:	12

Interval	Cumulative Frequency
1–10	2
1–20	4
1–30	6
1–40	8
1–50	10
1–60	12
Total:	12

Notice that the frequency table records that there are two scores in each interval. The cumulative frequency table, on the other hand, records that there are two scores less than or equal to 10, 4 scores less than or equal to 20, and so on. The numbers in the cumulative frequency column must increase from interval to interval, because each interval includes the interval before it.

Example

5. Using the data from exercise #4, construct a cumulative frequency table.

   Refer to the frequency table from exercise #4.

Interval	Frequency
71–75	3
76–80	6
81–85	3
86–90	3
91–95	4
96–100	5
Total:	24

Interval	Cumulative Frequency
71–75	3
71–80	9
71–85	12
71–90	15
71–96	19
71–100	24
Total:	24

Two changes must be made to convert a frequency table to a cumulative frequency table. First, the intervals must be changed: Each interval's upper limit remains unchanged, but the lower limit of all the intervals must be made equal to the lowest data value.

Second, the numbers in the cumulative frequency column are generated by starting with the lowest interval, which is the same in both tables, and adding the numbers in the corresponding intervals of the frequency table.

EXERCISES

Find the mode or modes of each of the following sets. If the set has no mode, indicate that.

1. 8, 3, 0, 2, 4, 7, 9, 1, 5, 6

2. 1, 2, 3, 2, 3, 1, 1, 2, 3, 2

3. 34, 37, 39, 32, 34, 36, 35, 37

4. 0, 4, 2, –3, 1, 6, –4, 3, 0, 9

The heights of a group of students in centimeters are 141, 143, 167, 182, 170, 148, 184, 179, 160, 147, 162, 174, 182, 169, 172, 180, 162, 153, 148, and 157. Use these data values to complete the following tables:

5.

Interval	Frequency
141–149	
150–158	
159–167	
168–176	
177–185	
Total:	

6.

Interval	Cumulative Frequency
141–149	
141–158	
141–167	
141–176	
141–185	
Total:	

The frequency table at right shows the number of errors made on a driving test by group of students. Refer to the table to answer the following.

Errors Made	Frequency
0	1
1	6
2	5
3	4
4	3
5	3

7. What is the mode number of errors made?

8. What is the median number of errors made?

9. What is the mean number of errors made?

10. How many students are represented in the table?

11. How many students scored above the 75th percentile for their group?

12. Construct a cumulative frequency table for the data.

14.3 HISTOGRAMS

A histogram is a kind of bar graph used to display frequency or cumulative frequency. In a histogram, the bars are vertical, and there is no space between them.

Here are frequency and cumulative frequency histograms for the tables you constructed in the previous section:

Interval	Frequency
71–75	3
76–80	6
81–85	3
86–90	3
91–95	4
96–100	5
Total:	24

FINAL AVERAGES IN HISTORY CLASS

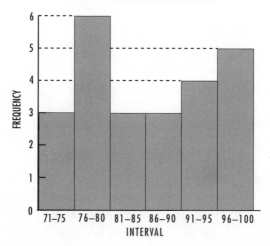

Interval	Cumulative Frequency
71–75	3
71–80	9
71–85	12
71–90	15
71–96	19
71–100	24
Total:	24

FINAL AVERAGES IN HISTORY CLASS

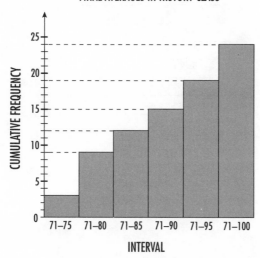

Test your understanding of histograms with the following exercises.

EXERCISES

Construct (a) a frequency histogram and (b) a cumulative frequency histogram for the data in each of the following tables.

1.

Interval	Frequency
1–10	4
11–20	2
21–30	0
31–40	3
41–50	5
51–60	1

2.

Interval	Frequency
1–3	1
4–6	1
7–9	3
10–12	4
13–15	5

3.

Interval	Cumulative Frequency
25–28	2
25–32	2
25–36	7
25–40	15
25–44	22
25–48	25

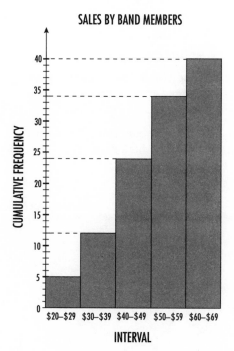

SALES BY BAND MEMBERS

The cumulative frequency histogram above shows the sales made by the members of the school band who participated in the Saturday Candy Sale. Refer to the histogram to answer the following questions.

4. How many band members participated in the sale?

5. How many band members had sales in the $50–$59 range?

6. The median amount of sales for a band member falls in what interval?

7. Construct (a) a frequency table and (b) a cumulative frequency table for the sales data shown in the histogram.

SUMMARY

- $\text{mean} = \dfrac{\text{sum of values}}{\text{number of values}}$
- The *median* of a set of numbers is the number in the middle when the numbers are arranged in order. If the set contains an even number of elements, so that no one number is in the middle, then the median is the average of the two middle values.

- The *lower quartile* is the median of the numbers below the set's median. The *upper quartile* is the median of the numbers above the set's median.

- The *mode* of a set of numbers is the number that occurs most frequently.

- An ordinary frequency table shows the frequency with which scores occur in a certain interval. A cumulative frequency table shows the frequency with which scores occur **below** certain values.

- A histogram is a kind of bar graph used to display frequency or cumulative frequency. In a histogram, the bars are vertical, and there is no space between them.

Answers
to Exercises

CHAPTER 1

SECTION 1.1

1. statement
2. statement
3. open sentence
4. open sentence
5. open sentence
6. open sentence
7. statement
8. statement

SECTION 1.2

1. Eight is not an odd number. OR It is not true that eight is an odd number.
2. Gold is not heavier than lead. OR It is not true that gold is heavier than lead.
3. Marie Curie did not discover radium. OR It is not true that Marie Curie discovered radium.
4. My pants are on fire. OR It is not true that my pants are not on fire.
5. Venus is not the planet nearest the sun. OR It is not true that Venus is the planet nearest the sun.
6. Zero is a negative number. OR It is not true that zero is not a negative number.
7. $2 + 3 \neq 5$
8. $7 - 4 \neq 3$
9. $7 \leq 3$ OR $7 \not> 3$
10. $3 \times 4 = 1.2$

SECTION 1.3

1. $b \wedge \sim a$
2. $\sim b \wedge a$
3. $b \wedge a$
4. $\sim a \wedge \sim b$
5. F
6. F
7. T
8. F

9.

p	q	$p \wedge q$
T	T	T
T	F	F
F	T	F
F	F	F

10.

p	q	$\sim q$	$p \wedge \sim q$
T	T	F	F
T	F	T	T
F	T	F	F
F	F	T	F

11.

p	q	$p \wedge q$	$\sim(p \wedge q)$
T	T	T	F
T	F	F	T
F	T	F	T
F	F	F	T

12.

p	q	$\sim p$	$\sim q$	$\sim p \wedge \sim q$
T	T	F	F	F
T	F	F	T	F
F	T	T	F	F
F	F	T	T	T

SECTION 1.4

1. $p \vee r$
2. $p \wedge q$
3. $p \vee (q \wedge r)$
4. $\sim q \vee p$
5. T
6. F
7. F
8. T

9.

s	$\sim s$	$s \vee \sim s$
T	F	T
F	T	T

10.

s	t	$\sim t$	$s \vee \sim t$
T	T	F	T
T	F	T	T
F	T	F	F
F	F	T	T

11.

s	t	$s \vee t$	$\sim(s \vee t)$
T	T	T	F
T	F	T	F
F	T	T	F
F	F	F	T

12.

s	t	$\sim t$	$s \wedge \sim t$	$t \vee (s \wedge \sim t)$
T	T	F	F	T
T	F	T	T	T
F	T	F	F	T
F	F	T	F	F

SECTION 1.5

1. $l \rightarrow n$
2. $n \rightarrow \sim m$
3. $(m \vee l) \rightarrow n$
4. $(l \wedge \sim n) \rightarrow m$
5. F
6. T
7. T
8. F

9.

p	$\sim p$	$p \rightarrow \sim p$
T	F	F
F	T	T

10.

p	q	$\sim p$	$\sim q$	$\sim q \rightarrow \sim p$
T	T	F	F	T
T	F	F	T	F
F	T	T	F	T
F	F	T	T	T

11.

p	q	$p \rightarrow q$	$\sim p$	$(p \rightarrow q) \vee \sim p$
T	T	T	F	T
T	F	F	F	F
F	T	T	T	T
F	F	T	T	T

12.

p	q	$p \wedge q$	$p \vee q$	$(p \wedge q) \rightarrow (p \vee q)$
T	T	T	T	T
T	F	F	T	T
F	T	F	T	T
F	F	F	F	T

Section 1.6

1.

c	$c \to c$
T	T
F	T

Yes, the statement is a tautology.

2.

c	d	$c \wedge d$	$(c \wedge d) \to d$
T	T	T	T
T	F	F	T
F	T	F	T
F	F	F	T

Yes, the statement is a tautology.

3.

d	$\sim d$	$d \to \sim d$
T	F	F
F	T	T

No, the statement is not a tautology.

4.

c	d	$c \vee d$	$\sim d$	$(c \vee d) \vee \sim d$
T	T	T	F	T
T	F	T	T	T
F	T	T	F	T
F	F	F	T	T

Yes, the statement is a tautology.

5.

c	d	$\sim c$	$\sim d$	$c \to d$	$\sim d \to \sim c$	$(c \to d) \vee (\sim d \to \sim c)$
T	T	F	F	T	T	T
T	F	F	T	F	F	F
F	T	T	F	T	T	T
F	F	T	T	T	T	T

No, the statement is not a tautology.

Section 1.7

1. *converse:* If I get hungry, I see peaches.
inverse: If I don't see peaches, I don't get hungry.
contrapositive: If I don't get hungry, I don't see peaches.

2. *converse:* If Holly is lost, then Holly is not on the bus.
inverse: If Holly is on the bus, then Holly isn't lost.
contrapositive: If Holly is not lost, then Holly is on the bus.

3. *converse:* If the camel is not dangerous, then the camel doesn't spit at you.
inverse: If the camel spits at you, then the camel is dangerous.
contrapositive: If the camel is dangerous, then the camel spits at you.

4. (Original statement is equivalent to "If it is dark, then I do not go swimming.")
converse: If I do not go swimming, then it is not dark.
inverse: If it is not dark, then I go swimming.

contrapositive: If I go swimming, then it is not dark.

5. *converse:* $s \to r$
   inverse: $\sim r \to \sim s$
   contrapositive: $\sim s \to \sim r$

6. *converse:* $s \to \sim r$
   inverse: $r \to \sim s$
   contrapositive: $\sim s \to r$

7. *converse:* $(s \wedge t) \to r$
   inverse: $\sim r \to \sim (s \wedge t)$
   contrapositive: $\sim (s \wedge t) \to \sim r$

8. *converse:* $\sim (s \wedge t) \to (q \vee r)$
   inverse: $\sim (q \vee r) \to (s \wedge t)$
   contrapositive: $(s \wedge t) \to \sim (q \vee r)$

9. F

10. T

11. T

12. F

Section 1.8

1. $p \leftrightarrow r$

2. $r \leftrightarrow (p \wedge q)$

3. $(q \to p) \wedge (p \to q)$ OR $p \leftrightarrow q$

4. $(\sim r \wedge q) \leftrightarrow p$

5. D

6. A

7. C

8. B

9.

a	b	$\sim b$	$a \vee \sim b$	$(a \vee \sim b) \leftrightarrow a$
T	T	F	T	T
T	F	T	T	T
F	T	F	F	T
F	F	T	T	F

No, the statement is not a tautology.

10.

a	b	$a \to b$	$b \to a$	$(a \to b) \leftrightarrow (b \to a)$
T	T	T	T	T
T	F	F	T	F
F	T	T	F	F
F	F	T	T	T

No, the statement is not a tautology.

11.

a	b	$a \wedge b$	$\sim(a \wedge b)$	$\sim a$	$\sim b$	$\sim a \wedge \sim b$	$\sim(a \wedge b) \leftrightarrow (\sim a \vee \sim b)$
T	T	T	F	F	F	F	T
T	F	F	T	F	T	T	T
F	T	F	T	T	F	T	T
F	F	F	T	T	T	T	T

Yes, the statement is a tautology. In other words, the statements $\sim (a \wedge b)$ and $\sim a \vee \sim b$ are logically equivalent.

12.

a	b	$\sim a$	$a \wedge b$	$a \vee b$	$(a \wedge b) \to (a \vee b)$	$(a \wedge b) \to (a \vee b) \leftrightarrow \sim a$
T	T	F	T	T	T	F
T	F	F	F	T	T	F
F	T	T	F	T	T	T
F	F	T	F	F	T	T

No, the statement is not a tautology.

CHAPTER 2

Section 2.1

1. $4 \times x$; $4 \cdot x$; $4(x)$; $(4)(x)$; $4x$
2. $a \times b$; $a \cdot b$; $a(b)$; $(a)(b)$; ab
3. $x \times y \times z$; $x \cdot y \cdot z$; $(x)(y)(z)$; xyz
4. $4 \times m \times n$; $4 \cdot m \cdot n$; $(4)(m)(n)$; $4mn$
5. 10^6
6. x^4
7. $z \cdot z \cdot z \cdot z \cdot z \cdot z \cdot z \cdot z$
8. $5 \cdot 5 \cdot 5$
9. $\dfrac{5}{3}$
10. $\dfrac{x}{y}$
11. $\dfrac{n+5}{8}$
12. $\dfrac{x+y}{x-y}$

Section 2.2

1. $5 - 2 + 3 = 6$
2. $4 \times 3 - 2 = 10$
3. $6(-2) + 3 = -9$
4. $10(5 - 3) = 20$
5. $4^2 - 6 \div 2 = 13$
6. $(7 - 5)^3 \times 3 = 24$
7. $(6 \times 4 \div 2)^2 = 144$
8. $\dfrac{8 - 3^2}{5 - 3} = -\dfrac{1}{2}$

Section 2.3

1. $\{3, 4, 6, 5, 7, 9\}$
2. {all factors of 60}
3. $\{..., -3, -2, -1, 0, 1, 2, 3,...\}$ or {all integers}
4. $\{30\}$
5. $\{ \ \}$ or $\varnothing$
6. $\{0, 1, 2, 3,...\}$ or {whole numbers}
7. $\{4\}$
8. $\{4\}$
9. $\{7, 9\}$
10. $\{ \ \}$ or $\varnothing$

Section 2.4

1. D
2. B
3. rational
4. rational
5. rational
6. irrational
7. rational (because $\sqrt{64} = 8$)
8. rational
9. rational $\left(0.\overline{66} = \dfrac{2}{3} \right)$
10. irrational

Section 2.5

1. 18
2. $-4x$
3. -30
4. $15n$
5. 27
6. -3

Section 2.6

1. $\dfrac{9}{5}$
2. $\dfrac{3}{11}$
3. $\dfrac{25}{4}$
4. $\dfrac{2}{15}$
5. 0.375
6. $\dfrac{37}{25}$
7. $\dfrac{47}{40}$
8. $\dfrac{5}{24}$
9. $\dfrac{3x}{28}$
10. $\dfrac{15}{12}$ or $\dfrac{5}{4}$
11. $\dfrac{1}{64}$
12. $\dfrac{24}{35}$

Section 2.7

1. 1
2. -125
3. $\dfrac{1}{81}$

4. $\dfrac{1}{8}$
5. x^{-3}
6. n^{7}
7. a^{20}
8. m^{-6}
9. 3.4×10^{3}
10. 1.9×10^{-3}
11. 5.31×10^{5}
12.

Section 2.8

1. -14
2. 1
3. $\dfrac{1}{32}$
4. $-\dfrac{1}{2}$
5. a
6. x
7. s
8. 8
9. The commutative property of multiplication.
10. The distributive property.
11. The associative property of multiplication.
12. The associative property of addition.

CHAPTER 3

Section 3.1

1. $x + 5$
2. $z - 12$

3. $6b$

4. $\dfrac{n}{8}$

5. $\dfrac{y}{2} + 20$

6. $2(m + 1)$

7. $7a + 2$

8. $5c - 3$

9. $100d$

10. $7(n + 1)$, or $7n + 7$

11. $g - 7$

12. $n - 12$

13. $2p$

14. $12 - 1.5x$

15. $450 + 20t$

16. $23 - m$

Section 3.2

1. equivalent
2. not equivalent
3. not equivalent
4. equivalent
5. $x = 5$
6. $b = 13$
7. $c = -16$
8. $y = 7$
9. $n = -598$
10. $p = -1$
11. $t = -19$
12. $h = 1$

Section 3.3

1. $v = 2$
2. $b = 9$
3. $n = 0$
4. $x = -8$

5. $a = -\dfrac{1}{17}$

6. $g = 13$

7. $t = 35$

8. $l = -0.2$

9. $f = 35$

10. $r = 15$

11. $-\dfrac{9}{8}$

12. $n = 8$

Section 3.4

1. $x = 5$
2. $a = -6$
3. $y = -4$
4. $b = 3$
5. $t = 4$
6. $n = 42$
7. $x = 24$
8. $s = -33$
9. $k = 15$

10. $m = \dfrac{7}{2}$

11. $h = -33$

12. $j = \dfrac{1}{6}$

Section 3.5

(It doesn't matter what letter you choose for your variable.)

1. Let p = Pooky's age now.
   $p + 7 = 22$

2. Let t = the number of toys purchased.
   $3.50t = 42.50$

3. Let n = the unknown number.
   $6n = -78$

4. Let x = the number.
$x - 32 = -12$

5. *Variable:* Let x = money Kaiser must earn.
Equation: $86 + x = 120$
Solution: $x = 24$
Answer: Kaiser must earn $24.00.

6. *Variable:* Let c = the cost of one ride
Equation: $5c = 12.5$
Solution: $c = 2.5$
Answer: One ride on the Ferris wheel costs $2.50.

7. *Variable:* Let j = Jamal's age now.
Equation: $j - 3 = 16$
Solution: $j = 19$
Answer: Jamal is 19 years old.

8. *Variable:* Let x = the stereo's original price.
Equation: $\frac{1}{2}x + 10 = 46$
Solution: $x = 72$
Answer: The original price of the stereo is $72.00.

9. *Variable:* Let l = Lucy's money after 8 weeks.
Equation: $360 + 8(20) = x$
Solution: $x = 520$
Answer: Lucy will have $520.00 after 8 weeks.

10. *Variable:* Let h = hours until the candle is 2.5 inches tall.
Equation: $10 - 1.5h = 2.5$
Solution: $h = 5$
Answer: The candle will be 2.5 inches tall after 5 hours.

11. *Variable:* Let e = Ellen's age. Then $e + 2$ = Jeff's age and $2e$ = Tyler's age.
Equation: $(e + 2) + e + 2e = 26$
Solution: $e = 6$
Answer: Ellen is 6 years old.

12. *Variable:* Let l = the length of the longest side.
Then $\frac{l}{2} + 2$ = the second side and $l - 4$ = the third side.
Equation: $l + \left(\frac{l}{2} + 2\right) + (l - 4) = 33$
Solution: $l = 14$
Answer: The length of the longest side is 14 inches.

Section 3.6

1. *Variable:* Let x = the smaller integer.
Then $x + 1$ = the larger integer.
Equation: $x + (x + 1) = 17$

2. *Variable:* Let n = the smaller integer.
Then $n + 2$ = the larger integer.
Equation: $n + (n + 2) = 140$

3. *Variable:* Let y = the smallest integer.
Then $y + 1$ = the middle integer, and $y + 2$ = the largest integer.
Equation: $y + (y + 1) + (y + 2) = -24$

4. *Variable:* Let b = the smallest number.
Then $b + 6$ = the middle number, and $b + 12$ = the largest number.

Equation: $b + (b + 6) + (b + 12) = 54$

5. *Variable:* Let x = the smaller integer.
   Then $x + 1$ = the larger integer.
   Equation: $x + (x + 1) = 31$
   Solution: $x = 15$
   Answer: The smaller integer is 15.

6. *Variable:* Let t = the smallest integer.
   Then $t + 2$ = the middle integer, and $t + 4$ = the largest integer.
   Equation: $t + (t + 2) + (t + 4) = 48$
   Solution: $t = 14$
   Answer: The integers are 14, 16, and 18.

7. *Variable:* Let p = the smaller number.
   Then $p + 3$ = the larger number.
   Equation: $p + (p + 3) = -51$
   Solution: $p = -27$
   Answer: The numbers are −27 and −24.

8. *Variable:* Let w = the smallest integer.
   Then $w + 1$ = the middle integer, and $w + 2$ = the largest integer.
   Equation: $w + (w + 1) + (w + 2) = 132$
   Solution: $w = 43$
   Answer: The largest of the three integers is 45.

Section 3.7

1. $d = -1$
2. $x = -6$
3. $y = 6$
4. $x = -1$
5. $n = -14$
6. $h = 7$
7. The equation is an identity. Its solution set is the set of real numbers.
8. The equation has no solution.
9. *Variable:* Let n = the smaller number.
   Then $n + 7$ = the larger number.
   Equation: $n + (n + 7) = 25$
   Solution: $n = 9$
   Answer: The two numbers are 9 and 16.
10. *Variable:* Let x = Janet' age now.
    Then $x - 2$ = her age two years ago, and $x + 5$ = her age in five years.
    Equation: $x - 2 = \frac{1}{2}(x + 5)$
    Solution: $x = 9$
    Answer: Janet is 9 years old now.
11. *Variable:* Let c = the smaller integer.
    Then $c + 1$ = the larger integer.
    Equation: $3(c + c + 1) = c - 17$
    Solution: $c = -4$
    Answer: The integers are −4 and −3.

12. *Variable:* Let p = the number of pennies.
    Then $16 - p$ = the number of nickels.
    Equation: $1p + 5(16 - p) = 44$
    Solution: $p = 9$
    Answer: There are 9 pennies in the collection.

CHAPTER 4

SECTION 4.1

1. It increases by a factor of 2.
2. It increases by a factor of 4.
3. It remains the same.
4. It is multiplied by a factor of $\frac{1}{4}$.
5. $n = 59$
6. $a = 50.24$
7. $V = 240$
8. $x = -44.1$
9. $W = 7x$
10. $C = 2.25p + 1.5s$
11. $C = 1g + 4h$
12. $A = \dfrac{a+b+c+d}{4}$

SECTION 4.2

1. $t = \dfrac{d}{r}$
2. $w = \dfrac{P-2l}{2}$, or $w = \dfrac{P}{2} - l$
3. $h = \dfrac{2A}{b}$
4. $a = \dfrac{2x}{t^2}$

5. $v = \dfrac{p}{m}$
6. $r = \sqrt{\dfrac{A}{\pi}}$

SECTION 4.3

1. $x < 4$
2. $x \geq -1$
3. $x \leq -3$
4. $x > 0$
5. $x \neq 6$
6. $x \geq 5$
7. *Variable:* Let n = the number.
   Inequality: $2n > n + 5$
8. *Variable:* Let n = the number.
   Inequality: $3n + 12 \leq 20$
9. *Variable:* Let n = the smaller integer.
   Then $n + 2$ = the larger integer.
   Inequality: $n + (n + 2) > -11$
10. *Variable:* Let g = Gerald's age.
    Inequality: $g - 7 < \dfrac{1}{2}g$
11.
12.
13.
14.

Section 4.4

1. $n \geq 6$

2. $x < -6$

3. $b < 5$

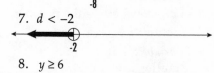

4. $t \leq 8$

5. $w > -3$

6. $z > -8$

7. $d < -2$

8. $y \geq 6$

9. $\{0, 1, 3, 5\}$

10. $\{-3, -2\}$

11. $\{-3, -2, 0, 1\}$

12. $\{\}$ or $\varnothing$

Section 4.5

1. $-3 < x < 2$ or $(-3 < x) \wedge (x < 2)$

2. $(f \leq 4) \vee (y \geq 10)$

3. $-5 \leq w < 0$ or $(-5 \leq w) \wedge (w < 0)$

4. $(h \leq -2) \vee (h > 4)$

5. $0 \leq x < 4$

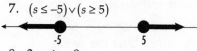

6. $-4 < r < -1$

7. $(s \leq -5) \vee (s \geq 5)$

8. $3 < t < 8$

9. $(y < 3) \vee (y \geq 7)$

10. $-4 \leq n \leq -4$, or $n = -4$

Section 4.6

(It doesn't matter what letters you choose for your variables.)

1. *Variable:* Let x = the smaller number.
   Then $3x$ = the larger number.
   Inequality: $x + 3x \geq 52$
   Solution: $x \geq 13$ and $3x \geq 39$
   Answer: The smallest possible integers are 13 and 39.

2. *Variable:* Let n = the smallest number.
   Then $n + 4$ = the middle number, and $n + 8$ = the largest number.
   Inequality: $n + (n + 4) + (n + 8) \leq -48$
   Solution: n -20
   Answer: The greatest possible numbers are -20, -16, and -12.

3. *Variable:* Let w = the rectangle's width.
   Then $5w$ = the rectangle's length.
   Inequality: $2w + 2(5w)$ 36
   Solution: $w \leq 3$
   Answer: The greatest possible width of the rectangle is 3.

4. *Variable:* Let d = the number of dimes.
   Then $d + 2$ = the number of quarters, and $d + 4$ = the number of nickels.
   Inequality: $10d + 25(d + 2) + 5(d + 4) = 140$
   Solution: $d = 3$
   Answer: Vance could have at most 15 coins (3 dimes, 5 quarters, and 7 nickels).

5. *Variable:* Let x = the integer.
   Inequality: $\dfrac{x+8}{x+47} \leq \dfrac{1}{4}$, or
   $4(x + 8)$ $1(x + 47)$
   Solution: x 5
   Answer: The greatest allowable integer is 5.

6. *Variable:* Let s = the triangle's shortest side.
   Then $s + 1$ = the middle side, and $s + 2$ = the longest side.
   Inequality: $s + (s + 1) + (s + 2) < 42$
   Solution: $s < 13$
   Answer: The greatest possible length of the triangle's longest side ($s + 2$) is 14.

7. *Variable:* Let p = the number of parcels.
   Inequality: $180 + 40p \leq 1000$
   Solution: p 20.5
   Answer: The greatest allowable number of parcels is 20.

8. *Variable:* Let n = the integer.
   Inequality: $\dfrac{n+5}{n+14} < \dfrac{1}{2}$, or
   $2(n + 5) < 1(n + 14)$
   Solution: $n < 4$
   Answer: The greatest allowable integer is 3.

CHAPTER 5

Section 5.1

1. 0
2. 1
3. 2
4. 3

5. 3

6. 6

7. $8y$

8. $-5bc$

9. $-2x^2$

10. $4a^2 - 4a + 4$

11. $6n^5m^3 + 4$

12. $-5a^2b + 3ab - a$

Section 5.2

1. x^8

2. $3n^3$

3. $-15y^3$

4. $2a^2b^3$

5. $6x^4y^5$

6. $\sqrt{35c^3d^2}$

7. g^6

8. a^2b^2

9. $-27x^6y^3$

10. $32n^3$

11. $4r^6s^{10}$

12. $-x^8$

13. $5b^4$

14. xy

15. $\dfrac{1}{x^2}$

16. $\dfrac{4nm^2}{3}$

17. $\dfrac{b^4}{4a^2c}$

18. $3r^2st^3$

Section 5.3

1. 1

2. 3

3. 3

4. 12

5. binomial

6. trinomial

7. monomial

8. trinomial

9. $-6p + 8$

10. $5x + 4$

11. $3w^3 + 5w - 15$

12. $4y^3 + 6y^2$

13. $-n^2 + 15n + 12$

14. $c^2 + 2c$

Section 5.4

1. $4d - 4$

2. $x^2 + x - 3$

3. $-3t^2 + 3t + 9$

4. $3x^2 + 2x + 3$

5. $7x + 3y + 8z$

6. $-2b^2 - 7b + 5$

7. $5t - 11$

8. $-4a - b$

9. $x^2y - 6xy + 5xy^2$

10. $-s^2 + 4s + 8$

11. $2y^2 + 5y - 5$

12. $x^3 - 4x + 3$

Section 5.5

1. $y^3 - 3y^2 + 4y$

2. $8ad^3 - 14a^2d^2$

3. $-12m^3n^2 + 3m^2n^2 - 15m^2n^3$

4. $5x^4y^2z - 7x^3y^3z + 2x^3y^2z^2$

5. $x^2 + 2x - 3$

6. $h^2 + h - 42$

7. $2a^2 + 5ab - 12b^2$

8. $p^2 - 10p + 25$

9. $r^2 - 49$

10. $t^2 - 5$

11. $2x^3 + 2x^2 - 11x + 3$

12. $6n^4 - 14n^3 + 9n^2 + 7n - 6$

13. $a^5 - 1$

14. $z^3 + 6z^2 + 12z + 8$

Section 5.6

1. $2c - 3$

2. $5x^2 - 2x$

3. $8cd - 2$

4. $6x^2y - xy + 7xy^2$

5. $s^3 - s^2 + s - 1$

6. $4n^2m^3 - 9nm^2$

7. $4f - g + 5fg$

8. $s - k + 1$

9. $x \neq 0$

10. $a \neq 0, 3$

11. $s \neq \dfrac{8}{3}$

12. $f \neq 0, g \neq -\dfrac{3}{2}$

CHAPTER 6

Section 6.1

1. GCF = 7

2. GCF = 11a

3. GCF = 3

4. GCF = $4n^2m$

5. $5(x - y)$

6. $2c(d + 1)$

7. $9(3c^2 - 2)$

8. $3n^2(1 + 2n^3)$

9. $g^2h(1 + g)$

10. $s(r + t + u)$

11. $5(2x^2 - 3x + 11)$

12. $4t^2(3t^2 - 4t + 1)$

Section 6.2

1. $x^2 - 36$

2. $b^2 + 6b + 9$

3. $9n^2 - 16$

4. $a^2 - b^2$

5. $t^4 - 81$

6. $25 - 144p^2$

7. $(d + 4)(d - 4)$

8. $(n + m)(n - m)$

9. $(3t + 10)(3t - 10)$

10. $(11 + 2y)(11 - 2y)$

11. $6(2x + 3)(2x - 3)$

12. $b(b + 3)(b - 3)$

13. $(x^2 + y^2)(x + y)(x - y)$

14. $(r^2 + 4)(r + 2)(r - 2)$

Section 6.3

1. $(x + 2)(x + 3)$
2. $(a - 3)(a - 4)$
3. $(n - 5)(n + 4)$
4. $(d - 3)(d + 5)$
5. $(y - 2)(y - 2)$
6. $3(q - 5)(q - 4)$
7. $(r^2 + 3)(r^2 + 5)$
8. $2(g - 6)(g + 2)$
9. $(a + 2b)(a + 3b)$
10. $(2t + 5)(t - 4)$
11. $(4n + 3)(n - 1)$
12. $(3y - z)(y - z)$

Section 6.4

1. $3(x + 4)(x - 4)$
2. $n(n + 3)(n + q)$
3. $6(d - 3)(d - 3)$
4. $2(t - 7)(t - 7)$
5. $\frac{1}{3}(p + 2)(p - 2)$
6. $(3s - 7)(s + 2)$
7. $4(m - 5)(m - 5)$
8. $2(5a - 4)(a + 1)$
9. $y(x - 3y)(x + 4y)$
10. $3(1 + n)(1 - n)$ or $-3(n + 1)(n - 1)$
11. $(z^2 + 1)(z + 1)(z - 1)$
12. $(t^2 + 3)(t + 2)(t - 2)$

Section 6.5

1. $\{-3, 0\}$
2. $\{-6, 8\}$
3. $\{-2, 5\}$

4. $\{0, 9\}$
5. $\{-4, 3\}$
6. $\left\{\frac{1}{3}, 1\right\}$
7. $\{-5, 0, 1\}$
8. $\{-2, 0, 2\}$
9. $\left\{-\frac{1}{2}, -4\right\}$
10. $\{-4, 4\}$
11. $\{-5, 4\}$
12. $\{-1, 1\}$

Section 6.6

1. The number is –1 or 5.
2. The rectangle is 4 by 9.
3. The integer is 6.
4. The number is –8 or 3.
5. The number is –8.
6. The numbers are 5 and 6.
7. The numbers are –9 and –2.
8. The numbers are 10 and 11.

CHAPTER 7

Section 7.1

1. $\frac{3}{1}$
2. $\frac{-6}{1}$
3. $\frac{1}{2}$
4. $\frac{5}{4}$
5. $\frac{-25}{3}$
6. $\frac{3}{8}$
7. $\frac{4}{25}$

8. $\dfrac{12}{1}$

9. $\dfrac{20}{1}$

10. $\dfrac{2}{3}$

Section 7.2

1. rational: $\dfrac{37}{99}$

2. irrational

3. rational: $\dfrac{17}{9}$

4. irrational

5. irrational

6. rational: $\dfrac{2}{1}$

7. irrational

8. irrational

9. rational: $\dfrac{17}{1}$

10. rational: $\dfrac{1}{10}$

11. rational: $\dfrac{3}{5}$

12. rational: $\dfrac{2}{1}$

Section 7.3

1. 40
2. 13
3. −9
4. 17, −17
5. 6
6. −11
7. 8, −8

8. $\dfrac{2}{5}$

9. $\dfrac{7}{3}$

10. $\dfrac{6}{20}$, or $\dfrac{3}{10}$

11. $\dfrac{1}{13}$, $-\dfrac{1}{13}$

12. $-\dfrac{5}{14}$

Section 7.4

1. $4\sqrt{2}$

2. $10\sqrt{3}$

3. $3\sqrt{14}$

4. $-3\sqrt{10}$

5. x^2

6. $n^3\sqrt{n}$

7. $ab\sqrt{a}$

8. $30\sqrt{2}$

9. $\sqrt{13}$

10. $2f\sqrt{11f}$

11. $6xy\sqrt{5yz}$

12. $6v^2w^2\sqrt{2w}$

Section 7.5

1. $4\sqrt{3}$

2. $16\sqrt{7}$

3. $7\sqrt{14}-2\sqrt{7}$

4. $7\sqrt{6}+12$

5. $\sqrt{35}$

6. −6

7. $80\sqrt{5}$

8. $28\sqrt{22}-21\sqrt{33}$

9. $\sqrt{5}$

10. 2

11. $3\sqrt{10}$

12. $3\sqrt{2}$

Section 7.6

1. $x = \sqrt{34}$

2. $x = \sqrt{113}$

3. $x = \sqrt{65}$

4. $x = \sqrt{57}$

5. $2\sqrt{6}$

6. $5\sqrt{2}$

7. $6\sqrt{5}$

8. 17

9. 20 feet

10. $\frac{\sqrt{2}}{2}$

11. B

12. D

CHAPTER 8

Section 8.1

1. False

2. True

3. False

4. True

5. True

6. True

7. point T

8. points R, S, and T

9. point U

10. line l

11. line segment RS

12. $\varnothing$

Section 8.2

1. acute; 50°

2. obtuse; 100°

3. right; 90°

4. acute; 80°

5. obtuse; 130°

6. straight; 180°

7. obtuse; 140°

8. acute; 40°

Section 8.3

1. $x = 36$

2. $x = 20$

3. $x = 22.5$

4. $x = 18$

5. $x = 12$

6. $x = 68$

7. $x = 18$

8. $x = 30$

9. 150°

10. 30°

11. 34°

12. $-3x + 196$

Section 8.4

1. $x = 124$

2. $x = 13$

3. $x = 25$

4. $x = 8$

5. $x = 65$

6. $x = 13$

7. $x = 20$

8. $x = 12$

9. parallel

10. not parallel
11. not parallel
12. parallel

Section 8.5

1. C
2. A
3. D
4. 108°
5. 120°
6. 135°
7. 144°
8. $x = \dfrac{(n-2)180}{n}$

Section 8.6

1. True
2. False
3. False
4. True
5. $x = 65$
6. $x = 17$
7. $x = 45$
8. $x = 36$
9. $x = 13$
10. $x = 108$
11. $x = 53$
12. $x = 103$

Section 8.7

1. C
2. B
3. $x = 76$
4. $x = 36$
5. $x = 112$
6. $x = 127$

7. $x = 15$
8. $x = 28$
9. $x = 90$
10. $x = 85$
11. 10
12. $5\sqrt{2}$

CHAPTER 9

Section 9.1

1. $3 : 1$
2. $1 : 8$
3. $2 : 3$
4. $4 : 25$
5. 15
6. 48
7. 240
8. 21
9. 132
10. 30°, 45°, 105°
11. 10
12. 6, 18, 24

Section 9.2

1. $x = 6$
2. $x = 3$
3. $x = 20$
4. $x = 36$
5. $x = 6$
6. $x = -3$
7. $x = 5$
8. $x = -12$

Section 9.3

1. $x = 21$
2. $n = 15$

3. $y = 15$

4. $s = 12$

5. $a = 9$

6. $x = 5.5$

7. $m = 9.6$, $n = 10.4$

8. $j = 5.8\overline{3}$, $k = 6.6\overline{6}$

9. 15

10. 4.5 feet

11. 21 feet

12. 56

CHAPTER 10

SECTION 10.2

1. 14

2. 120

3. 28

4. 8

5. 35

6. 63

7. 60

8. 30

9. 3

10. 60

11. width = 7 feet, length = 12 feet

12. $x = 11$

13. 13

14. 32

SECTION 10.3

1. 3

2. 25

3. 16π

4. 18π

5. $\dfrac{12}{\pi}$

6. $\sqrt{\dfrac{25}{\pi}}$, or $5\sqrt{\dfrac{1}{\pi}}$

7. $\pi x^2 - 6\pi x + 9\pi$

8. 36π square meters

9. 2,000,000 miles

10. $A = \dfrac{c^2}{4\pi}$

11. $36 - 9\pi$

12. $9\pi - 18$

13. $200 - 50\pi$

14. $32 - 8\pi$

SECTION 10.4

1. 60

2. 343

3. $x^3 + 4x^2 - 5x$

4. $6x^3$

5. 160

6. 84

7. 40

8. $125 + \dfrac{125}{3}$, or $166.6\overline{6}$

9. $\dfrac{1}{8}$

10. 1.5

11. 5

12. $\dfrac{16}{3}$, or $10.6\overline{6}$

SECTION 10.5

1. 45π

2. 28π

3. 15π

4. $\dfrac{64\pi}{3}$, or $21.3\overline{3}(\pi)$

5. $90\,\pi$

6. $\dfrac{36}{\pi^2}$

7. $\dfrac{243\pi}{2}$, or $121.5\,\pi$

8. $63\,\pi$

9. 4

10. $1 : 2$

11. $\dfrac{4\pi^4}{3}$

12. 1.5

CHAPTER 11

SECTION 11.1

1. $(3, 3)$
2. $(0, 4)$
3. $(-2, -6)$
4. $(-1, 2)$
5. $(3, -2)$
6. $(0, -4)$
7. quadrant IV
8. quadrant I
9. quadrant II
10. y-axis
11. quadrant III
12. x-axis
13. 6
14. 22.5
15. 40
16. 18

SECTION 11.2

1. 1

2. -1

3. $\dfrac{3}{4}$

4. 13

5. $\dfrac{1}{11}$

6. -2

7. $-\dfrac{13}{12}$

8. $-\dfrac{1}{3}$

9. C

10. D

11. A

12. A

SECTION 11.3

1. A
2. D
3. B
4. C
5. parallel
6. skew
7. parallel
8. skew
9. D
10. C
11. A
12. B

SECTION 11.4

1. $y \geq -x + 3$

2. $y < -\dfrac{2}{5}x + 2$

3. $y \geq 4x - 2$

4. $y < -\dfrac{3}{2}x$

5. $y \leq \dfrac{4}{5}x - 3$

6. $y > -1$

7. $y \leq \dfrac{4}{3}x + 1$

8. $y > \dfrac{1}{6}x + \dfrac{3}{2}$

9.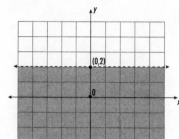

10.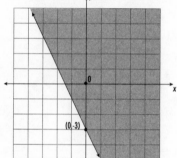

11.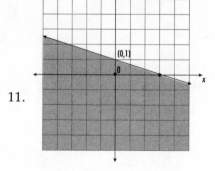

12.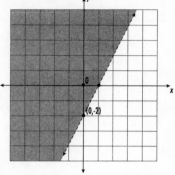

SECTION 11.5

1.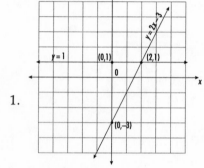

Solution set: (2, 1)

2.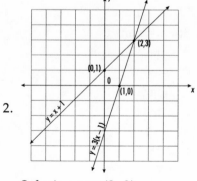

Solution set: (2, 3)

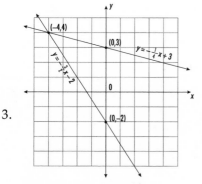

3.

Solution set: (–4, 4)

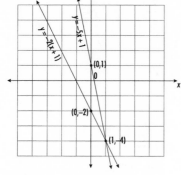

4.

Solution set: (1, –4)

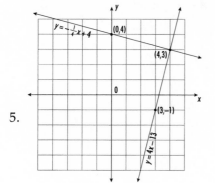

5.

Solution set: (4, 3)

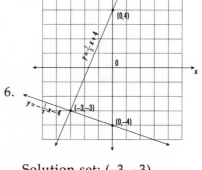

6.

Solution set: (–3, –3)

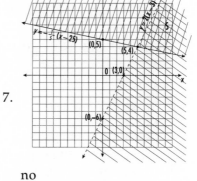

7.

    no

8. no

9. no

10. yes

Section 11.6

1. $x = 1, y = 4$

2. $x = 3, y = -1$

3. $x = 14, y = 4$

4. $x = 8, y = 7$

5. $x = 3, y = 2$

6. $x = -2, y = 4$

7. $x = -2, y = -1$

8. $x = 4, y = 2.25$

9. *System:* $n + d = 12$
$5n + 10d = 85$
Solution: $n = 7$, $d = 5$
Answer: The bag contains 7 nickels and 5 dimes.

10. *System:* $4b + 2s = 15$
$2b + 3s = 13.5$
Solution: $b = 2.25$, $s = 3$
Answer: A burger costs $2.25, and a slush-drink (whatever that is) costs $3.00.

11. *System:* $l = 2w - 2$
$2l + 2w = 38$
System: $w = 7$, $l = 12$
Answer: The rectangle's width is 7 and its length is 12.

12. *System:* $s + l = 500$
$2.5s + 3.5l = 1400$
Solution: $s = 350$, $l = 150$
Answer: Manny's Joint sold 350 small and 150 large goopy drinks (whatever they are) that day.

CHAPTER 12

SECTION 12.1

1. *D*
2. *J*
3. *G*
4. Angle *LKJ*
5. Segment *IH*
6. Quadrilateral *ABCD*
7. yes; 4
8. yes; 1
9. no

10. yes; 1
11. no
12. yes; 2

SECTION 12.2

1. no
2. yes; 180°
3. yes; 90°, 180°, 270°
4. no
5. no
6. yes; 120°, 240°
7. yes; 72°, 144°, 216°, 288°
8. yes; 60°, 120°, 180°, 240°, 300°
9. A
10. C
11. D
12. C

SECTION 12.3

1. translation
2. reflection
3. rotation
4. dilation
5. reflection
6. rotation
7. reflection
8. dilation
9. D
10. B

CHAPTER 13

SECTION 13.1

1. $\dfrac{1}{6}$

2. $\frac{3}{6}$

3. $\frac{2}{6}$

4. $\frac{1}{6}$

5. $\frac{5}{6}$

6. $\frac{3}{6}$

7. $\frac{4}{52}$

8. $\frac{13}{52}$

9. $\frac{1}{52}$

10. $\frac{1}{52}$

11. $\frac{2}{52}$

12. $\frac{20}{52}$

13. $\frac{3}{8}$

14. 80

Section 13.2

1. $\frac{1}{6}$

2. $\frac{2}{7}$

3. $\frac{2}{5}$

4. $\frac{3}{6}$

5. B

6. C

7. $\frac{4}{12}$

8. 0

9. $\frac{7}{12}$

10. $\frac{8}{12}$

11. 2

12. $\frac{16}{24}$

Section 13.3

1. $\frac{2}{6}$

2. $\frac{4}{6}$

3. $\frac{4}{6}$

4. $\frac{4}{6}$

5. $\frac{4}{6}$

6. $\frac{3}{6}$

7. $\frac{2}{9}$

8. $\frac{5}{9}$

9. $\frac{7}{9}$

10. 1

11. 0.61

12. $\frac{16}{52}$

Section 13.4

1. 56

2. 270

3. 24

4. 216

5. $\frac{1}{216}$

6. $\frac{6}{216}$

7. (*a*) (H, H), (T, H)
(H, T), (T, T)

(*b*)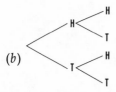

8. (*a*) (1, H), (2, H), (3, H),
(4, H), (5, H), (6, H)
(1, T), (2, T), (3, T), (4, T),
(5, T), (6, T)

(*b*)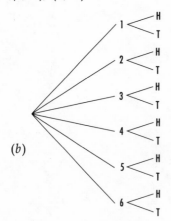

9. (*a*) (C, H), (O, H) (A, H),
(T, H)
(C, A), (O, A) (A, A), (T, A)
(C, T), (O, T) (A, T), (T, T)

(*b*)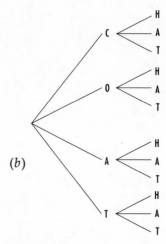

10. (*a*) (M, I), (I, M), (C, M),
(E, M)
(M, C), (I, C), (C, I), (E, I)
(M, E), (I, E), (C, E), (E, C)

(*b*)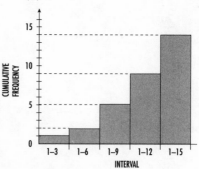

Section 13.5

1. $\frac{12}{49}$

2. $\frac{16}{49}$

3. $\frac{9}{49}$

4. $\frac{25}{49}$

5. $\frac{33}{49}$

6. $\dfrac{24}{49}$

7. $\dfrac{12}{2652}$

8. $\dfrac{156}{2652}$

9. $\dfrac{624}{2652}$

10. $\dfrac{16}{2652}$

Section 13.6

1. 5040
2. 120
3. 720
4. 120
5. 12
6. 128
7. 24
8. 600
9. 840
10. 120
11. 11880
12. 990

CHAPTER 14

Section 14.1

1. (*a*) 3
   (*b*) 3
2. (*a*) 1.3
   (*b*) 1.2
3. (*a*) 1001
   (*b*) 2
4. (*a*) 4
   (*b*) 2.5
5. 83
6. 77.5

7. 86.5
8. 83
9. 99
10. 45.5
11. 28
12. (*a*) $\dfrac{2}{8}$
    (*b*) 0
    (*c*) $\dfrac{3}{8}$

Section 14.2

1. no mode
2. 2
3. bimodal: 34, 37
4. 0

5.
Interval	Frequency
141-149	5
150-158	2
159-167	4
168-176	4
177-185	5
Total:	20

6.
Interval	Cumulative Frequency
141-149	5
141-158	7
141-167	11
141-176	15
141-185	20
Total:	20

7. 1
8. 2
9. 2.5
10. 22
11. 3

12.

Errors Made	Frequency
0	1
0-1	7
0-2	12
0-3	16
0-4	19
0-5	22

(b)

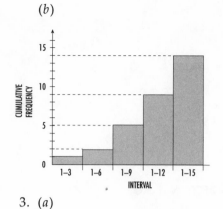

SECTION 14.3

1. (a)

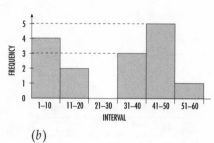

(b)

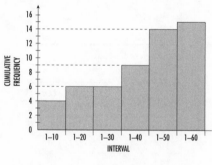

2. (a)

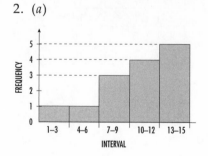

3. (a)

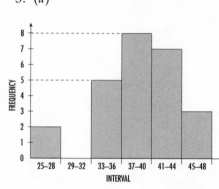

(b)

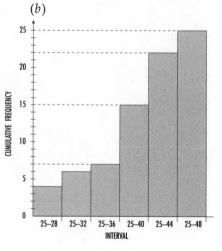

4. 40

5. 10

6. $40-$49

7. (*a*)

Interval	Frequency
$20-$29	5
$30-$39	7
$40-$49	12
$50-$59	10
$60-$69	6

(*b*)

Interval	Cumulative Frequency
$20-$29	5
$30-$39	12
$40-$49	24
$50-$59	34
$60-$69	40

16

Sample Exams

SAMPLE EXAM I

Part I

Answer 30 questions from this part. Each correct answer will receive 2 credits. No partial credit will be allowed. Write your answers in the spaces provided on the separate answer sheet. Where applicable, answers may be left in terms of π or in radical form.

1 If the probability of snow tomorrow is $\frac{2}{5}$, what is the probability of no snow tomorrow?

2 Let p represent "Today is Monday" and let q represent "I am tired." Using p and q, write in symbolic form: "Today is Monday and I am not tired."

3 If a letter is chosen at random from the ten letters in the word "SEQUENTIAL," find the probability that the letter chosen is an "E."

4 In six computer games, Olga scored 122, 138, 130, 98, 102, and 124. What was the mean of her scores?

5 Solve for x: $1.4x - 0.9 = 3.3$

6 Let p represent "The triangle is equilateral" and let q represent "The triangle is a right triangle." Using p and q, write in symbolic form: "If the triangle is a right triangle, then it is not equilateral."

7 If 25% of a number is 12, find the number.

8 Solve for x: $\frac{7}{10}x + 2 = 16$

9   In the accompanying diagram $\overleftrightarrow{AB}$, $\overleftrightarrow{CD}$ and intersect at E.
    If $m \angle AED = 2x + 11$ and $m \angle CEB = 5x - 19$, find the
    value of x.

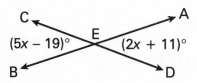

C

(5x − 19)°   E   (2x + 11)°

B   D

10 The area of a circle is 25π. What is the length of a radius
    of the circle?

11 A girl 5 feet tall casts a shadow of 2 feet. At the same
    time, a nearby tree casts a shadow of 24 feet. Find the
    number of feet in the height of the tree.

12 If x varies directly as y and when $x = 8$, when $y = 4$, find
    x when $y = 16$.

13 Find the value of $5xy^2$ if $x = -2$ and $y = -3$.

14 In the accompanying diagram, parallel lines $\overleftrightarrow{AB}$ and $\overleftrightarrow{CD}$
    are intersected by transversal $\overleftrightarrow{EF}$ at G and H,
    respectively. If $m \angle CHG = x + 20$ and $m \angle DHG = 3x$,
    find the value of x.

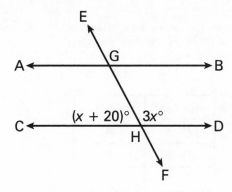

15 Expressed in radical form, what is the product of
    $2\sqrt{7}$ and $3\sqrt{5}$?

16 The larger of two supplementary angles has a measure of 20° more than the measure of the smaller angle. Find the number of degrees in the measure of the *smaller* angle.

17 In the accompanying diagram, $m \angle A = x + 20$, $m \angle B = 3x$, $m \angle BCD$ is an exterior angle formed by extending $\overline{AC}$ to point D, and $m \angle BCD = 120$. Find the value of x.

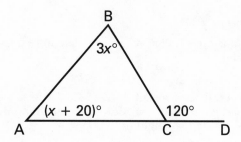

18 Solve for x: $9x - 4(x - 3) = 72$

19 Solve the following system of eqations for y:
$$2x + y = 12$$
$$-2x + 3y = -4$$

20 What is the inverse of $-\dfrac{a}{2}$?

21 The test scores for 20 students in a Spanish class are shown in the frequency table below. In which interval does the upper quartile lie?

Interval	Frequency
90–99	4
80–89	6
70–79	5
60–69	4
50–59	1

Directions (22–35): For *each* question chosen, write on the separate answer sheet the *numeral* preceding the word or expression that best completes the statement or answers the question.

22 What is the quotient of $\dfrac{26x^4y^2}{13xy}$, $x \neq 0$, $y \neq 0$?

(1) $2x^4y^2$ (3) $2x^3y$

(2) $13x^5y^3$ (4) $13x^3y$

23 The two acute angles in an isosceles right triangle must measure

(1) 30° and 60°   (3) 40° and 50°

(2) 35° and 55°   (4) 45° and 45°

24 What is the value of $_5P_1$?

(1) 1   (3) 24

(2) 5   (4) 120

25 The perimeter of a square is $20x - 4$. Which expression represents a side of the square in terms of x?

(1) $5x$ (3) $8x - 16$

(2) $10x - 2$ (4) $5x - 1$

26 Which number is *not* a member of the solution set of the inequality $4x \geq 18$?

(1) 4.4   (3) 4.6

(2) 4.5   (4) 4.7

27 What is the sum of $\dfrac{x-1}{3}$ and $\dfrac{x+3}{5}$?

(1) $\dfrac{x+1}{4}$ (3) $\dfrac{8x+4}{15}$

(2) $\dfrac{8x+2}{15}$ (4) $\dfrac{x^2+2x-3}{15}$

28 Which figure *cannot* have both pairs of opposite sides parallel?

(1) parallelogram   (3) rhombus

(2) rectangle   (4) trapezoid

29 Which is a rational number?

    (1) $\sqrt{7}$ (3) $\sqrt{49}$

    (2) $\sqrt{18}$ (4) $\sqrt{20}$

30 If each side of a rectangle is doubled, the area of the
    rectangle will
    (1) double
    (3) be multiplied by 4
    (2) be divided by 2
    (4) remain the same

31 The accompanying diagram shows a right triangle.

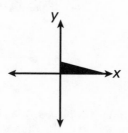

    If the triangle is rotated 90° counterclockwise about the
    origin, what will the image be?

(1)    (3)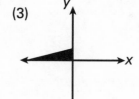

(2) 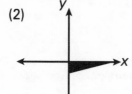   (4)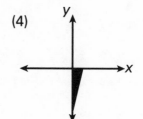

32   Which statement is true about the graph of the line
     whose equation is $y = 8$?
     (1) The line is parallel to the x-axis.
     (3) The line is parallel to the y-axis.
     (2) The line passes through the origin.
     (4) The line has a slope of 8.

33   The solution set of $x^2 - 5x + 6 = 0$ is
     (1) {1,5}   (3) {2,3}
     (2) {-1,-5}   (4) {-2,-3}

34   The length of the hypotenuse of a right triangle is 20
     centimeters and the length of one leg is
     12 centimeters. The length of the other leg is
     (1) 8 cm   (3) 32 cm
     (2) 16 cm   (4) $\sqrt{544}$ cm

35   Which sentence illustrates the associative property for
     multiplication?
     (1) $ab = ba$
     (3) $a(bc) = (ab)c$
     (2) $a \bullet 1 = a$
     (4) $a(b + c) = ab + ac$

Part II

Directions: Answer four questions from this part. Clearly indicate the necessary steps, including appropriate formula substitutions, diagrams, graphs, charts, etc. Calculations that may be obtained by mental arithmetic or the calculator do not need to be shown.

---

36   James is four years younger than Austin. If three times
     James' age is increased by the square of Austin's age, the
     result is 28. Find the ages of James and Austin. [*Only an
     algebraic solution will be accepted.*]

37   Write an equation or a system of equations that can be
     used to solve each of the following problems. In each
     case, state what the variable or variables represent.
     [*Solution of the equations is not required.*]
     a   The sum of two numbers is 240. The larger number is 6 less
           than twice the smaller. Find the numbers.

     b   In the accompanying diagram of isosceles trapezoid *ABCD*,
           $AB = CD$. The measure of $\angle B$ is 40° more than the measure
           of $\angle A$. Find m$\angle A$ and m$\angle B$.

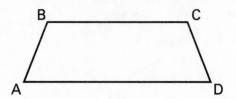

38 A jar contains four balls. Each ball has one letter printed on it. The letters are *A*, *E*, *D*, and *G*. One ball is drawn from the jar and its letter is noted. A second ball is then drawn without replacing the first and its letter is noted.

 a Draw a tree diagram or list the sample space showing all possible outcomes.

 b Find the probability that the letters printed on the two balls drawn consist of

   (1) *at least* one vowel
   (2) no vowels
   (3) the same letter

39 Construct and complete the truth table for the statement

$\sim(q \wedge \sim p) \leftrightarrow (p \vee q)$.

40 *a* On the same set of coordinate axes, graph the following system of inequalities:

$y \leq -4x + 6$

$y > \dfrac{2}{5}x - 5$

 b Based on the graph drawn in part *a*, write the coordinates of a point in the solution set of this system.

41 Use any method—algebraic, trial and error, making a table—to solve this problem. A written explanation of how you arrived at your answer is also acceptable. Show all work.

There are two pairs of integers that satisfy both of these conditions:

The smaller integer is 10 less than the larger integer.

The sum of the squares of the integers is 250.

 a Find the two pairs of integers.

 b Show that one pair of integers found in part *a* satisfies both given conditions.

42 Pentagon *RSTUV* has coordinates *R*(1,4), *S*(5,0), *T*(3,–4),
    U(–1,–4), and *V*(–3,0).

   a On graph paper, plot pentagon *RSTUV*.

   b Draw the line of symmetry of pentagon *RSTUV* and label the
       line *b*.

   c Find the area of
       (1) triangle *RVS*
       (2) trapezoid *STUV*
       (3) pentagon *RSTUV*

ANSWER KEY

Part I

1. $\dfrac{3}{5}$

2. $p \wedge \sim q$

3. $\dfrac{2}{10}$

4. 119
5. 3
6. $p \rightarrow \sim q$
7. 48
8. 20
9. 10
10. 5
11. 60
12. 32

13. −90
14. 40
15. $6\sqrt{35}$
16. 80
17. 25
18. 12
19. 2
20. $\dfrac{a}{2}$
21. 80–89
22. 3
23. 4
24. 2

25. 4
26. 1
27. 3
28. 4
29. 3
30. 2
31. 1
32. 1
33. 3
34. 2
35. 2

Part II

36.   Analysis

       1 and 5

37. a   Larger number = $2x - 6$

       Smaller number = x

       $x + 2x - 6 = 240$

37. b   m$\angle A = x$

       m$\angle B = x + 40$

       $x + x + 40 = 180$

38. b   (1) $\dfrac{10}{12}$

       (2) $\dfrac{2}{12}$

       (3)   0

41. a   5,15 and −15,−5

42. c   (1)   16

       (2)   24

       (3)   40

SAMPLE EXAM 2

Part I

Answer 30 questions from this part. Each correct answer will receive 2 credits. No partial credit will be allowed. Write your answers in the spaces provided on the separate answer sheet. Where applicable, answers may be left in terms of π or in radical form.

---

1   The sections of a spinner are shaded in blue and yellow. The probability that the spinner will land on a blue

   section is $\frac{4}{9}$. What is the probability that the spinner will

   not land on a blue section?

2   The Earth is approximately 93,000,000 miles from the Sun. If this distance is expressed as 9.3×10^n, what is the value of n?

3   Solve for x: $0.5x + 3 = 4.5$

4   If the scores 18, 20, 25, 11, and x have a mean of 19, what is the value of x?

5   In the accompanying diagram, $\overleftrightarrow{BC}$, $\overleftrightarrow{BAD}$, and $\overleftrightarrow{CAE}$ intersect to form $\triangle ABC$. If $m\angle ABC = 25$ and $m\angle C = 90$, find $m\angle DAE$.

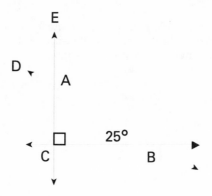

6   Factor: $y^2 - 100$

7   Two adjacent sides of a rhombus are represented by
    $5x + 7$ and $6x - 1$. Find the value of x.

8   If two angles are supplementary and one angle is twice
    as large as the other, find the number of degrees in the
    measure of the smaller angle.

9   Solve for x: $\dfrac{x}{7} - 5 = -4$

10 If y varies directly as x and $y = 24$ when $x = 4$, find the
    value of y when $x = 9$.

11 In the accompanying diagram of $\triangle ABC$, $\overline{AC}$ is extended
    to D, $m\angle BCD = 140$, and $m\angle ABC = 85$. Find $m\angle BAC$.

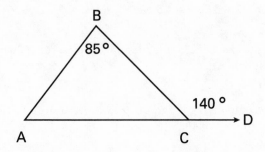

12 The sides of a triangle measure 9, 15, and 18. If the
    shortest side of a similar triangle measures 6, find the
    length of the longest side of this triangle.

13 In the accompanying diagram, *K* is the image of *A* after a translation. Under the same translation, which point is the image of *J*?

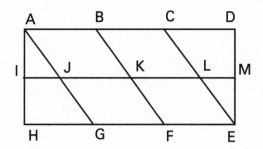

14 Write in symbolic form the inverse of $\sim\!e \rightarrow p$.

15 Point $(k,-2)$ lies on the line whose equation is $x - 3y = 7$. What is the value of *k*?

16 In the accompanying diagram, transversal $\overleftrightarrow{GH}$ intersects parallel lines $\overleftrightarrow{AB}$ and $\overleftrightarrow{CD}$, $m\angle DGH = x$, and $m\angle BHG = 2x - 30$. Find the value of *x*.

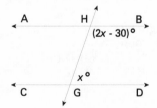

17 Solve for *x* in terms of *a*, *b*, and *c*:
$$ax - 3b = c$$

18 Express $\dfrac{3x}{4} - \dfrac{x}{5}$ as a single fraction in simplest form.

Directions (19–35): **For each question chosen, write on the separate answer sheet the numeral preceding the word or expression that best completes the statement or answers the question.**

19 If $n + 8$ represents an odd integer, the next larger odd integer is represented by
(1) $n + 10$ (3) $n + 7$
(2) $n + 9$ (4) $n + 6$

20 The product of $(-3xy^2)(5x^2y^3)$ is
(1) $-8x^3y^5$ (3) $-15x^2y^5$
(2) $-15x^3y^5$ (4) $-15x^3y^6$

21 What is the value of x in the equation $4(2x + 1) = 27 + 3(2x - 5)$?

(1) 21   (3) $7\frac{1}{2}$

(2) 9   (4) 4

22 Which letter has a point of symmetry?
(1) **E**   (3) **H**
(2) **C**   (4) **T**

23 The line whose equation is $y = 4x + 2$ has a y-intercept whose coordinates are
(1) (0,0)   (3) (4,0)
(2) (0,2)   (4) (0,4)

24 Which graph represents the inequality $-1 \le x < 4$?

(1)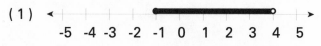

(2)

(3)

(4)

25 The expression $\dfrac{12z^4 + 20z^3 - 4z^2}{-4z^2}$, $z \neq 0$ is eqivalent to

(1) $-4z^2$ (3) $-3z^2 - 5z + 1$
(2) $-3z^2 - 5z$ (4) $3z^2 - 5z - 1$

26 Which equation represents the line parallel to the y-axis and 4 units to the left of the y-axis?

(1) $x = 4$ (3) $y = -4$
(2) $x = -4$ (4) $y = 4$

27 What is the greatest number of two-letter arrangements that can be formed from the letters G, R, A, D, and E if each letter is used only once in an arrangement?

(1) 120 (3) 20
(2) 60 (4) 5

28 If two angles of a triangle each measure 70°, the triangle is described as

(1) right (3) obtuse
(2) scalene (4) isosceles

29 What is the value of the expression $2x^2 - 5x + 6$ when $x = -2$?

(1) 32 (3) 24
(2) -24 (4) 4

30 The value of $(7 - 2)!$ is

(1) 5 (3) 2520
(2) 120 (4) 5038

31 The expression $\sqrt{200}$ is equivalent to

(1) $2\sqrt{10}$ (3) $100\sqrt{2}$
(2) $10\sqrt{2}$ (4) $2\sqrt{100}$

32 Which statement has the same truth value as $\sim m \rightarrow p$?

(1) $m \rightarrow \sim p$ (3) $\sim p \rightarrow \sim m$
(2) $p \rightarrow \sim m$ (4) $\sim p \rightarrow m$

33 Which ordered pair is the solution set for this system of equations?

$$x + y = 8$$
$$y = x - 3$$

(1) (2.5,5.5)　　　　　　　(3) (4,4)
(2) (4,1)　　　　　　　　　(4) (5.5,2.5)

34 What is the solution set of the equation $x^2 - 7x - 18 = 0$?
(1) {9,−2}　　　　　　　　(3) {−6,3}
(2) {−9,2}　　　　　　　　(4) {6,−3}

35 When $a^2 + a - 3$ is subtracted from $3a^2 - 5$, the result is
(1) $2a^2 - a - 2$　　　　　(3) $-2a^2 + a + 2$
(2) $2a^2 - a + 2$　　　　　(4) $4a^2 + a - 8$

Part II

Answer four questions from this part. Clearly indicate the necessary steps, including appropriate formula substitutions, diagrams, graphs, charts, etc. Calculations that may be obtained by mental arithmetic or the calculator do not need to be shown.

---

36. a On the same set of axes, graph the following system of inequalities. Label the region that represents the solution set with an S.

$$y \geq 3x$$
$$x + y < 8$$

　　b Write the coordinates of a point that satisfies the inequality $y \geq 3x$ but does not satisfy the inequality $x + y < 8$.

37 Solve the following system of equations algebraically and check:

$$2x = 5y + 8$$
$$3x + 2y = 31$$

38   Find four consecutive positive integers such that the product of the first and fourth is four less than twice the first muliplied by the fourth. [Only an algebraic solution will be accepted.

39   A restaurant sells large and small submarine sandwiches. Rolls for the sandwiches are ordered from a baker. The roll for a large sandwich costs $0.25 and the roll for a small sandwich costs $0.15. Melissa, the manager of the restaurant, ordered 130 more large rolls than small rolls. What was the greatest number of large rolls she received if she spent less than $63? [Show or explain the procedure used to obtain your answer.

40   The frequency table below shows the scores on a science quiz.

Interval	Frequency
90–99	6
80–89	8
70–79	10
60–69	4
50–59	2

a   Based on the frequency table, which interval contains the median?

b   Which interval contains the 70th percentile?

c On your answer paper, copy and complete the cumulative frequency table below.

Interval	Cumulative Frequency
50-99	
50-89	
50-79	
50-69	
50-59	2

d On graph paper, using the cumulative frequency table completed in part c, construct a cumulative frequency histogram.

41   In the accompanying diagram, ABCD is an isosceles trapezoid with bases $\overline{AB}$ and $\overline{CD}$, $\overline{BA}$ is extended to E, and $\overline{DE} \perp \overline{EB}$. Side $\overline{BC}$ is a diameter of semicircle O, AB = 4, AE = 3, DE = 4, and DC = 10.

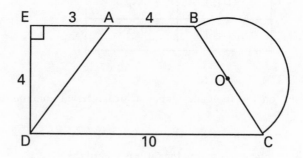

a Find the length of the hypotenuse.

b Find the area of the entire figure to the nearest integer.

42　　Let p represent "It is raining" and let q represent "I am going swimming."

a　Write each of these sentences in symbolic form.

(1) It is not true that if it is raining, then I am going swimming.

(2) It is raining and I am not going swimming.

b　Construct a truth table for the two sentences written in part a to determine whether or not the sentences are logically equivalent. Justify your answer.

ANSWER KEY

1. $\dfrac{5}{9}$

2. 7
3. 3
4. *21*
5. *65*
6. *(y + 10)(y –10)*
7. 8
8. 60
9. 7
10. 54
11. 55
12. 12
13. F

14. $e \rightarrow \sim p$
15. 1
16. 70
17. $\dfrac{c + 3b}{a}$
18. $\dfrac{11x}{20}$
19. 1
20. 2
21. 4
22. 3
23. 2
24. 1

25. 3
26. 2
27. 3
28. 4
29. 3
30. 2
31. 2
32. 4
33. 4
34. 1
35. 1

37. x = *9*, y = *2*
    Check

38. Analysis

    1, 2, 3, 4

39. 206

40. a   70–79

  b   80–89

  c

Interval	Cumulative Frequency
50–99	30
50–89	24
50–79	16
50–69	6
50–59	2

41. a   5

  b   44

42. a   (1) $\sim(p \rightarrow q)$
       (2) $p \wedge \sim q$

Glossary

abscissa

The *x*-coordinate of a point on the coordinate plane.

absolute value

The positive difference of a number and zero. The absolute value of a positive number is itself. The absolute value of a negative number is its opposite.

$$|5| = 5$$

acute

Having a measure of less than 90°. An acute angle is smaller than a right angle, and an acute triangle is one whose angles all measure less than 90°.

additive inverse

The opposite of a number. The sum of a number and its additive inverse is zero. For example, the additive inverse of 2 is –2. The additive inverse of –14 is 14.

adjacent	Side-by-side, or touching. In a polygon, neighboring angles are called adjacent angles. Sides that meet at a vertex of the polygon are called adjacent sides.
altitude	A line drawn perpendicularly from the base of a polygon to its highest point. Used to find the areas of triangles, trapezoids and parallelograms.

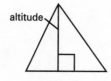 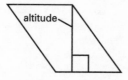 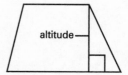

antecedent	The first part of a conditional statement. In the statement , the antecedent is p. Also called the "hypothesis."
associative property	The associative property for multiplication states that it doesn't matter how you group values when you multiply them together; you always get the same product. In other words,
a(bc) = (ab)c	The associative property for addition states that it doesn't matter how you group values when you add them together; you always get the same sum. In other words, $a + b = b + a$
average	The sum of a set of values divided by the number of values. Also called the mean or arithmetic mean.
base	**1.** In a polygon, the side from which an altitude is drawn. Its length is used to find the areas of triangles, trapezoids, and parallelograms.

 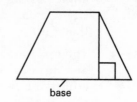

2. In exponential expressions, the number being raised to a given power. In the expression 3^4, for example, the base is 3 and the exponent is 4.

base angle   In a triangle, the two angles adjacent to the base of the polygon.

biconditional   A statement of the form, *"p if and only if q."* Represented symbolically by $\leftrightarrow$. A biconditional statement is true when both of its parts have the same truth value.

binomial   An expression having two terms, like x + 5 or $3n^4 - 5n^2$.

circumference   The perimeter a circle. Given by the formula $C = 2\pi r$, where r is the circle's radius, or by the formula $C = \pi d$, where d is the circle's diameter.

clockwise   The direction in which the hands of a clock rotate:

collinear   Lying along a straight line.

commutative property   The commutative property states that the order in which you add or multiply numbers doesn't matter.
The commutative property for addition:
$a + b = b + a$
The commutative property for multiplication:
$ab = ba$

complementary angles   A pair of angles whose measures add up to 90°.

compound statement   A logical statement having more than one part, like $p \rightarrow q$ or $p \vee q$.

conclusion   The second part of a conditional statement. For example, in the statement $p \rightarrow q$, the conclusion is q. In the statement "If it rains, then I will get wet," the conclusion is "I will get wet."

conditional statement	A statement of the form, "If p, then q." Its symbolic representation is $p \rightarrow qx$. A conditional statement is always true except when its hypothesis (p) is true and its conclusion (q) is false.
congruent	Identical in shape and measure.
conjunction	A compound statement of the form "p and q." Represented symbolically by $p \wedge q$. A statement of conjunction is true only when both of its parts are true.
consecutive	In order, without skipping. Consecutive positive integers: 1, 2, 3, 4, 5. Consecutive multiples of 4: 4, 8, 12, 16, 20.
constant	A numeral whose value is not subject to change, unlike a variable.
contradiction	A compound statement that is always false, regardless of the truth values of its component statements.
contrapositive	A conditional statement formed by negating both parts of a conditional statement and interchanging them. The contrapositive of $p \rightarrow q$ is $\sim p \rightarrow \sim q$. The contrapositive of a conditional statement is logically equivalent to the original statement.
converse	A conditional statement formed by interchanging the parts of a conditional statement. The converse of $p \rightarrow q$ is $q \rightarrow p$.
counterclockwise	The rotational direction opposite to the direction in which the hands of a clock rotate:

cumulative frequency	The sum of all frequencies from the bottom of the range to a given data point.
cumulative frequency histogram	
	A bar chart whose bars represent the cumulative frequencies for various intervals.
decimal form	The standard form of a number. The numbers 34, 5.0, and 137.58 are in decimal form.

denominator	The number on the bottom of a fraction.
diameter	A line drawn through the center of a circle between two points on the circle's edge. A circle's diameter is twice as long as its radius.
difference	The result of a subtraction. The difference of two numbers is found by subtracting the smaller from the larger.
dilation	A transformation in which a figure increases or decreases in size without changing in shape or position.
direct variation	A mathematical relationship in which two quantities increase or decrease together, always maintaining the same ratio. If x varies directly as y, then the fraction $\dfrac{x}{y}$ will always have the same value.
disjunction	A compound statement of the form "p or q." Expressed symbolically as $p \vee q$. A statement of disjunction is always true unless both of its parts are false.
distribution	A set of data values.
distributive property	The distributive property states that adding two numbers together and multiplying the sum by a third number is equivalent to multiplying both numbers by the third number and then adding the products. In other words, for any real numbers a, b, and c, $a(b + c) = ab + ac$
domain	The set of values that may replace a variable without violating any law of mathematics.
equilateral triangle	A triangle with three equal sides and three equal angles. Each angle has a measure of 60°.
exponent	A number that indicates how many times another number (called the base) should be multiplied by itself. In the expression 5^3, the exponent (3) indicates that the base (5) should be multiplied by itself three times: $$5^3 = 5 \times 5 \times 5 = 125$$

exterior angle	An angle outside the vertex of a polygon.

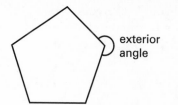 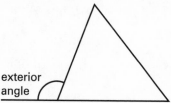

factorial	Expressed as $n!$, for any positive integer n, and equal to the product of every integer from n to 1, inclusive. The expression $6!$, which is read as "six factorial," is equivalent to $6 \times 5 \times 4 \times 3 \times 2 \times 1$, or 720.
fair coin	An ordinary coin, marked "heads" on one side and "tails" on the other, which, when flipped, has an equal probability of landing on either side.
fair die	An ordinary die (as in a pair of dice), whose six sides are numbered 1–6. It is shaped so that, when rolled, it has an equal probability of landing on any given side.
FOIL	A mnemonic formula for multiplying two binomials together. The letters stand for First, Outside, Inside, Last.
frequency	The number of times a given value appears in a distribution.
frequency table	A table listing the frequency with which values occur in certain intervals.
hexagon	A six-sided polygon.
histogram	A vertical bar graph with no space between the bars. It's used to display frequency or cumulative frequency for a data set.

horizontal line symmetry

A figure has horizontal line symmetry when it can be folded divided by a horizontal line into two halves that are reflections of each other.

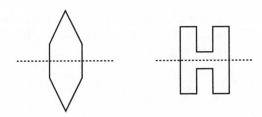

hypotenuse

The longest side of a right triangle, opposite the right angle.

hypothesis

The first part of a conditional statement. In the statement $p \rightarrow q$, the hypothesis is p. Also called the "antecedent."

inequality

A sentence comparing two expressions using one of the following relationships: > (greater than), < (less than), ≥ (greater than or equal to), or ≤ (less than or equal to).

integer

A member of the set containing positive and negative numbers divisible by 1, and zero. These are integers: {...–3, –2, –1, 0, 1, 2, 3...}.

interior angle

An angle on the interior of a polygon.

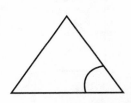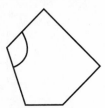

interval

The range of values between one data point and another, including the endpoints. In a set of integer values, the interval 3–6 includes the values 3, 4, 5, and 6.

inverse

A conditional statement formed by negating both parts of a conditional statement. The inverse of the statement $p \rightarrow q$ is $\sim p \rightarrow \sim q$.

irrational number A number that cannot be expressed as the quotient of two integers. Square roots that cannot be resolved, such as $\sqrt{5}$, and the number π are also irrational.

isosceles triangle A triangle having two equal sides and two equal angles. The two equal sides are opposite the two equal angles.

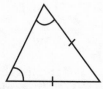

leg One of the two sides in a right triangle that are adjacent to the right angle.

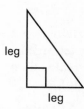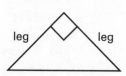

line symmetry A figure has line symmetry when it can be divided by at least one line into equal halves that are reflections of each other.

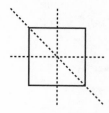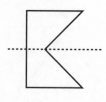

logical connectives The four logical relationships which can connect two statements: conjunction ($\wedge$), disjunction ($\vee$), conditional ($\rightarrow$), and biconditional ($\leftrightarrow$).

logically equivalent Two statements are logically equivalent when they always have the same truth value. For example, a conditional statement ($p \rightarrow q$) and its contrapositive ($\sim p \rightarrow \sim q$) are logically equivalent.

lower quartile	The point one-fourth of the way from the bottom of a range of values. In a distribution, the lowest 25 percent of the values in the distribution are at or below the lower quartile.
mean	The sum of a set of values divided by the number of values. Also called an average.
median	The middle value in a set when the values are arranged in order. If a set contains an even number of values, the median is the average of the two middle values.
mode	The value that occurs most often in a set. If no value occurs more often than every other value in a set, then the set has no mode.
monomial	An expression having a single term, such as 6, x, or $-8ab$.
multiplicative inverse	The reciprocal of a number. The product of a number and its multiplicative inverse is always 1. The multiplicative inverse of 5 is $\frac{1}{5}$. The multiplicative inverse of $-\frac{1}{3}$ is -3.
negation	The logical opposite of a statement. The negation of the statement p is denoted by $\sim p$.
numerator	The number on the top of a fraction.
obtuse	Having a measure of more than 90°. An obtuse angle measures between 90° and 180°. An obtuse triangle has an angle that measures more than 90°.
octagon	An eight-sided polygon.
open sentence	Any equation or inequality including one or more variables.
order of operations	The order in which arithmetic operations should be performed in complicated expressions: **P**arentheses, **E**xponents, **M**ultiplication and **D**ivision, **A**ddition and **S**ubtraction. Remembered by the mnemonic word PEMDAS.
ordinate	The y-coordinate of a point on the coordinate plane.

origin	On a number line, the point having the coordinate zero. On the coordinate plane, the point where the x-and y-axes intersect, having the coordinates $(0, 0)$.
parallel	Having the same slope. Parallel lines never intersect.
parallelogram	A quadrilateral in which opposite sides are parallel. The two smaller angles are equal and the two larger angles are equal. The measures of a smaller angle and a larger angle add up to 180°. A parallelogram can have right angles. Rectangles and squares are parallelograms.

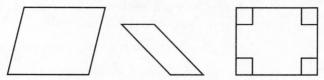

PEMDAS	A mnemonic device representing the order of operations: **P**arentheses, **E**xponents, **M**ultiplication and **D**ivision, **A**ddition and **S**ubtraction.
pentagon	A five-sided polygon.
percentile	The point in a data set beneath which a certain percentage of the values in the set are found. The 80th percentile of a set, for example, is the value at or below which 80 percent of the values in the set lie.
perimeter	The sum of the lengths of a polygon's sides.
permutation	An ordered arrangement of items.
perpendicular	At right angles. Adjacent sides of a square are perpendicular, because an angle of 90° separates them.
point symmetry	A figure has point symmetry when its appearance is not changed when the figure is turned upside down (rotated 180° in the plane of the page).
polygon	A closed shape formed by line segments joined end-to end. Polygons include triangles, squares, pentagons, and so on.

prime	A number is prime when it has only two factors: 1 and the number itself. For example: 2, 3, 5, 7, 11. All prime numbers are positive. The smallest prime number is 2.
probability	The number of ways in which an event can happen divided by the total number of possible outcomes.
product	The result of multiplication. The expression $(x + 4)(x - 7)$ is the product of two binomials.
Pythagorean theorem	The formula relating the lengths of the sides of a right triangle: $a^2 + b^2 + c^2$, where a and b are the lengths of the legs and c is the length of the hypotenuse.
quadrant	One of the four sections into which the coordinate plane is divided by the x-and y-axes. They are numbered counterclockwise from the upper right.

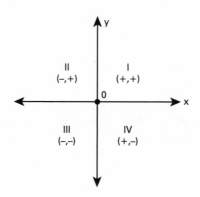

quadratic equation	An equation of the form $ax^2 + bx + c = 0$, where a, b, and c are constants.
quadratic formula	A formula for finding the roots of a quadratic equation of the form:

$$x = \frac{-b \pm \sqrt{b^2 - 4ac}}{2a}$$

quadrilateral	A polygon having four sides.

quotient	The result of division, or the expression of division. A fraction, for example, can be described as a quotient, because the fraction bar indicates division.
radical	The symbol indicating a square root: $\sqrt{}$.
radicand	The number under a square root. In the expression $2\sqrt{5}$, the radicand is 5.
radius	A line segment extending from the center of a circle to the circle's edge.

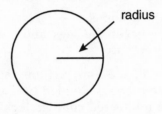

ratio	A comparison of two numbers by division. The ratio of 2 to 5, for example, is $\frac{2}{5}$. The ratio can also be written as 2:5.
rational number	A number that can be expressed as the quotient of two integers.
rotational symmetry	A figure has rotational symmetry when it can be rotated through some angle less than or equal to 180° so that its image is identical to the original figure.

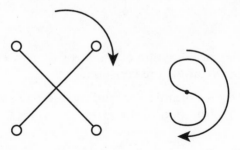

real number	All numbers except the square roots of negative numbers.
reciprocal	The result of dividing 1 by a given number. The

reciprocal of n is $\dfrac{1}{n}$. The reciprocal of $\dfrac{1}{n}$ is n.

rectangle
A quadrilateral with four right angles. Opposite sides in a rectangle are parallel and equal in length. The diagonals of a rectangle are also equal in length. A rectangle whose length and width are equal is a square.

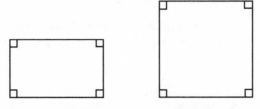

reflection
An image produced by flipping a figure over a line of reflection.

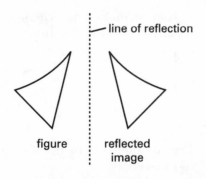

regular
A regular polygon is one whose sides are all of equal length and whose angles are all of equal measure.

rhombus
A quadrilateral with four sides of equal length. Opposite angles in a rhombus are equal. Adjacent angles are supplementary.

right angle

An angle measuring 90°. Denoted by a square marking:

right triangle

A triangle having one right angle. The sides of a right triangle can be related by the Pythagorean theorem:

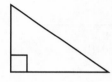 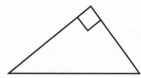

rotation

A transformation in which an image is turned around a point of rotation.

sample space

The complete set of possible outcomes for a series of events.

scalene triangle

A triangle with three angles of different measures and three sides of different lengths.

scientific notation

A system of notation in which a number is expressed as the product of a number between 1 and 10 rounded to the nearest tenth and a power of 10. The number 1,000 in scientific notation is 1.0×10^3. The number 0.0024 in scientific notation is 2.4×10^{-3}.

similar

Similar polygons have identical shapes but may be different in size. Corresponding angles of similar polygons are equal. Corresponding sides of similar polygons are proportional.

slope	The ratio of the vertical increase to the horizontal increase of a line. Slope can be described as "rise over run," and is found using the formula $$m = \frac{y_2 - y_1}{x_2 - x_1}$$ The slope of a horizontal line is zero. The slope of a vertical line is undefined.
slope-intercept form	A linear equation in the form $y = mx + b$ is in slope-intercept form, where m is the line's slope and b is the line's y-intercept.
solution set	The set of all values that satisfy an equation or system of equations.
square	A rectangle with four sides of equal length.
square root	The square root of a number n is the number that must be squared to produce a value of n.
standard notation	The familiar, everyday way of writing a number down. The numbers 5, –26, and 35.48 are all in standard notation.
sum	The result of addition, or the expression of addition. The expression $x + y$ is the sum of x and y.
supplementary angles	A pair of angles whose measures add up to 180°.
symbolic form	A representation of logical sentences in which statements are represented by letters such as p and q, and logical connectives (like "and," "or," and "if...then") are represented by symbols such as $\wedge$, $\vee$, and $\rightarrow$.
system	A set of equations or inequalities whose solution set contains all values that satisfy all of the equations or inequalities.
tautology	A statement which is always true, regardless of the truth values of its premises.
transformation	A change in a figure produced by moving each point in the figure according to a given rule.

translation	A transformation in which a figure is displaced in a given direction without rotating or changing in size.

transversal	A line that intersects two other lines at distinct points.
trapezoid	A quadrilateral having two parallel sides and two sides that are not parallel.

tree diagram	A diagram mapping the possible outcomes of a series of events, and the probability of each event.
trinomial	An algebraic expression having three terms.
truth table	A chart showing the truth values of a series of statements. Usually used to construct a list of the truth values of a sentence for all possible combinations of the truth values of its component statements.
truth value	The quality of being true or false, represented by the letter T or the letter F.
undefined	A fraction is considered "undefined" when its denominator is zero, because it is meaningless to divide a number by zero.
upper quartile	The value a quarter of the way from the top of a range of values. In a set of values arranged in order, 25 percent of the values in the set are found at or above the upper quartile.
vertex	A corner of a polygon, where two sides meet.

vertex angle   In an isosceles triangle, the vertex angle is the angle formed by the equal sides.

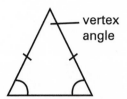

vertical angles   Opposite angles formed by the intersection of two lines. Vertical angles have equal measures.

vertical line symmetry   A figure has vertical line symmetry when it can be divided by a vertical line into two halves that are reflections of each other.

volume   A measure of the space contained within a solid.

x-axis   The horizontal axis of the coordinate plane.

y-axis   The vertical axis of the coordinate plane.

y-intercept   The y-coordinate at which a graph intercepts the y-axis.

Index

H

hexagon 142
histograms 276
hypotenuse 122, 147
hypothesis 8

I

identity 57
image 233
imaginary 117
impossibility 248
inequalities 64, 68
inequalities word problems 74
integers 25
interior 131
intersection 23
inverse 12
irrational numbers 25, 111, 114
isometries 242
isosceles triangle 146

L

lateral faces 186
like monomials 80
line of reflection 233
line segment 128
line symmetry 234
linear equations 206
linear term 101
listing outcomes 255
logic 1
logical connectives 4
logical equivalency 12
lower quartile 267
lowest common denominator 31

M

mean 265
measure of an angle 131
measure of central tendency 266
median 266
middle quartile 267
mode 270
monomials 79
multiplying binomials 89
multiplying monomials 81
multiplying polynomials 88, 90

multiplying probabilities 257
multiplying radicals 120

N

n-gon 143
natural numbers 24
negation 3
negative exponents 36
negative integers 25
negative radicands 117
negative square root 116
no mode 270
non-negative integers 25
null set 23

O

obtuse angle 133
obtuse triangle 147
octagon 142
open sentence 1, 2, 17
opposite angles 135
opposites 28
order of operations 20
order property of numbers 27
ordered pair 198
ordinate 198
origin 27, 197
outcome set 254

P

parallel lines 137
parallelograms 150
parentheses 21
PEMDAS 21
pentagon 142
percentiles 269
perfect square 113, 116
perimeter 171
permutations 261
perpendicular 139
perpendicular lines 139
planes 127
point symmetry 237
points 127
polygons 142
polyhedrons 186
polynomials 79, 85

T

tautology 10
terminating decimals 112
terms 80
transformations 233
translating English into
  algebra 41
translation 241
transversals 137
trapezoids 152
tree diagram 256
triangle 142, 145
trinomial 85
truth table 4
truth value 2

U

undefined terms 127
union 22

V

variable 17
vertex 129, 188
vertex angle 146
vertical angles 135
volume
  of a cone 192
  of a cube 187
  of a cylinder 191
  of a pyramid 188
  of a rectangular solid 187
  of a right prism 186
  of a sphere 192

W

whole numbers 24
word problems 52, 74, 106, 228

X

x-axis 197
x-coordinate 198

Y

y-axis 197
y-coordinate 198

Z

zero exponent 35
zero product property 105

MATH I

ANSWER SHEET

Your answers to Part I should be recorded on this answer sheet.

Part I

1	11	21	31 ....
2	12	22	32 ....
3	13	23	33 ....
4	14	24	34 ....
5	15	25	35 ....
6	16	26	
7	17	27	
8	18	28	
9	19	29	
10	20	30	

Your answers for Part II should be placed on the next page.

Part II

MATH I

ANSWER SHEET

Your answers to Part I should be recorded on this answer sheet.

Part I

1	11	21	31 ....
2	12	22	32 ....
3	13	23	33 ....
4	14	24	34 ....
5	15	25	35 ....
6	16	26	
7	17	27	
8	18	28	
9	19	29	
10	20	30	

Your answers for Part II should be placed on the next page.